Roman Britain

Roman Britain

John Wacher

Book Club Associates
London

This edition published 1978 by
Book Club Associates
By arrangement with J. M. Dent & Sons Ltd.

First published 1978
Reprinted 1980
© John Wacher 1978

Printed and Bound in Great Britain by
Butler & Tanner Ltd
Frome and London
1005147096
This book is set in VIP Baskerville 11 on 12 point

Contents

IN MEMORIAM
N. M. W.

Plates

Figures

Preface

This book is an attempt to collect together the great mass of evidence, accumulated down to the end of 1976, relating to the Roman period of British history and to present it in a form which will be of use to the widest possible range of readers. The material has been gathered in an essentially non-historical way, although a broad outline of chronological development has been followed within each topic selected for discussion. Emphasis has been placed on the activities of the population; consequently the core of the book deals with their work and leisure.

I am most grateful to all those people and institutions, mentioned individually above, for their kindness in making available the photographs and other material used for the illustrations. Tony McCormick spent many laborious hours producing the excellent line-drawings, sometimes from indifferent or difficult sources, while Cheryl McCormick lavished great care on the production of an error-free typescript. To both I must record my indebtedness. Marius Cooke was responsible for producing some first-rate photographs and prints. Mark Hassall devoted much time to reading through the whole typescript, as the result of which it has been, in places, greatly improved: my grateful thanks to him. But, as is usual, I must reserve to myself any errors of omission or commission, especially where, owing to my own stubbornness, I have retained arguments with which he disagreed.

Leicester
March 1977

Fig. 1 The Roman Empire at the time of Trajan

Chapter 1

Britain before the Romans

In 55 BC the first formal intervention by Rome in British affairs took place with the expedition of Julius Caesar. Contacts by traders from Gaul and the Mediterranean had, however, been made before, but it is to Caesar that we owe the first moderately full description of Britain and the Britons. Nevertheless, we must remember that his personal experience was restricted to the south-east, where he described Kent as a thickly populated area and the people as the most civilized, differing little from the Gauls. His information on the interior is more hazy and often at odds with the modern archaeological record.

In Caesar's day much of Britain was culturally in the Iron Age, although a wide and complex variety of developments could then have been detected, owing to the differing backgrounds of many of the original Iron Age migrants.

Undoubtedly, as Caesar infers, the most advanced cultures, both socially and technologically, lay in the south-east, where the more recent migrants from Gaul had landed and then spread inland to assert their presence in Kent, Surrey, East Anglia, Hertfordshire and Berkshire. In some cases these migrants had been fleeing from Caesar's activities in Gaul. In the main, however, they had crossed to Britain in a succession of waves from about 150 BC onwards, coming mainly from the northern part of Gaul. They are collectively known as the Belgae and represent the third, and last, principal Iron Age cultural group, Iron C, to reach Britain before the final Roman conquest in AD 43. But when the Belgic migrants arrived in Britain they found a country which already possessed a long tradition of earlier Iron Age cultures. Arriving first about the seventh century BC two cultural mainstreams can be detected thereafter, referred to usually as Iron A and Iron B.

Iron A migrations seem mainly to have affected south and east Britain. It is likely that small parties of migrants, on making a land-fall on the coast, would carry on until they reached a part not yet settled by their fellows, or, similarly, make their way up suitable rivers. In this way they reached Yorkshire in the north-east and the Severn valley in the west, while more isolated parties ventured further up the west coast to Wales and beyond, ultimately reaching Scotland. In time their numbers became great enough to impress their distinctive cultural achievements on the indigenous Bronze Age people of Britain, with whom they ultimately merged. The cultural way of life of these people is often called after the name of its principal European site, where excavations first revealed its nature: Hallstatt, in Austria.

To begin with, apart from their use of iron and their ability to fashion better quality pottery, these new immigrants to Britain are scarcely distinguishable from the late Bronze Age inhabitants. Agriculture was their mainstay, being based on individual farms and small communities. However, it is now recognized that the later Bronze Age saw the development of hill fortifications, so that, while most farms and villages were still left undefended or at best surrounded by a stockade in the Iron Age, some fortified sites developed along already established lines, and parallel with similar developments on the other side of the Channel. In time, hill-forts with a single rampart and ditch became much more frequent, although regional distinctions can be made. In Wessex and areas immediately north and west, hill-forts of this type are comparatively common, but in the eastern parts of the country they become rarer and far fewer examples are known.

As yet, no satisfactory explanation of the relationships between hill-fort and hill-fort, hill-fort and village, hill-fort and farm, and village and farm, has been put forward, although many views have been canvassed, and we are only now beginning to realize the full complexities of the problems involved. The construction of hill-forts must represent a growing sense of insecurity and the start of corporate actions on the part of communities. In turn it is probable that local chieftains emerged to control them, and we can detect the early beginnings of an organized society.

An acceleration in the rate of hill-fort construction in the third and fourth centuries BC can probably also be partly ascribed to increasing pressure of migrations from a new source. These groups, with their new and different life-styles, are usually referred to as Iron B and their cultural characteristics as La Tène styles. One of the most spectacular developments of this culture was the emergence of a highly distinctive, ornamental metalwork, much of it carried out on articles of war, such as sword-scabbards, shields, helmets and horse-harness. This could well point to the existence among the immigrants of an aristocratic warrior class who could commission these weapons from specialist craftsmen. Judging from the appearance in Britain of elaborate horse-harness, we may conclude that continental chariot-warfare had also been introduced, which may account for the apparent ascendancy gained by these people over the indigenous population. Yet, to start with, the areas they first occupied tended not to be those settled earlier by Iron A

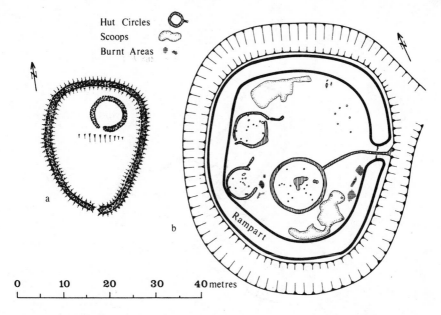

Hut Circles
Scoops
Burnt Areas

a

b

Rampart

0   10   20   30   40 metres

Fig. 2 Pre-Roman farms at: a) Ells Knowe, Northumb; b) Draughton, Northants

migrants. But as time went on the Iron B peoples spread, in many places amalgamating their culture with that of Iron A to produce a distinctively British product.

Another development of this period can be seen in the construction of multiple defences for many existing, and some new, hill-forts, especially in the west and south-west. There is, however, a tendency for the overall number of hill-forts in commission to decline, whereas the size and strength of the remainder are often increased, perhaps pointing to a concentration of local power in fewer hands.

Yet, in many spheres, the way of life of the majority of the inhabitants of Britain can have changed but little in the five hundred or so years of Iron Age migrations that we have been dealing with. It would have depended entirely on agriculture, with individual farms largely based on family units or nucleated communities of varying size sometimes surrounded, at first, by a stockade. If situated on a suitable hill-top, these rudimentary defences often developed into full hill-fort fortifications. The houses themselves were usually circular and constructed of wood with mud-covered walls; the roofs were most likely of thatch or turf. In areas where plentiful stone abounded, such as the south-west, Wales or the northern hill-country, rough, drystone walls replaced some of the timber and mud. From time to time, square or rectangular timber-framed buildings have been identified during exca-

Fig. 3 Pre-Roman village settlement at Cheselbourne, Dorset

vations, but it is not certain if these are dwelling-houses or granaries for the storage of wheat, barley, rye or even beans – the main cereal and pulse crops. In some areas, notably Wessex, grain seems also to have been stored in pits dug in the ground and probably originally lined with basketwork or skins. But this method could only be used after the grain had been dried or roasted over a low fire, to prevent germination and rotting. Recent experiments in storing grain in this way show that it releases certain gases which do much to prevent the growth of fungi and insects. It is probable that, on some occasion, water seeped into such a storage pit which fortuitously contained certain yeasts and enzymes, so forming an amber-coloured, slightly frothy alcoholic liquid: ale has been brewed in Britain ever since. It was apparently the favourite beverage of the people of north-western Europe.

The fields in which these crops were grown were often squarish, or broad rectangular plots, ranging in size from 0.1 to 0.5 ha., although far more irregular units have been observed in many river valleys. The boundaries were usually marked by a ditch or low bank; the latter, on hillside sites, were emphasized by ploughing. It is possible that hedges and fences were also used between fields, since grazing stock must have been kept from growing crops. Since the first hedge was undoubtedly the result of a farmer using green wood for a fence and so inadvertently striking cuttings, hedges would almost certainly have been a feature of the Iron Age cultivated landscape.

Cows and sheep were the principal domestic animals, although pigs were probably fattened in woods and forests and goats provided not only meat and milk but also a long-staple wool. As in most primitive societies where winter fodder is in short supply, an autumn slaughter of surplus stock would have taken place, leaving only the breeding animals to be fed, and incidentally providing a supply of smoked, dried or salted meat for winter use. Salt was extracted by the evaporation of sea-water on many coastal sites such as those identified around the Kent and Essex marshes and the Fens. It would have been valuable not only for preserving meat, but also in the curing of skins to make leather.

It is also probable that greater emphasis was placed on cattle and sheep rearing in the hill-country of the north and west, although the existence of certain types of enclosures and linear ridge dykes, in some southern parts, encourages belief in the existence of large-scale grazing areas. Furthermore, these are often found to show little or no trace of cultivation.

As already briefly noted above, a series of new migrations to eastern Britain began about 150 BC; they are normally referred to as Iron C or the Belgae. Like their Iron B ancestors, they came from much the same areas of northern Gaul between the Seine, the Marne and the Rhine, and they were to affect Britain more radically than any of their predecessors. Culturally and politically they were more advanced, making use of a primitive currency based primarily on gold and silver, later on copper, coins, and possessing a definable tribal structure. However, it must be remembered that their apparent importance in the development of Britain is perhaps mainly due to the fact that we know more about them, either from contemporary classical sources, or from characteristics surviving into the better documented Roman period. If we did not possess such additional information, it is probable that we would compare earlier settlements more favourably with them. Yet, as the main agents in the shaping of Britain immediately before the Roman conquest, they are worthy of greater consideration in the present context.

In the early stages of their migrations, the pattern of coastal landings and subsequent dispersals inland is obtained almost entirely from an analysis of the coin distributions. The distributions reflect a complex sequence of movements which primarily affected south-east Britain. The coins themselves, at first imported, later gave rise to British issues, indicating the presence of centralized authorities capable of controlling tribal areas and running the necessary mints, of which a number of examples have been identified, such as those at Verulamium, Colchester and Silchester. It is also probably right to equate these mints with the existence of tribal capitals, and in time several sites appear which are, unlike hill-forts, usually situated in plains and valleys and are defended both by natural features and by one, or often more, great dykes enclosing large areas of land. These fortified centres were being modified and extended down to the Roman invasion, a factor which tends to show the insularity of Britain: such dykes, consisting of massive banks and ditches, were probably intended as defences in a mobile form of warfare employing chariots. In 1940, southern Britain was again criss-crossed by similar dykes to counter tanks and motorized infantry carriers. Yet in the first century BC chariot-warfare had largely become obsolete in continental Europe, although it appears to have survived in Britain. Indeed, Caesar seems to have been somewhat surprised when he was opposed by chariots on his first landing.

The increase in the number of Belgic settlers in Britain produced more changes than a developing political maturity. Technically they were far more advanced than the indigenous Iron Age people, being able to produce good quality wheel-turned pottery and a much wider range of iron tools. Their leaders also pursued patronage of British bronzesmiths and high quality decorative metalwork continued to be produced. In consequence, farming benefited by the introduction of tools and equipment which enabled more heavily forested land to be cleared and cultivated. Indeed, the growing agricultural prosperity of south-eastern Britain is perhaps best represented by the devices later adopted and imprinted on their coins by two rival tribes: a vine-leaf and an ear of corn (or barley), each a clear indication of the source of tribal wealth.

The fraternal groups which now existed on both sides of the English Channel also led to greatly increased trade between Britain and Gaul. Wine was imported in large amphoras, together with glassware, pottery and metalwork, being paid for no doubt by British agricultural produce. This trade reached its peak, as might be expected, in the

1 Grimes Dyke
2 Heath Farm Dyke
3 Prettygate Dyke
  and Triple Dyke
4 Lexden Moat Farm
  Dyke
5 Sheepen Dyke
6 Berechurch Dyke
7 Gosbecks

Fig. 4 The Iron Age oppidum at Camulodunum, Colchester

century or so that elapsed between Caesar's expeditions and the Claudian invasion, and it is to this period that the oft-quoted passage of the contemporary geographer, Strabo, refers; in it, he gives a detailed list of British imports and exports. As in most cases throughout history where a culturally, or technically, more advanced society is trading with a more primitive one, British exports consisted of basic raw materials or agricultural produce, while the imports were largely of manufactured goods.

Different strata in Belgic society can be identified by a study of their burials. In these practices they differed from earlier Iron Age immigrants by cremating their dead and interring them in large cemeteries. Frequent use seems to have been made of square 'barrows', or enclosures, and great clusters of them have now been identified at such places as Stevenage and Welwyn in Hertfordshire and at Burton Fleming, a La Tène 'Arras' culture cemetery, in east Yorkshire. Each 'barrow' appears to contain a 'master' burial with 'satellite' burials surrounding it; they may represent family groups. A person's position in society was normally indicated by the richness of the grave goods buried with him: fire-dogs, an amphora stand, vessels of pottery or even silver, amphoras of wine, bronze mirrors and personal trinkets. Such burials would represent the aristocratic upper classes. In some places even more elaborate single tombs, often surmounted by a circular barrow, may represent the burial of a member of a royal house. Such a barrow at Lexden, a short distance west of Colchester, contained, beside the usual collection of pottery vessels and pieces of metalwork, a folding stool, a bronze table and a medallion of the emperor Augustus, no doubt presented by a visiting embassy.

The diminishing quality and quantity of grave goods indicates the slide down the social scale, the bottom being reached where the ashes of the cremation are gathered into a single vessel, often hand made in the older traditional manner, or even deposited in the earth without any detectable container at all. It must not be forgotten either that Iron Age society was slave-owning, a practice indicated by the slave-chains and neck-shackles found on a number of sites; slaves would have been a spoil of inter-tribal war. As a class they have probably left less detectable evidence in the form of burials than any other.

Another aspect of the developing society of the Belgic period can be detected by observing the much wider range of 'consumer' goods available. There must have been professional bronzesmiths in the earlier Iron Age, but by now they had been joined by professional blacksmiths and potters and possibly by other craftsmen such as carpenters, together perhaps with shopkeepers and merchants. So, to some extent, the foundation was already being laid for the adoption of an altogether more complex way of life, to which they were shortly to be introduced.

When Caesar arrived in Britain, the Belgic political structure had not fully developed. According to his account, where, for the first time, we learn of British personalities by name, his principal opponent was the tribe of the Catuvellauni, inhabiting modern Hertfordshire, with their main centre at Wheathampstead. He also mentions the Trinovantes of Essex and east Hertfordshire as being one of the strongest tribes in the south-east. Yet, despite their supposed strength, the Trinovantes sought Caesar's help against their western neighbours, and in this apparent paradox lies concealed many of the explanations for what was to come after. It is, in reality, the starting point from

100 m contour

Fig. 5 Tribal areas of Iron Age Britain

which, inevitably, permanent Roman intervention in British affairs ultimately became necessary.

The Britain that Caesar left behind in 54 BC can therefore be described summarily as follows. Except for some remote areas in the hill-country of Wales, Scotland and northern England, it was an Iron Age country with different parts in various stages of cultural development. In the south-west and from there penetrating up the lower Severn valley, along the Jurassic zone of the Cotswolds and into Northamptonshire, Lincolnshire, parts of East Anglia and Yorkshire the culture had a pronounced Iron B flavour. In some places, this had merged with the underlying Iron A culture, while in others it overlay it. Iron A itself had survived almost unchanged in many of the areas beyond.

In the south-east itself, then the most advanced region, both culturally and politically, small tribal groupings seemed to have formed the main stream of development with, as Caesar tells us, no less than four rulers in Kent. The Trinovantes, probably of predominantly Iron A stock, seem to have been the most closely knit community, with their territory extending through Essex into much of east Hertfordshire; and already there was the burgeoning power of the Catuvellauni.

The last group of Belgic migrants to reach Britain came after Caesar's expeditions, and they are usually associated with his erstwhile friend, and later foe, Commius, of the Gallic tribe of the Atrebates.

The age of primary Belgic movement to Britain then appears to have ceased, to be replaced, from about 30 BC onwards, by a period of expanding influence among the chief tribal groups, which ultimately reached out to the Severn in the west and the Trent in the north. Then, for the first time also, it is possible to recognize most of the tribal names and territories which ultimately came to be crystallized under the Roman system of local administration. We have already mentioned the Catuvellauni and the Trinovantes. In Gloucestershire and Somerset lay the Dobunni, derived from Commius' Atrebates who themselves inhabited Hampshire, Berkshire and west Sussex; in Dorset there were the Durotriges; in Norfolk and north Suffolk, the Iceni. North-west of the Catuvellauni lay the Coritani, and beyond them again the Cornovii and Brigantes.

The emergence of reasonably unified tribal kingdoms did not, however, prevent a power-struggle from taking place, and the principal aggressor was the tribe of the Catuvellauni.

After their defeat by Caesar, the Catuvellauni, ruled by Cassivellaunus, were forbidden by the terms of their submission to molest the Trinovantes. Yet a generation or so later, under a new king, Tasciovanus, and with a new tribal capital at Verulamium, these terms were being ignored. We do not know why the site of the capital was changed. Perhaps the old one at Wheathampstead was still tainted by the humiliation inflicted by Caesar, and only the selection of a new site would have helped to erase a memory which could have no part in their growing scheme of aggression.

About AD 10, the Trinovantes were totally submerged beneath Catuvellaunian domination, and moreover, as if to emphasize the completeness of the conquest, a new Catuvellaunian capital was founded adjacent to, and superseding, that of the Trinovantes at Colchester. From this site, the Catuvellaunian king, Cunobelin, proceeded to expand his empire. By then also, Rome itself had undergone major convulsions. Augustus had emerged as the sole effective ruler in 27 BC, and had attempted to place the Roman empire on a sounder footing. In the west the final submission of Spain and Gaul were secured, and it is said that he even considered taking up the option, left by Caesar, of occupying Britain. If military action was contemplated by Augustus in Britain, it surely would have been in the years leading up to AD 10, with the shattering of Trinovantian security and with Caesar's treaty in ruins. But by then Augustus had other worries, notably the loss in AD 9 of three legions and their general in Germany. It is perhaps rash, but nevertheless interesting, to ackı.ɔwledge the ideal timing of Cunobelin's move to Colchester.

If Augustus was embarrassed by Cunobelin's actions, he could take consolation in the alliance he had much earlier formed with the Atrebatic king, Tincommius, Commius' son and successor. Although Tincommius was expelled from his kingdom, perhaps by his brother Eppillus, the Roman alliance held and seems to have played an important part in Augustus' policy towards Britain. So long as there was a pro-Roman power to balance the unfriendly, if not openly hostile, Catuvellauni, Augustus was saved from taking direct action. Yet Cunobelin's moves can hardly have passed without diplomatic protest.

When Tiberius followed Augustus as emperor, he seems to have pursued the latter's policy and allowed British affairs to drift, taking action neither to prevent further Catuvellaunian expansion, nor to strengthen Atrebatic confidence. Consequently Cunobelin's empire extended over most of Kent and also beyond the Thames into northern Atrebatic territory. Moreover, feelers may already have been put out into the upper Thames valley and into the midlands. Only the Iceni appear to have been immune, but whether from lack of interest on the part of the Catuvellauni or from successful resistance is not known, since little more than border encroachments took place.

Despite the veiled hostility of the Catuvellauni towards Rome, however, trade greatly expanded in the decades leading up to the invasion of AD 43, and the number of Italian, Gallic, German or Spanish traders visiting Britain increased with it. As a by-product, knowledge of British geography and life-styles became more widely disseminated in the Roman world and must increasingly have influenced imperial thinking.

The precedent set by Augustus and followed by Tiberius with regard to Britain seems, during the middle years of the latter's reign, to have been matched by a lull in Catuvellaunian aggression. Cunobelin, perhaps growing older and wiser, and more of a statesman, appeared content with what he held. Perhaps, also, he knew the limits to which he could go before precipitating direct Roman action against him. But in his declining years, especially following the death of Tiberius in AD 37, power was increasingly transferred to his sons. One of these, Adminius, held pro-Roman views; his centre was probably at the old stronghold of Verulamium. Two others, however, Togodumnus and Caratacus, revived the old implacable hostility towards Rome. By the time Gaius had succeeded Tiberius as emperor, this pair had sufficient ascendancy over their father to cause Adminius' expulsion; he fled to Gaius for help and the latter mounted his abortive invasion campaign.

About AD 40, Cunobelin died and his two hot-headed sons succeeded to a position of absolute power, which they proceeded to use in order to expand the Catuvellaunian empire still further. A wedge was driven up the Thames valley into the Cotswolds, so as almost to sever the Dobunni. Here, in newly captured lands a puppet king, Boduoccus, was installed. The pressure which, for many years, had been maintained against the Atrebates was now greatly increased and, apparently without thought of the consequences (for had not Gaius' attempted invasion proved a fiasco?), they captured the last remaining Atrebatic strongholds in southern Sussex and expelled the king, Verica, who like Adminius before him, fled to Rome for help.

Verica was a Roman ally, perhaps even a client king, whose status would have been regulated by treaty. His defeat may well have been judged by the Catuvellauni as a suitable and final revenge for their earlier humiliation by Caesar. For a brief time, Togodumnus and Caratacus must have felt in a commanding position. They ruled all that was worth having in Britain; they were a match even for the Roman empire, which dared not touch them. Indeed, twice in the space of thirty years, Rome had been successfully defied. Catuvellaunian confidence was at its zenith and a demand for the extradition of Verica and his followers went out.

But Gaius had been replaced as emperor by Claudius, and the actions taken by the Roman empire were, more often than not, taken on the varying inclinations of individual emperors. Togodumnus and Caratacus had misjudged their man; Claudius was not Gaius.

The emergence of an entirely hostile power on their north-west frontier presented a new problem to Rome. Necessary retribution had also to be delivered for wrongs done to a Roman ally, for otherwise there would, in future, be little value in such alliances, and Rome then relied on allies to a very great extent to maintain peaceful frontiers.

With the benefit of hindsight, these problems can now be viewed in two ways. It could be argued that when an aggressor, in this case the Roman empire, intends to conquer new territory, a political motive can always be found to justify the necessity of the action. Since Caesar's day, emperors had been periodically contemplating the annexing of Britain. Had the time now come, and was the expulsion of Verica the political expedient for what was in reality a foregone conclusion? Alternatively, the invasion in AD 43 may be seen as the consequence of the coincidence of a number of factors, none of which had all occurred together before and might never have occurred together again. Throughout history, violent events have often been precipitated by just such conjunctions, although one factor alone often acts as the catalyst. Roman thinking may have been to some extent conditioned by the first explanation, but it is probable that in the second lies the real reason for the invasion, and we may consider the coincidental factors.

There had been for a long time in Rome the feeling that Caesar had left unfinished business in Britain, to the point where Britain was sometimes even considered as an unoccupied province of the empire. There was the very real political motive afforded by the expulsion of Verica and the need to inflict punishment on his transgressors. In addition, the occupation of Britain would be one further step towards the annihilation of the Druids, who were a source of much anti-Roman feeling in both Gaul and Britain. There was an emperor who sought military triumph and looked upon a British conquest as an easy and not too expensive way of obtaining it. There were the rumours, no doubt carefully fostered by merchants hoping to reap greater benefits after an occupation, of considerable natural wealth in Britain, especially of precious metals.

But probably the overriding reasons were those connected with the military strategy of the north-west empire. If Britain were to be left in the control of an aggressively anti-Roman power, some means would have had to be found for protecting the north-west frontier from attack. Static defences of the type required to keep out small raiding parties – since an all-out assault by the Catuvellauni need not have been contemplated – are notoriously expensive in terms of manpower. It has been claimed that no more men would have been required for a static frontier force along the Channel than were needed for the British invasion – some 40,000. But calculations based on later frontier requirements indicate that at least 85,000 men would have been needed for effective control of the north-west coast of Gaul. The massing of manpower at even the lesser figure along that coast would, moreover, have had undesirable side-effects. In the first place, large quantities of extra food would have had to have been provided by the Gallic provinces, a task which may have been beyond them, since they already had to feed the Rhine garrisons. Secondly, it would have caused a dangerous imbalance of army power between the western and eastern empire. Augustus had early realized that the key to his power lay in a loyal army, and that an over-large garrison under the command of an unscrupulous governor could be a threat to the emperor's security. This precept was overlooked several times in later years, with disastrous consequences for the Roman empire. But Augustus had initiated a system whereby the main units of the army were carefully spread between the provinces and already, under Claudius, the Rhine army was overweight, being a legacy of Gaius' futile military operations. To have added a Gallic army to it on the Channel coast would have been an act of extreme folly on the part of Claudius. However, the surplus army units on the Rhine could be used to advantage, an overall manpower saving could be effected, the commissariat problem could be solved and the danger of insurrection of an over-large garrison could be avoided, if the invasion of Britain took place, so placing the troops in safety beyond the Channel with an adequate supply of food from fresh sources.

The time was right. The unique conjunction of events had come about. An army consisting of four legions, Legio II, Legio XIV and Legio XX from the Rhine, Legio IX from the upper Danube, together with appropriate auxiliaries and support forces was assembled at Boulogne under the command of Aulus Plautius, recently governor of Pannonia. After a delay caused by a mutiny, the army embarked for Britain.

Chapter 2

Warfare and its Consequences

So far, only one landing place of the Roman army in AD 43 has been positively identified, at Richborough in Kent. There, a fortified beach-head, enclosing about 4 ha. within a double ditch, was constructed to protect them. Somewhere, a little further inland, has still to be found the large temporary camp, perhaps as large as 65 ha., where, after coming ashore, the concentration of troops took place. It may be, also, that detachments of the army landed on different parts of the coast, and one attractive theory has suggested that Verica was reinstated directly in west Sussex by a group detailed to retake his kingdom. Contrarily, it has been argued that the splitting of the invasion army into more than one division would have been bad tactics. Yet a force sent to restore Verica need not have been large, since it was landing in basically friendly territory. Politically and strategically a move of this sort, although possibly a risk, would, if successful, have had far-reaching effects on the Britons. It would be the type of action which, if it prospered, would have earned wide acclaim for the commanding general, but equally, if a failure, a wide degree of odium. There seems, however, little doubt that the principal force landed at Richborough and that the main actions thereafter took place in Kent. After some skirmishes in east Kent and a major battle at the river Medway, the Roman army arrived at the Thames and there awaited the emperor Claudius, as they had been instructed to do.

It would probably have taken Claudius at least six weeks to have reached Britain. It seems inconceivable that Aulus Plautius, having already inflicted serious defeats on the enemy, in one of which Togodumnus was killed, would have waited idly beside the Thames for his arrival. Although Plautius could take no official action which would appear to lessen the importance of Claudius' ultimate victory, a wise commander would have occupied his time in making sure that that same victory would be inevitable. Claudius remained in Britain for only sixteen days, but in that time the Catuvellaunian capital at Colchester was occupied and the surrender of a number of other tribes accepted.

With the departure of Claudius, the campaigns were resumed. Until

Fig. 6 Britain between AD 43 and AD 85

then, the army had fought in concert; now it was split into three battle groups (vexillations), while a fourth remained in reserve in a newly built fortress at Colchester. Each group had a legion at its core, supported by auxiliary cavalry and infantry, and each was commanded in the field by the legionary legate, who would be assisted as necessary, not only by his legionary staff officers, but also by the prefects or tribunes of the auxiliary units.

The legions themselves, at this stage in imperial history, were organized into ten cohorts, every cohort containing six centuries, each commanded by a centurion. A legion was also expected to be a fully self-contained fighting unit and therefore included in its strength a wide variety of specialists such as armourers, clerks, surveyors, medical orderlies, carpenters, stonemasons, hydraulic engineers, glaziers, even shipwrights and river pilots. The total strength was therefore in the region of 6000 men, although the actual fighting strength was probably nearer 5300–5600. All were Roman citizens and in this fact lay the prime distinction between legions and auxiliary regiments.

The Roman army as established in the republican period was composed entirely of citizens. In time, especially after the beginning of the principate, it was realized that the legions were the mainstay of imperial power. Consequently, the number of legions in being was carefully regulated and never exceeded thirty-five in number, seldom enough to guard the ever-widening frontiers. In order, therefore, to supplement the army, it early became the custom to recruit native troops, particularly from the frontier regions. These men did not hold Roman citizenship, although the honour could be conferred on them on discharge, or occasionally on a whole regiment for distinguished service. At first, these regiments were organized in quingeniary units (500 strong), either of cavalry *(ala)*, infantry *(cohors peditata)*, or of mixed composition *(cohors equitata)*. The took their names normally from the region in which they were originally recruited: *cohors VI Thracum equitata* (from Thrace), more rarely from where they were stationed, and occasionally, in the case of *alae*, from the name of their first commander. They were commanded by a Roman officer of the rank of prefect or tribune and were subdivided in the case of infantry units into centuries and in cavalry units into troops.

By the end of the first century, however, larger milliary regiments (1000 strong) were being recruited, although cavalry units of this strength remained rare because they were expensive to maintain. Other, more irregular units of native troops, such as *numeri* and *cunei*, also existed from the second century onwards, but they did not achieve real importance until the later empire, by which time the whole structure of the Roman army had changed radically.

Of the campaigns which followed the capture of Colchester, most is known about that in the south and south-west of Britain. There, Legio II Augusta, commanded by the future emperor Vespasian, had to wage a vicious war against the Durotriges, and another tribe, who had not surrendered to Claudius. Vespasian's biographer gives some details of his victories: the capture of the Isle of Wight and the reduction of over twenty hill-forts. Graphic evidence for some of these battles has come from excavations at the hill-forts of Maiden Castle and Hod Hill. At the former, a direct assault on the east gate had to be mounted before it was captured; at the latter, surrender seems to have been more quickly obtained by opening the attack with an artillery bombardment of *ballistae* (spring-guns) on the chieftain's house.

The two other advances, headed by Legio IX Hispana into the north midlands and by Legio XIV towards the west midlands, probably met less opposition as the territory of the Coritani in which they were moving had almost certainly been surrendered to Claudius at Colchester.

During the advances, the battle groups would have been accommodated in temporary campaign camps, each large enough to contain the whole force. The fortifications were slight, consisting of no more than a low bank surmounted by a palisade and fronted by a small ditch. The leather tents of the men were pitched in the interior. Unfortunately no campaign camps of the invasion period are yet known in south-east Britain, although many have been identified in the midlands, the north and in Wales, where they belong to the activities of later periods.

These initial successes of the army led naturally to a period of consolidation. One of the principal objectives of the invasion, the defeat and occupation of the Catuvellauni and their allies, had been achieved. Tribes friendly to Rome who had suffered from Catuvellaunian aggression, such as the Iceni, Trinovantes, Dobunni and Atrebates, were relieved and refugee princes probably reinstated. It is likely that, at this stage, no further occupation of territory was considered necessary by the Roman high command.

But the newly created province of Britannia had to be protected. It would appear that, in common with practice then in force on other frontiers, the natural boundaries of the rivers Severn and Trent were selected. Behind them was constructed an elaborate system of roads, forts and fortresses to give a deep, fortified zone extending from Devon to Lincolnshire. The main lateral line of communication was the road now known as the Fosse Way, sometimes incorrectly considered the frontier line. The key pivots in this system would have been the three main headquarters of Legio II, Legio XIV and Legio IX. Legio II probably constructed its first base on a site at Lake Farm near Wimborne in Dorset, where a fortress of appropriate size is at present undergoing excavation. Unfortunately, we cannot yet say with certainty where the equivalent base of Legio XIV lay; it may have been near Leicester. A fortress of 10.9 ha. at Longthorpe, Peterborough became the headquarters probably for Legio IX not later than AD 48; it is not yet known if it was preceded by one elsewhere.

These early vexillation fortresses, as they are best called, are a comparatively recent discovery in Roman Britain. Apart from those mentioned above, the sites of others, dating to the middle of the first

Fig. 7 Legionary fortresses at: a) Inchtuthil; b) Chester; c) Caerleon; d) Longthorpe

century, are known in outline. Excavations at Lake Farm and more especially at Longthorpe show that they lack the standardized planning of legionary fortresses of the late first and second centuries. They vary in size from 8–12 ha. and consequently could not accommodate a complete legion, which would normally require an area of 18–20 ha. It is most likely, therefore, that these fortresses represented a flexible approach on the part of the high command to the problem of British defence, accommodating the regional headquarters, a stores depot and quarters for a mixed force of legionaries and auxiliaries not stationed in minor forts elsewhere, and therefore providing a mobile reserve.

Scale

| 0 | 100 | 200 | 300 | 400 | 500 | 600 | 700 m |

| 0 | 500 | 1000 | 1500 | 2000 ft |

Rampart ━━ Ditch ▨ Quarry pit ▱

Fig. 8 Iron Age hill-fort at Hod Hill, with Roman fort in north-west corner

The fortress at Longthorpe was defended by twin parallel ditches and a turf or earth rampart, probably surmounted by a timber breast-work. The four gates were timber-framed; each had two carriageways flanked by projecting towers. The internal buildings, of which the headquarters building at the centre, some granaries, stores buildings and legionary and auxiliary barracks have been identified, were likewise constructed round timber frames, with the walling completed with interwoven wattle plastered with mud, or daub. This type of construction was invariably employed by the Roman army in Britain until the end of the first century, and less often later. The system had the advantage of flexibility, since many of the building-frames could be prefabricated and, if necessary, transferred from one site to another as the need arose, or stockpiled in a central depot. It does, however, imply the availability of an ample supply of seasoned timber, and the implications of this element of Roman army duties are considered below in Chapter 5.

Apart from the three main regional bases mentioned above, and in addition to the legionary fortress at Colchester, there were numerous auxiliary forts planted in the frontier region. Structurally they were similar to these bases, but were planned to suit the forces in garrison. A degree of nonconformity can therefore be expected according to whether they were constructed for legionary or auxiliary infantry, or cavalry detachments, or combinations of one with another.

One of the best-known forts of this period is that constructed in an unusual position in the north-west corner of the Iron Age hill-fort at Hod Hill. It contained a headquarters block, houses for two senior officers commanding, respectively, a legionary cohort and half a quingeniary cavalry regiment, and the necessary barracks, stabling and other ancillary buildings. Although the legionary detachment as a whole, being composed of citizens, would have taken precedence over the cavalry unit, the prefect of the latter would have ranked higher than a legionary centurion and would consequently have commanded the fort. These arrangements are reflected by the placing of the legionary barracks in the front half of the fort together with the more spacious house of the cavalry prefect.

Other forts of this general type are known at Great Casterton, near Stamford, Waddon Hill, on the Dorset coast near Bridport, Cirencester, and many other places in the frontier zone. They were served by a number of coastal supply bases such as Poole, London, Fishbourne, near Chichester, Fingrinhoe in Essex and Richborough, where the invasion beach-head was converted for this purpose by the construction of granaries. In the carriage of supplies inland use would not only have been made of the developing road system, but also of suitable rivers.

Within the new British province then set up, most of which was under military government, special administrative arrangements were, however, made in two areas: the client kingdoms of the Iceni and Atrebates, in East Anglia and southern England respectively.

Ever since mid republican days, Rome had made use of native monarchs both within and outside the boundaries of provinces. Such rulers, in return for protection, were allowed to retain a subordinate 'freedom', the level of which depended much on the strength of the individual kings. They were expected to be friendly allies, who would not treat with Rome's enemies. During Augustus' principate they were

Fig. 9 Forts at: a) Gelligaer; b) Fendoch; c) Mumrills; d) The Lunt;
e) Chesters

also being used to govern territory otherwise too difficult or too incon-
venient to administer directly. In essence, their creation and retention
was an economy on the part of the imperial government, saving manpower much needed elsewhere. In this respect, it is important to
remember that no great army of civil servants moved into Britain in the
wake of the invasion. During the first and second centuries the provincial administration was always small and, within closely prescribed
limits, the native people were allowed, indeed expected, to run their
own affairs (see below, Chapter 5).

It is probable that agreements made with the rulers, although incorporating certain basic precedents, varied from individual to individual; consequently, in the absence of firm evidence, it is difficult to envisage the arrangements made between the imperial administration and the Iceni and the Atrebates. It is possible to argue that the realm of the Atrebates under Verica's successor, Cogidubnus, became a client kingdom within the province, while that of the Iceni, first under Antedius, later under Prasutagus, and with its extensive coastal boundary on the North Sea, remained outside the provincial boundary. But in both the kings would have been expected to maintain order, to collect tribute and probably to provide a quota of recruits for the Roman army. Had these areas been dealt with in the same way as the rest of the province, extra garrisons would have been required. So, the effect of creating these client kingdoms, in ostensibly reliable territory, was to achieve an economy of manpower and the saving of trouble for the provincial governor and his small staff.

Roman strategy towards Britain began to show signs of weakness in the decades following the invasion. In the first place, Caratacus, sometime ruler of the Catuvellauni, had escaped from the campaigns of Aulus Plautius, found new allies in Wales and was clearly intent on carrying on the war. Although the queen of the tribe of the Brigantes in north Britain, Cartimandua, was a professed ally of Rome, she was unable to maintain peace there and was ultimately expelled as the result of civil war.

Although Caratacus was, in the end, captured with the aid of Cartimandua in AD 51, hostility continued in Wales and the north throughout that and the following decade. A number of campaigns were mounted, especially in Wales, but they were mostly ineffective, except in purely limited terms. Changes had also been made in military dispositions. The army had evacuated the immediate south-eastern area of Britain, in order to provide the necessary forces to extend the fortified frontier zone up to the Welsh border. This move had, in turn, led to the establishment of a purely civilian administration in the evacuated areas and included the foundation of the first Roman *colonia* at Colchester, a chartered town, for discharged legionary veterans.

Strife inside the province was not unknown and the traumatic experience of the Boudiccan rebellion in AD 60 nearly caused its loss. The pressures which erupted in that year had been growing for some time. An abortive rebellion by the Iceni a decade or so earlier had been caused by their compulsory disarmament, when they clearly considered themselves still a free people. The Trinovantes, freed from Catuvellaunian control, found to their surprise that their old capital was not to be returned to them. It was absorbed in the new *colonia* at

Colchester and, instead, they were fobbed off with a new site at Chelmsford which they did not want. It is probable also that a new generation of Catuvellaunians were growing up eager to revenge their earlier defeats. Harsh and unrealistic taxes and compulsory expenditure were being exacted. It only needed an excuse for violence and the rest would follow automatically.

The excuse came with death of the client king of the Iceni, Prasutagus, and the decision to absorb his tribe into the province. Moreover, Prasutagus, hoping to ensure the succession of his wife Boudicca, unwisely made the emperor Nero co-heir in his will. Nero often considered a half-share of an estate as evidence of ingratitude on the part of the testator and usually ended by taking all. To this mixture was then added the arrogance of the officers sent to secure the inheritance and incorporate the kingdom into the province. No doubt also they were met with equal arrogance from the Icenian royal household. Arrogance and inflexibility led directly to violence. The rebellion had started.

The absence of the governor, Suetonius Paullinus, with a large part of the army in north Wales, meant that at first the rebels were entirely successful. They sacked the new towns of Colchester, London and Verulamium and inflicted a major defeat on the nearest army unit, Legio IX. But the outcome must, to some extent, have been a foregone conclusion. A native rabble, no matter how large, was seldom a match for the ordered discipline of the Roman army, providing the encounter took place in relatively open country. Suetonius Paullinus gathered what forces he could and selected a good site for the battle, variously placed somewhere along Watling Street between Towcester and Atherstone. The rebels were defeated and fled in disorder; it is recorded that Boudicca committed suicide. Then followed a punitive expedition in East Anglia, only stopped when it was feared that future imperial revenue would be seriously depleted.

The consequences were far-reaching. The Iceni, deprived of much of their land, appear never to have fully recovered, always remaining a poor and backward area. The grievances of the Trinovantes seem partly to have been met by a local reorganization which enabled them to renew the use of their old capital as a religious centre. Overall, the Roman attitude to the native Britons was perhaps slightly softened.

A further consequence was the stalemate situation forced upon the Roman army, which lasted to AD69. No governor, acting either from his own inspiration or from official orders, was prepared to undertake the risk of removing garrisons from areas where open rebellion had flared so recently in order to subjugate and occupy Wales. Some must have realized the need to settle the Welsh problem, but were denied the extra army units required for its successful completion. Some had also realized that the original Severn-Trent frontier, facing hostile forces on two fronts, was no longer tenable. The time had come for a radical reassessment of the province's needs.

This reassessment was unfortunately delayed by a serious civil war in the empire, following the suicide of Nero. Within little more than a year three emperors were created in succession, only to be removed with equal rapidity. Finally Vespasian, then commanding an army in Judaea, succeeded where the others had failed.

The principate of Vespasian saw a new and more vigorous policy begun in Britain. In succession three governors, Petillius Cerealis, Julius Frontinus and Julius Agricola, completed the occupation of Wales and advanced the northern frontier to the fringes of the Scottish highlands. Of the three governors, the last, Cnaeus Julius Agricola, is perhaps deservedly the best known, as the result of the biography left by his son-in-law, Tacitus; it was Agricola who placed the seal on the Roman occupation of Britain.

But before the military occupation of Wales and the north could take place, troops in garrison in the midlands had to be released for service. In consequence, this period saw not only the extension of the frontiers in Britain, but also the consolidation, under civilian administration, of what is usually referred to as the civil zone of the province: an area bounded by the Welsh border on the west and the Trent-Dee line approximately on the north (see Chapter 5 below). Beyond these limits, military government was still firmly ensconced, based on a series of new forts and fortresses.

In the period before Vespasian became emperor, various changes in military dispositions, including the temporary removal of Legio XIV, had led to the foundation of new legionary fortresses at such places as Lincoln, Wroxeter, Gloucester and Exeter. Now, hand in hand with the fresh advances a new generation of fortresses were required in addition to numerous auxiliary forts, and work started at York, Caerleon, Chester and Inchtuthil – the most northerly of all. The logistic problems facing these governors must have been formidable when it is remembered that apart from the fortresses just mentioned, at least eighty new auxiliary forts were constructed as well as over 3000 km. of new roads. The implications of these figures are considered more fully below (Chapters 5 and 6).

Although some forts were still being constructed, as in the earlier period, for mixed units or regiments, most now became standardized on a basic layout, making use occasionally of innovations to increase the strength of the fortifications. In general, however, the materials of construction – wood, earth, turf, wattle and daub – remained the same;

nevertheless, masonry was appearing regularly for building bath-houses. Examples of military construction of this period are the legionary fortress at Inchtuthil on the river Tay, probably built by, and for, Legio XX, and the auxiliary fort at Fendoch at the entrance to the Sma' Glen further south.

The fortress at Inchtuthil is exceptional in having no modern buildings obscuring any part of it, for it lies in open meadow-land beside the river. Moreover, since the fortress was only occupied for a short time, its excavated remains were not confused by later alterations to buildings, and it presents a single-phase plan almost unique in the empire. The defences, consisting of a single ditch and a stone wall backed by a turf rampart, enclosed an almost square area of just over 21 ha. The fortifications were pierced by double-span gates, one to each side. Within the fortress the regular planning of the streets can be observed with the headquarters building in the centre. Other buildings which have been identified are granaries, a large workshop, a hospital, a drill-shed, staff officers' houses, and numerous store sheds. The barracks are arranged in ten groups of six representing the ten cohorts of the legion and their six constituent centuries. It is interesting that the commanding legate's house was never constructed, although the site for it beside the headquarters block had been levelled and prepared. Internal provisions for the distribution of fresh water had been made, although they had never been connected to an aqueduct; drainage was also taken care of. Outside the fortress to the south-east lay a small bath-house of masonry. There was, in addition, an external stores compound containing a barrack and an office block.

The auxiliary fort at Fendoch, built for a milliary cohort of infantry, presents, as might be expected, many of the features of the legionary fortress but in a miniature and simplified form. The headquarters block, the commandant's house, the hospital, two granaries, stores and workshops and ten barracks, one for each century, can readily be identified within the regular street plan. Here, provision for piped running water was completed and adequate arrangements for drainage were also made. Cooking-ovens, a considerable fire-risk in a fort constructed largely of wood, were placed against the back of the rampart.

The military system of which this fortress and fort were a part was not destined to last for long without change. Within ten years of Agricola completing his dispositions in Britain, events elsewhere in the empire enforced changes. With no central reserve of troops, Domitian, who was now emperor, could only turn to peaceful provinces for reinforcements. Britain was peaceful and had to provide one legion, Legio II Adjutrix, which had earlier replaced Legio XIV, and numbers of auxiliaries for campaigns in Dacia and Moesia. Although Wales could still be held, the northern frontier had to be drawn back, first to the Forth-Clyde line and ultimately, by about AD 105, to the Tyne-Solway line, so that all lowland Scotland was abandoned. This last withdrawal may have been caused partly by a renewed call for reinforcements from Britain by the emperor Trajan and partly by enemy action, as some forts, including Corbridge, a fort on the river Tyne, were burnt. For the next decade the northern frontier of Britain must have remained in a state of uneasy peace.

This same decade, however, also saw the consolidation of the three remaining, principal army bases in Britain – the legionary fortresses at York, Chester and Caerleon for Legio IX, Legio XX and Legio II Augusta respectively. The defences were made stronger and more permanent by the addition of stout masonry walls, equipped with internal towers, while inside buildings were also reconstructed in masonry. A number of auxiliary forts were treated similarly. The decision to carry out this work must have represented, yet again, a radical reappraisal of the military requirements of the British province. The replacement of prefabricated, easily dismantled, timber-framed buildings by permanent masonry structures can only indicate that the period of mobile warfare, of conquest and advance was considered to be over for the foreseeable future. Static defence increasingly came to replace mobile attack, and these changes are inevitably reflected in military architecture and strategy.

The end of this decade, which coincided with the death of Trajan and the accession of Hadrian as emperor, was marked by a serious war in northern Britain. It was, however, successfully concluded and in AD 122, Hadrian himself visited Britain as part of an extended tour of the provinces. By now, also, the idea of linear fortified frontiers to replace garrisoned zones defending natural barriers was gaining ground, having been tried in Germany and Moesia under Domitian. Probably because of the more hostile and unsettled nature of northern Britain, it was decided to build a much stronger barrier, stronger indeed than anywhere else in the empire.

Hadrian's Wall seems closely to have followed the earlier line of Trajan's frontier, since some isolated watch-towers of earlier build than the Wall itself have been identified. As first envisaged, the new frontier was to consist of a masonry wall equipped with small fortlets at every mile – milecastles – with two turrets between each pair, and with the whole work fronted by a large ditch. To the rear were a number of garrison forts connected by the road known as the Stanegate. Work started in AD 122, under the governor A. Platorius Nepos, and proceeded westwards from Newcastle. Its construction, however, caused considerable irritation to the tribes it was intended to separate, those to

Legend:
- ★ Legionary fortress
- ▲ Fort
- × Probable fort
- ||||| Military zone
- Roads
- Civitates
- Coloniae

0   100   200 Km

Fig. 10 Hadrianic frontiers, civitates and roads

the south being as hostile as those to the north, so much so that, by the
time it was finished, many modifications had been incorporated. Chief
among them were the removal of the garrisons from the rear to the Wall

itself, the reduction in thickness of the barrier west of the North Tyne from 3 m. to just under 2.5 m., the extension of the Wall eastwards from Newcastle to Wallsend and ultimately the completion in turf of the section westwards from the river Irthing. In places also the digging of the ditch in front of the Wall proved impossible or unnecessary owing to the hardness of the rock or the presence of cliffs. Moreover, since building work was carried out in short lengths by gangs from the three British legions, II, VI and XX, it proceeded at a somewhat uneven pace from one part to another. Consequently the frontier, when completed in its first stage, must have presented a decidedly patchwork appearance. Travelling from east to west, one would see first a length of narrow wall, 2.5 m. wide, from Wallsend to Newcastle, then the wide wall, 3 m. wide, as far as the North Tyne. From there to the river Irthing, the narrow wall lay atop the wide foundation, as work on laying the foundations had proceeded faster than the building of the superstructure. From the river Irthing to its termination at Bowness-on-Solway, construction was of turf with, as elsewhere, forts and turrets of masonry, but with the milecastles built of turf and wood instead of stone.

A number of reasons have been argued for these alterations, notably that a geological fault west of the Irthing caused a complete lack of readily available limestone to burn for mortar. Yet this factor seems only partly to explain the change from masonry to turf and does nothing to account for the narrowing of the masonry wall. Ultimately, the turf wall was replaced by masonry, so the supply of mortar was not an insuperable problem. The main cause would seem to lie in speed; it became increasingly necessary to hasten the work and economies had to be made. It is known that the greatest threat was posed at the west end of the barrier for there was placed the senior officer on the frontier, commanding a milliary ala of cavalry at Stanwix. Such units were rare in the Roman army; only one is known to have served in Britain, so they were placed where need was greatest. Moreover, the frontier itself in this part was strengthened by the placing of three outpost forts at Birrens, Netherby and Bewcastle, to give advanced warning of attacks. In addition the western flank beyond the end of the Wall was protected by a series of mileforts, towers and forts extending along the Cumberland coast. Between Bowness and Cardurnock the mileforts seem to have been placed between parallel ditches and stockades for extra protection, a system somewhat reminiscent of the German frontier.

Once the garrison forts, fifteen in number, had been sited on the Wall, a military zone was marked out to the rear by means of an earthwork known as the Vallum, a ditch running between two parallel mounds of earth and turf. Hardly defensive in structure, it was probably intended to mark a prohibited area for the local natives. A military road, giving lateral communication between the forts and milecastles, ran within this zone.

The forts of Hadrian's Wall were constructed throughout in masonry, with their size and the nature of their buildings dictated by the type of unit occupying them. In one respect, however, some differed from the normal pattern to be expected for such forts. Those in which cavalry regiments were stationed were so planned that the whole front part of the fort, including three of the gates, projected beyond the line of barrier, to enable rapid deployment of the troops in the outfield. Consequently an extra pair of gates had to be introduced in the rear of the fort to accommodate the military way. The milecastles contained at most two small barracks, with gates to front and rear, while the turrets would have provided shelter for patrols and facilities for signalling.

It is perhaps appropriate to review at this point the strength of the Roman army in Britain, since the garrisons for the new frontier were obtained by withdrawing regiments from south Wales and northern England. In doing this, Hadrian probably took a calculated gamble, removing military control completely from the tribal territories of the Silures, Demetae and Parisi and partly from Brigantia: east of the Pennines. The counterpart of this move, would, as before, have required the setting up of suitable local civilian authorities.

The army in Britain underwent considerable changes in composition between the times of Claudius and Hadrian. Reinforcements of legionaries and ten auxiliary regiments were brought to Britain after the Boudiccan rebellion, but the overall garrison strength was probably temporarily reduced before, and again at the time of, the Civil War in AD 69, when Legio XIV finally departed from Britain. Its place was taken in the early 70s by Legio II Adjutrix which, however, was withdrawn again, together with auxiliaries, by AD 90. Further temporary withdrawals, or exchanges, of auxiliary units took place towards the end of the first or the beginning of the second century, followed almost immediately by the arrival of reinforcements. By AD 122, Legio VI had arrived in Britain, ultimately to replace Legio IX, and for a long time it was considered that the latter had either been destroyed or disgraced during the war of AD 117. But evidence more recently obtained, although still tenuous, suggests that it was withdrawn from Britain, possibly before that war, to reside for a short time in Holland before probably being sent to an eastern province to perish ultimately in the Jewish rebellion of AD 132. The army in Britain under Hadrian, therefore, consisted of three legions and probably something of the order of fifteen milliary and fifty quingeniary auxiliary regiments, giving a total of about 53,000 men, an overall increase of perhaps

Fig. 11 Antonine frontiers

Key:
* — Legionary fortress
Δ — Fort 140 - 158
♦ — Fort 140 - 200
▲ — Fort 165 - 200
? — Probable occupation
● — Naval base

≡ Military zone 140 - 158
||| Military zone 165 - 200
~ 100 m contour

0   100   200 Km

10,000 since the Claudian army landed in Britain. Moreover, it was an increase which had been brought about solely by auxiliaries at the expense of the legions and indicates the changing relative importance accorded to these two fighting arms, a change which, in time, altered the whole structure of the Roman army.

The frontier of Hadrian is generally accorded to have been a tactical success but a strategical and political failure, since, although it could

control the troublesome tribes of south-west Scotland and northern
England, it was politically divisive and it was too distant from the
warlike people of Caledonia. Its completion, about AD 130, seems to
have been marked by a renewal of serious hostilities, in which the
Brigantes were involved, in addition probably to tribes beyond the
frontier. Certainly forts in the north-eastern Pennines were reoccupied
at this time, and an experienced general, Julius Severus, was sent to
govern Britain.

The death of Hadrian and the accession of Antoninus Pius in AD 139
brought with it a review of the British northern frontier, which acknowledged its strategic weakness, and the decision to reoccupy lowland
Scotland was taken. Lollius Urbicus, the governor appointed to the
task, had won the necessary victory over the Scottish tribes by AD 143 to
enable him to establish the new frontier controls on the Forth-Clyde
line, the narrowest neck of land in the whole of mainland Britain. Twice
before in the first century the northern frontier had rested there. It was
not, therefore, unknown country. Yet, when construction took place, a
reversion to earlier, almost obsolete, techniques somewhat surprisingly
occurred. The barrier itself was built of turf laid on an unmortared,
cobble foundation, with a massive ditch in front of it, while in the forts a
combination of structural techniques employed masonry, turf, timber
and clay. As with Hadrian's Wall, the work was carried out entirely by
detachments of the three legions then present in Britain.

The other chief differences between the old and new frontiers can be
summarized briefly. The Antonine barrier possessed no continuous
system of milecastles and probably no turrets. The garrison forts were
placed much closer together, there being nineteen forts and at least
three fortlets spread over about half the distance of the earlier frontier.
A number of these forts are, however, of substandard size and their
internal arrangements show some variation. It is probable that manpower shortages were compelling the Roman command to split units
between two or three small forts. The same economies were practised in
lowland Scotland which, once more within the empire, required garrisons. Again the stations in Wales and Brigantia were thinned, since the
overall size of the provincial army had not changed appreciably since
the Hadrianic period.

The methods and materials used on the new frontier might be taken
to imply the construction of only a temporary barrier, perhaps as an
experiment. For a hundred years now, the Roman army had been
attempting to find, often at great cost, a stable northern frontier in
Britain, which could be held without too great a drain on manpower.
No less than six different positions had been successively tried; none
had so far provided the answer. It would not be extraordinary, there-

Fig. 12 Fortlets at: a) Chew Green; b) Bar Hill; c) Poltross Burn milecastle

fore, if the line of the new Scottish frontier was viewed with some cautious reserve and the greatest economy practised in its construction. Would a further forward movement be possible, or would a withdrawal to the Hadrianic line prove necessary? For the time being, the Hadrianic frontier was freely opened, with new crossing-places being made over the Vallum and with gates removed from milecastles. The forts, however, were kept in good order, perhaps indicating yet another of the uncertainties in the minds of the army staff.

There are, perhaps, some slight suggestions of a forward movement. At least four earlier Agricolan forts were reoccupied between the Forth and the Tay. But it may be that they were intended as no more than outpost forts, of the type used at the western end of Hadrian's Wall.

The new frontier appears to have held until the early 150s, when, as frequently happened, events within the province and not pressure from outside, compelled its abandonment.

In AD 154, a serious rebellion in Brigantia took place. The effect was immediate and could only be met by a planned withdrawal from Scotland. A new governor, Julius Verus, was sent to Britain with reinforcements for all three legions in Britain; he succeeded in stabilizing the situation. His governorship saw the recommissioning of Hadrian's Wall and the rebuilding of some forts further south in Brigantia as might be expected.

The rebellion settled and the Brigantes under firmer military control, the return to Scotland was made, probably in AD 159–60. But the reoccupation of Scotland coupled with that of Brigantia placed intolerable strains on the already stretched manpower. By about AD 163 withdrawal from the Antonine Wall had again taken place, and Hadrian's Wall once more became the accepted frontier, served as before by outpost forts which were now increased in number.

The last half of the second century was a turbulent period in Britain. Apart from the events detailed above, there was possibly a revolt in Wales and further assaults on the northern frontier took place, in one of which the Antonine Wall may have been partly reoccupied and in another Hadrian's Wall itself may have been breached. The century terminated, however, in an altogether more serious disaster.

The emperor Commodus was assassinated in AD 192, and there broke out in the empire another civil war, in which the governor of Britain, Clodius Albinus, was a contestant. By AD 196 he and Septimius Severus were the only survivors in the struggle and Albinus must have realized that he could not succeed to the purple by remaining in Britain. Accordingly he collected together the army in Britain and crossed to Gaul where, near Lyons, he was defeated by the superior legionary strength of Severus.

In the meantime, northern Britain had been invaded, the hill-men of Brigantia had again rebelled, in addition probably to some tribes in Wales. They set on the empty forts and burnt them to the ground, and in places even dismantled the Wall itself. Knowing little of imperial politics, they probably considered that the hated invader had departed for good; they could not wait to start removing the most obvious traces of the occupation.

Among the sites which suffered equally were the civilian villages, the *vici*, which had in many cases grown up alongside forts. This process had been a natural one, although regulated by the Roman army. The local population, with an eye to the main chance, early realized that the soldiers were far wealthier than their fellow natives, and hastened to

Buried features visible on aerial photographs
• Well
—·—·— Modern fences

Fig. 13 Vicus at Housesteads

turn this wealth to their own account. They could supply goods and
services not normally catered for in the military regime, and to do so
built themselves shops, houses and workshops as close to the forts as
was permitted by the local commander. So thriving settlements had
grown, sometimes to be given a purely local autonomy to run their
affairs. In the south, where military occupation had ceased in the last
decades of the first century, many of these villages had been developed
to form sizeable towns, capable of independent existence and growth,
long after the initial reason for their presence had gone.

In the north and in Wales many of these villages had grown in close
juxtaposition to forts. Even during the short occupation of the Antonine

*   Legionary fortress

▲   Fort

?   Probable occupation

■   Shore fort

●   Naval base

◊   Walled town

‒‒‒   **100**m contour

0   100   200 Km

Fig. 14 Third-century Britain

Wall properly constituted vici had been established. Their inhabitants were people determined to make the best of things under an alien rule, and even after Scotland had been evacuated, goods from the province continued to circulate, for people there had acquired a taste, in that short time, for Roman-style pottery, metalwork, coinage and other products. But the pacifying effects of trade were not fully to be felt until the fourth century.

During the second century these northern villages were rudimentary affairs with simple, timber-framed buildings providing the necessary accommodation. Neither were they, except in one or two instances, of great extent, usually with the shops and houses lining one or more of the roads leading to the fort. For protection they relied on the neighbouring troops; with those removed, as in AD 197, they suffered the same fate as the forts. Yet, with the recovery of Britain in the early third century and, additionally, because of constitutional changes then introduced, these villages were refounded and prospered, being provided with good masonry buildings, proper streets and other amenities, and often grew to considerable size.

Severus restored order in Britain by degrees. It was no easy matter and ultimately required the presence of the new emperor, who set up his headquarters at York in AD 208. By then, most of the wrecked military installations in Britain up to the Wall and its outposts had been restored. There followed a series of ineffective campaigns aimed at punishing the Caledonians. There may have been some intention to reoccupy parts of southern Scotland, and a new fortress, about 13 ha. in extent, was built at Carpow on the Tay apparently for a vexillation of Legio VI. Severus was, however, a sick man and he died at York in AD 211, to be succeeded by his elder son, Caracalla, who was with him in Britain. Despite hostile accounts of Caracalla's actions in the province, which may indeed conceal the truth, it was he who brought the Caledonian war to a successful conclusion, imposing terms which were acceptable to both sides. Their effectiveness can be judged by the almost unbroken period of peace on the northern frontier which followed and which lasted until the end of the third century. These actions also effectively stilled the Brigantes. Since their first major defeat at the hands of Petillius Cerealis in the early 70s, almost every new generation that arose made its attempt to throw out the Roman army, resulting, as we have seen, in a series of costly wars throughout the second century.

Other important changes also occurred at this time. In order to prevent a provincial governor, commanding a large army, from being hailed as a pretender, the British province was split in two – Britannia Superior and Britannia Inferior. Superior contained London, Caerleon and Chester, and its governor, of consular rank, had control of two legions and some auxiliaries in Wales. Inferior included a capital at York, Lincoln and the northern frontier, and its governor, of lower, praetorian rank, commanded only one legion, but many more auxiliaries. Similar divisions were made in Syria and Pannonia.

A further change, of even greater significance for the two new provinces, was the proclamation by Caracalla, in 212, that all free-born men and women should be Roman citizens. This immediately demolished many of the distinctions which had existed between legions and auxiliary regiments and between chartered and non-chartered towns. In many cases it increased the taxes payable to the imperial government, but also conferred privileges. Moreover, serving soldiers were now legally allowed to marry and also to hold land which could be farmed. This last provision exercised the greatest benefit on the northern vici, since soldiers could now buy farms or houses with the prospect of retirement and, in some cases, were even given grants of land. It was only slowly, however, that these constitutional innovations produced any visible effects, but it is probably right to say that they were ultimately responsible for altering the whole character of the empire.

The successful pacification of northern Britain has, nevertheless, to be viewed in conjunction with a growing threat to another part of the province. Seemingly from the late second century, there had been the menace of piratical marauders on the east coast. Coming mostly from northern Germany, they were probably at first only a threat to the considerable volume of coastal shipping plying between the continent and rich centres like York and London. Growing bolder, they may from time to time have landed on the coast and plundered where they could. Hitherto, the British fleet had been stationed at ports on both sides of the Channel, chiefly at Boulogne, Dover and Lympne, although east coast bases at Rochester, Caistor-by-Yarmouth and Brough-on-Humber were probably also used. With the increasing threat to coastal shipping in the North Sea, greater emphasis was placed on the latter sites, and the defences were further strengthened by the provision of forts for auxiliary garrisons at appropriate points, presumably to deal with any raiders who had managed to escape the sea-patrols and make a landing.

A glance at a physical map of Britain will show that there are three main points of entry on the eastern seaboard of Britain: the Thames, the Wash and the Humber. Together they give access to river systems which penetrate the whole of central Britain from the North Downs to the Pennines and stretching almost to the Welsh Border. Here lay the danger points which had to be protected. Accordingly, new masonry forts were constructed at Reculver on the north Kent shore and probably also at Brancaster, on the Norfolk side of the Wash, in the early third century. Furthermore, the naval base at Brough-on-Humber was rationalized in size and provided with fresh defences of turfwork and new internal buildings of masonry.

The forts at Reculver and Brancaster represent developments in

P	Principia	M	Medieval Structures
B	Baths	R	Roman Features

Fig. 15 Saxon Shore forts at: a) Reculver; b) Richborough; c) Pevensey; d) Burgh

military architecture introduced to meet changing conditions. They are larger than the normal auxiliaries' forts of the second century, about 3 ha. in area, and therefore probably accommodated naval units as well as the cohorts or alae assigned to them. The gates are smaller, normally containing only one portal.

By the middle of the third century, the whole empire was approaching a state of anarchy. A succession of emperors was put forward by the garrisons of different provinces and the civil war and strife which resulted seriously undermined the structure of society. In addition, a series of barbarian invasions damaged many provinces, including Gaul and Germany, while mounting monetary inflation caused chaos to the economy. Yet, to a great extent, Britain stayed remote from all these convulsions, with the exception of inflation. Outwardly, the resulting loss of confidence in the central government was seemingly expressed in a reluctance to spend money, and little new building work took place. For a time, between AD 259 and 274, Britain, together with Spain, became part of the independent Gallic empire, but this secession can hardly have altered the daily life of the provinces concerned.

Soon after the middle of the century, the earlier threat to the east coast reached more serious proportions, and work was now started on additional forts to combat the menace. For a start, the great triumphal monument, erected at Richborough late in the first century to com-memorate the addition of the British province to the empire, was stripped of its ornaments and trophies to become a lookout tower against sea-raiders. It was surrounded by a rampart and triple ditches for protection, but before the work had been completed, the plans were changed and a large rectangular masonry fort was erected on the site. Other similar forts were started in East Anglia and on the south coast, so that by the time Carausius, a prefect of the British fleet specifically appointed to combat piracy, rebelled and proclaimed himself emperor in Britain, a considerable chain of coastal forts had been established, later to be known as the Saxon Shore defences.

Carausius seems to have received popular support not only in Britain but also in Gaul and Germany. He stemmed the inflationary cycle by a new issue of better quality coins and apparently reduced the activities of sea-raiders.

But the manpower crisis worsened during the third century. Never easily resolved, it had probably been exacerbated by a number of serious epidemic diseases and by civil war and rebellion. Increasingly, therefore, the Roman army was being strengthened, and at the same time diluted, by troops recruited even more from beyond the frontiers. Particularly in the western provinces they came from free Germany. Their training was undoubtedly poorer and discipline more lax. Today they would be called foreign mercenaries and they probably enlisted more from a desire to obtain as much as they could for themselves, including land settlements, than to protect the empire. Their presence in the Roman army, although necessary due to circumstances beyond imperial control, had a weakening effect.

At about the same time as Carausius took office in Britain, Diocletian had become emperor in Rome and succeeded in reuniting the empire, except for Britain, under his control. He suppressed anarchy, defeated invaders and put down rebellions. His main failure was his inability to defeat Carausius; his chief value was as an administrator. He early realized that the burden of running an increasingly complex empire was too great for one man to carry, so he appointed Maximianus, a colleague, as co-Augustus with special responsibility for the western provinces, while he, himself, remained in charge in the east. From this act grew the system known as the Tetrarchy, whereby each Augustus appointed a Caesar as heir and after a number of years abdicated in his favour, so hoping to ensure a peaceful and smooth succession instead of civil war.

In the west, Maximianus appointed Constantius Chlorus as Caesar, and it was he who, in the end, retook Britain after Carausius had been murdered. When Constantius Chlorus led the expedition to Britain, he was met by an army taken mainly from the northern garrisons. As in AD 196 when troops had been withdrawn, so in AD 296, an invasion occurred in which the Picts, by which name some Caledonian tribes were now known, inflicted damage to the frontier installations and villages. There followed the usual programme of punitive expeditions and restorations, in which damage from neglect was also made good. With the return of Britain to the empire confidence was restored and prosperity returned.

Among other administrative reforms, introduced by Diocletian to shore up the disintegrating fragments of empire, were many that touched Britain. Civil and military commands were now separated; the governor of a province was no longer commander-in-chief, but only head of a burgeoning civil service, which was greatly expanded, since many of the tasks, once left voluntarily in the hands of responsible classes of society, or carried out by army staff, were now assumed by career civil servants organized in a carefully graded hierarchy.

When Constantius Chlorus, now senior Augustus, died at York in AD 306, his son was hailed emperor in his place. Within six years the Tetrarchy was at an end and Constantine virtually undisputed sole ruler of the whole empire. It was probably then that Britain was again divided, this time into four provinces, each with a governor, but under the unified diocesan control of a *vicarius,* who, in turn, was responsible to the pretorian prefect of Gaul. It is usually assumed that Britannia Superior became Maxima Caesariensis and Britannia Prima, with London and Cirencester as their respective capitals, while Britannia Inferior became Flavia Caesariensis and Britannia Secunda, with capitals at York and Lincoln. Other provinces were similarly subdivided in the early fourth century, a process which must have led to a multiplication of posts in the imperial civil service. Indeed, we might be forgiven for wondering if, as today, some of the multiplication was caused by the necessity of providing an adequate career structure for the growing number of government officials, for only in that way would there have been enough senior posts to make promotion possible.

Constantine's reign was a long one, lasting until AD 337, and, as far as Britain was concerned, apparently peaceful. After his death, however, events began to take a graver turn. Renewed attacks seem to have been made on the northern frontier, while increased activity in the Saxon Shore forts, together with the addition of another at Pevensey, suggests that Saxon raiders were again becoming more than a nuisance; it was probably then that these coastal defences were reorganized under a new officer, the Count of the Saxon Shore. It is also possible that units of the mobile field army, a comparatively new introduction, were now in Britain. They were normally billeted in towns and so have left little evidence for their presence, although a unit may for a time have been stationed at Catterick.

The fort at Pevensey was the last major addition to the Saxon Shore. These forts, as already indicated above, showed marked differences from earlier auxiliary forts. Most were larger and often, as in the case of Dover and Pevensey, irregular in shape. Composite stone walls and earth banks were, in all the later examples, replaced by defences of massive masonry walls up to 4.5 m. thick; square angles replaced rounded corners. The gates were narrow and, at some, of unusual design; they were normally protected by massive external towers. Similar towers of varying patterns projected also from the lines of the walls, to provide better deployment of artillery, now used to enfilade the entire length of the fortifications so as to keep an enemy at a distance.

It is unfortunate that all too little is known about the internal arrangements of these forts. Possible headquarters buildings and bath-houses have been identified at Richborough and Lympne, but in the main, barracks and other buildings appear to have been constructed with wooden frames, an interesting return to older methods.

Indeed the Roman army had by now assumed a very different structure from what it had once been. Although some units still retained their old titles, including many of the legions, most were now organized simply in vexillations of cavalry – *equites* – or infantry – *milites*. The legions themselves, despite retaining their original names and titles, were greatly reduced in strength with perhaps no more than 1000 men, but their number was increased. They no longer held precedence over auxiliaries. Now the distinction lay between the static frontier forces, the *limitanei*, and the mobile field armies of *comitatenses*. The former were not expected to fight at any distance from their bases, which they had to defend. Since their wives and families, homes and farms surrounded the forts they occupied, they had an incentive to do so, but in doing so they took yet another step along the path which ultimately led to their being little better than a local militia. The élite were therefore the mobile field army, often including heavily armoured cavalry, who were expected to fight in any of the provinces within a given command, according to where the need arose.

These new units, then, may have been serving in Britain by AD 342, when a visit by the emperor Constans in person was considered necessary to restore order. Eight years later Constans was ousted by a usurper Magnentius. Magnentius came of barbarian stock, showing the extent to which such people had penetrated the upper social orders of Rome, often to achieve high office, but he lasted only three years, early suffering defeat by Constans' co-emperor, Constantius II. He appears to have taken what troops he could from Britain, where he had been welcomed, to sustain his cause. For supporting the usurper, people in Britain suffered severe reprisals, and it would seem that the British garrisons remained below strength for some time to come.

Certainly when the next external threat materialized about AD 360, the army in Britain was in no fit state to repel it, and there followed a series of raids by Picts from beyond the Forth, Scots from northern Ireland, Attacoti probably from the western isles, and Saxons. Neither the east nor west coasts, nor the northern frontier were safe, and the raids culminated in the famous barbarian conspiracy of AD 367, when all combined to attack the province.

The effect was disastrous. Hadrian's Wall fell, despite the presence of its garrison, and the commander-in-chief of the northern frontier, the Duke of the Britains, was immobilized and probably besieged at York. The Count of the Saxon Shore was killed in action. The morale of the army seems to have been at a low ebb and many deserted, while the frontier patrol scouts, who should have given the alarm, proved treacherous, so enabling the attack to be a surprise.

This chaotic state lasted almost two years before the emperor Valentinian was able to dispatch Count Theodosius, with four regiments of the field army, to put the provinces in order. Fortunately by then most of the invaders had probably returned home laden with loot and Count Theodosius was only met by small marauding groups. An amnesty for deserters enabled much of the army to be reformed. Then an extensive programme of restoration followed, in which numerous changes in organization can be detected. The frontier forts were reconstructed, probably with the help of labour from civilian areas in the south, and with the standard of masonry showing a marked decline. The numerous villages, sacked at the same time as their parent forts, were not however rebuilt, and the new arrangements inside the forts show that all now lived within their protection.

The failure of the frontier scouts led to their disbanding and to new arrangements, or treaties, being made with tribes beyond the Wall,

Fig. 16 Signal stations at: a) Roper Castle; b) Scarborough; c) Gask

who may have been given improved status of clients or confederates, and who would be expected to play their part in frontier defence. Count Theodosius also improved the coast defences of Yorkshire and Durham by providing a chain of signal stations at suitable points. This element suggests that part at least of the Pictish attack had been seaborne and descended on the coast south of the eastern extremity of the Wall. The new stations contained a high masonry tower placed within a small fortlet and were sited so as to be able to signal the position of raiders to ships at sea.

A natural phenomenon was also creating difficulties. A relative rise in sea-level, which seems to have begun at some time in the third century, was influencing coastal sites, among them forts and harbours of the Saxon Shore. Certainly Brough-on-Humber could no longer operate and it is possible that Portchester and Lympne were likewise affected; a new fort at Bitterne on the river Itchen may have been designed to replace Portchester.

In the hinterland of the Wall and on the west coast work was also put in hand with several forts being rebuilt in a more regular manner, together with an additional naval base at Holyhead. The latter, of a new design already in use on the Rhine and the Danube, was walled only on the three landward sides, so providing a protected beach on which ships could be safely drawn up.

It is probable also that Theodosius was responsible for stationing regular troops for the first time as permanent garrisons in towns, villages and also some villas (see Ch. 4 below), but apart from some characteristic items of equipment which bespeak their presence, no evidence has yet been found of specific accommodation; they were most likely billeted among the townspeople.

One further reorganization seems to have been the creation of a fifth British province, Valentia, either in the northern area or in Wales, with Carlisle or Chester as its capital.

Theodosius, when he left Britain, was able to leave behind him a restored, peaceful and ordered diocese, and so matters remained until AD 383, when Magnus Maximus, probably Duke of the Britains at the time, rebelled against the central authority. As had happened so often before, Maximus took a large part of the remaining British garrisons, chiefly from the north-west, and including Legio XX from Chester, to support his claim to be emperor of the west, in which he was successful, until put to death by Theodosius I, son of Count of Theodosius, in AD 388. But the regiments taken by him to the continent never returned, and consequently Britain in the next decade was subjected to increased raids, particularly this time by the Irish on the Welsh coast, where they were beginning to form permanent settlements. In the north, however, the confederate tribes beyond the Wall, together with its surviving troops, appear to have held the Picts at bay.

In AD 396, another attempt was made to reorganize the defences of Britain, by the general Stilicho, a Vandal by birth, which seems to have been temporarily successful. But by now, pressure was mounting against the central empire, with Alaric, the Gothic leader, campaigning in Italy and threatening Rome. Yet more regiments were taken from Britain.

The inability of the central government to care for Britain threw up its own solution. The remaining units of the regular army elected in turn three usurper emperors, of whom only the last, Constantine III, survived long enough to take action. But the action he took did not meet with British approval since, in order to protect the Channel coast, he collected together what was left of the army and crossed to Gaul, where serious disturbances were taking place. Despite the fact that he was largely successful, and was recognized by the true emperor, Honorius, he fell into the trap of meddling in central politics and was executed.

Britain was now deprived of any protection by the regular army. In disgust at the activities of Constantine III, the people dismissed his civil servants and, in AD 410, addressed a petition for help to Honorius. Still heavily pressed by the Goths in Italy he was unable to respond, and, in his famous rescript, told the British towns to defend themselves.

We must remember that the Roman army had been withdrawn from Britain before, and there could have been nothing in the circumstances of AD 410 which did not suggest to the inhabitants that, as before, this was but a temporary interruption, to be made good when the situation improved. Indeed there are some authorities who believe that the Roman army did return between AD 416 and 419, but there is no evidence from any British site to support such a view. Destiny ruled otherwise and formal Roman involvement in Britain ceased after 367 years. To view this time-span in perspective, it can be put in modern terms and likened to the period from the defeat of the Spanish Armada until after the First World War!

Complete collapse, however, did not take place immediately, and Roman institutions and way of life continued on a diminishing scale for several more generations.

We have seen from the preceding description that warfare was largely endemic in Roman Britain. Apart from periods in the third century and again in the first half of the fourth, the frontiers were rarely at peace for more than a decade, and it is not surprising, therefore, that Britain, for its size, contained the largest garrison of any province of the Roman empire. Yet behind the iron curtain of the frontier there developed a civilized and prosperous province, little touched by actual fighting. Moreover, the frontiers in Britain must be viewed in a wider context, for they were also the north-west frontiers of Gaul and Spain. Without them, Gaul certainly would have been at risk, as happened immediately before AD 43. Although more compact, they were therefore as important as the Rhine and Danube frontiers were to other parts of the empire, and warranted the same expenditure of manpower and resources.

What did the native Britons gain? It is probably true to argue that warfare can bring economic benefits to a population, providing the people themselves are not touched by the fighting or embroiled in its political effects. The presence of a large standing army in Britain would undoubtedly have been beneficial to many of the inhabitants. It would have put money in peoples' pockets of a value unheard of in the Iron Age. It would have brought foreign traders to Britain in increased numbers, so incidentally introducing the inhabitants to new or improved goods and technology. Even the compulsory supply of grain and food to the army, and taxes to the imperial government, will have acted as a stimulus to increase production and provided work for many hands. It is perhaps no coincidence that the Antonine period in the second century was one of the most prosperous, when that same period saw some of the bitterest and most continuous fighting on the frontiers, with the army probably at its greatest strength.

There was of course a darker side. Arbitrary military rule in the frontier areas cannot always have been pleasant. Recruitment into the army itself was probably not always voluntary. Slaves were bought and sold and exploited with few humanitarian feelings, although in this respect conditions probably differed little from the Iron Age. Life also must have become more burdensome towards the end of the empire, with the growing corruption in public affairs, taxes which did more than shear the sheep and unpleasant jobs made hereditary because there were too few applicants.

On balance, the British province was a success. Once committed to the project, the imperial government maintained it, with only slight faltering, and only yielded when the centre of the empire was itself threatened. Other provinces fared less favourably, being abandoned at an earlier date.

Chapter 3

Cities, Towns and Minor Settlements

The geographer Strabo, writing about the turn of the first century BC and first century AD, implied that the backwardness of western Europeans, outside Italy, was derived from their hunting, raiding way of life. Once they were converted to a settled, agricultural existence, urbanism would develop of its own accord.

From this, we might infer that there was nothing in Britain, before the Roman period, which Strabo would have recognized as a town, despite the fact that both he and Caesar respectively refer to fortified woods and forests in Britain as being called *poleis* and *oppida*. But they were presumably employing the nearest Greek and Latin equivalents for whatever Celtic word was used by the Iron Age people. We do not know, nor are we likely to find out, what that Celtic word was, so we cannot say what it was that such sites were called by the people who built and used them. They may have considered them towns, even if they were not to Roman eyes; in the country of the blind the one-eyed man is king. It follows, therefore, that any attempt to ascribe 'towns' to the pre-Roman period in Britain is bound to be subjective and to depend on arguments advanced by modern theoreticians. A hill-fort does not become a 'town' just because modern processes of analysis, which are by no means universally agreed, ascribe to it a dominating influence over a purely arbitrary area containing other hill-forts of lesser size. Here, as in all things, we must be extremely careful to distinguish between primary evidence and modern inference. We know, from contemporary sources, that towns – even cities – were established in Britain during the Roman period; we have no such basic information for the Iron Age. In this respect it is informative to compare archaeological opinion of some decades ago with that of today. There was a time when 'village', long used to describe certain types of ill-defined, prehistoric settlement, became a naughty word, used by an archaeologist at his peril. Now, quite suddenly within the last few years, not only has it again become respectable, but also fashion decrees that towns should now be introduced into the same period. Such is the swing of the archaeological pendulum, and it is likely to carry on for many years yet.

This is not to say that some major centres in the Iron Age did not exercise control over lesser ones. We have already seen in an earlier chapter how tribal capitals grew up by reason of developing political, social and economic needs. The argument, therefore, revolves not around their existence, but whether we can justifiably call those sites towns.

Most people nowadays in the so-called developed countries have fairly clear views in their own minds of what constitutes a town. Yet often one person's idea will conflict with another's, and there is probably no universal agreement over border-line cases. It is still possible to insult a resident of a seemingly marginal community by referring to it as a village, when the inhabitants think of it as a town. Indeed this has formed the basis for one of the most realistic definitions of a town: when the people living there think of it as a town, it becomes one. Unfortunately, it is seldom possible to use such an assessment in antiquity, particularly in the prehistoric period. Moreover, such an assessment is just as subjective as those objected to above.

How then are we to define towns in prehistoric and Roman Britain? Some definition is obviously necessary if confusion is to be avoided, and the problem is probably best approached by way of a qualitative, functional analysis. It is probably best to avoid quantitative methods, since there is not sufficient primary evidence available to give them accuracy. In this case, as with computers, if rubbish is put in, rubbish will come out. Locational analyses, for all their apparent scientific appearance, when applied to Roman Britain, too often project in a graphical form only the subjective views of the manipulator.

It is probably recognized generally now that nucleated settlements acquire certain functions, of which some grow with the settlement and others are conferred upon it by virtue of its nature. They can be listed: an economic function connected with trade and industry and its associated shops, factories and markets; an administrative function usually formed when the settlement is selected to act as the centre of some level of local or central government; a communications function often derived from the position of the settlement at an important road or river junction; a religious function represented by a major church or temple; an educational function seen in the provision of schools, colleges and apprenticeship schemes; a protective function generated simply by a concentration of people, but sometimes enhanced by physical fortifications; and a function which provides some degree of amenity and provision for amusements or cultural entertainments, such as theatres, sports stadiums, museums, piped water, sewage disposal systems, good roads and houses, public swimming-baths, etc.

To some extent, and with minor modifications, all these functions, probably together with others – the list is by no means exhaustive – can be applied to the towns and other settlements of antiquity. But if the list is examined more critically it will be seen that some overlap. Communications, for instance, are part of a good road or street system and therefore might be classed under amenities, or alternatively, under the function of trade since they are closely involved with it. Religious devotions can usually be practised anywhere; the provision of a church or temple might also be seen as an amenity; likewise education.

The original list can therefore be shortened to the basic functions: administrative, protective, economic and provision of amenities.

We might here usefully invoke the help of the second-century topographer, Pausanias, who in describing the Greek site, Panopeus, says of it: 'A city of the Phocians, if one can give the name of city to those who possess no government offices, no gymnasium, no theatre, no market-place, no water descending from a fountain, but live in base shelters just like mountain cabins, right on a ravine.' Pausanias clearly had well-established views on what does, or does not, constitute a city and, more helpfully than Strabo, links them to buildings with specific functions, which is useful for our own classification, as will be seen below.

Some of these functions can usually be observed in even the smallest hamlet; it may have a shop or pub, or piped water or drains, and it is protective simply by the concentration of people within its boundaries. In antiquity, even hill-forts may have provided facilities for entertainment or amusement, although any genuine amenities would appear pretty primitive to modern or even Roman eyes. But we must be careful not so to judge them. A hill-fort might have provided amenities lacking in an isolated farm of the period. It may also have been the centre of some sort of rudimentary administration.

How then are we to distinguish between a hill-fort, an 'oppidum', an Iron Age village, a Romano-British village or a Romano-British town? Clearly the assignment of raw functions alone is not enough. In order to refine the method it will become necessary to consider the *level* at which they are applied, and at this point the arguments are bound to become more subjective; one man's village is another man's town. Fortunately, when dealing with Roman Britain, a degree of conformity can be observed within certain classes of towns. There is also an important additional factor to be considered: an element of integrated planning appears in many instances.

However, further difficulties arise involving nomenclature. In the Roman world, as today, there were different classes of town, as well as a

500 m

R. Colne

⟶ N

——— Town wall

≡≡≡ " ditch

------- Fortress ditch

■■ Tower

* Public building

♦ Mosaic and tessellated
 pavements

Basilica

Temple

Fig. 17 Colchester

variety of Latin words used to describe nucleated settlements: *colonia,
municipium, vicus, oppidum, urbs, civitas,* and even a Greek word: *polis.* In
English we have town, city, county town, urban district, county
borough, borough, village, hamlet, although some of them have virtually disappeared with local government reorganization. Most of the
latter have clearly defined meanings within the modern administrative
system and cannot always be suitably matched against Latin or Greek
meanings.

Elsewhere, the present writer has argued against the use of the word
city to describe sites of antiquity and has suggested that 'town' should

alone be used to describe those above a certain functional level. This view has stimulated some reaction; so, if it is to be modified, let city be used to define those sites of Roman Britain which, like modern cities, received a charter of independence: the *coloniae* and *municipia*. Let it not be used as a synonym for town. Let it also be remembered that whereas all cities are towns, not all towns are cities.

The foundation of towns in Roman Britain followed, to some extent, precedents established elsewhere, especially in Gaul. It is quite clear from what came after that the Romans, when they arrived, saw nothing in Britain which even remotely resembled their idea of a town, let alone a city. The provincial government began, therefore, by setting an example to the natives, by the deliberate foundation in AD 49, at Colchester, of a chartered colonia, on the site of the abandoned legionary fortress. Thereby, they partly made use of land which had already been requisitioned and was in imperial ownership. As so often happened, its inhabitants were provided by a discharge of legionaries, probably from Legio XX. Each veteran would have been given a plot of land within the town, on which a house was built, and a somewhat larger plot of arable or pasture, the size commensurate with his rank, in the country surrounding the town. This land, the *territorium*, was considered part of the town, was administered from it, and might have been as much as 400 sq. km. in total extent. It is not entirely surprising that the expropriation of so much land in and around the sometime capital of the Trinovantes, was a principal cause of the rebellion in AD 60.

Later, in the closing decades of the first century, two more similar, chartered coloniae were founded at Lincoln and Gloucester, respectively the abandoned sites of legionary fortresses of Legio IX and Legio II Augusta. In both cases, extra land would have been required, and in this instance was probably obtained peacefully from the Coritani and Dobunni by the payment of adequate compensation.

Later still, a fourth, well-attested colonia appeared in Britain at York, but by a different process of advancement. It had become the custom, as time went on, to promote existing towns to higher grades. Normally, the first step was to municipium, of which there were two types. In Italy and in some of the more central provinces, where most of the inhabitants would have been Roman citizens, full Roman rights, in law, would be conferred on the town with its charter. In the remoter provinces, where few, if any, of the inhabitants possessed the citizenship, Latin rights were more usually given, with the magistrates alone being made Roman citizens. The principal distinction lay in the respective constitutions: a municipium with full Roman rights would have to abide by Roman law, but, in one with Latin rights, some native laws could probably still be retained.

When the legionary fortress was founded on the north-east bank of the Ouse at York, in the latter part of the first century, a civilian settlement began to grow on the opposite bank. Probably at first it was given the status of vicus; by the later second century it may have been promoted to the intermediate rank of municipium, and by AD 237 it had become a colonia, by which time also it was the provincial capital of Britannia Inferior.

The evidence for the existence of other coloniae and municipia in Britain is slight. It is likely that London, never part of the local government organization, became a municipium towards the end of the first century, for reasons which are outlined below (Chapter 5) and may even have been promoted to colonia in the early fourth century, when it received the additional honorary title of Augusta. It is difficult to conceive that a town, which was not only the largest in Britain, but also, in turn, the provincial capital of Britain, Britannia Superior and Maxima Caesariensis, and the seat of the diocesan vicar, was not so treated.

Verulamium also was probably given a municipal title in the first century. It is sometimes argued, additionally, that certain tribal towns, centres of local government administration, such as Canterbury, Dorchester (Dorset) and Leicester were similarly promoted, but there is no sound evidence to support these claims.

It is not difficult, therefore, to accept the four known British coloniae, the probable municipium at Verulamium, and possibly London, as towns, or even cities, if such a designation is considered more apt. They were chartered; no doubt exists about their status. Below this level, there are some two dozen major settlements which can properly be called towns, together with more numerous other sites, over which general agreement has not yet been reached by archaeologists; it is at this point that a return must be made to a consideration of functions.

The major settlements, which we are about to consider as towns, were those which grew to fulfil the need for centres of local government. The Roman approach to the problems of local administration was extremely flexible. If, in a freshly acquired province, some form of suitable divisions between areas already existed, it was retained and adapted to suit the new conditions. In the three north-western provinces of Gaul and in Britain, the Iron Age tribal structure provided these divisions. Consequently, when the time came for a civilian administration to be formed, it was based, with only minor alterations, on the tribal areas of pre-Roman Britain. Each area was given local autonomy as a *civitas*, a constitution of sorts, and carefully prescribed rights and duties. Each area naturally required an administrative centre, and in response to the need a number of towns appeared, usually referred to now as civitas capitals. By the mid second century,

Fig. 18 Verulamium: a) Claudio-Neronian; b) Flavian; c) late Antonine;
d) fourth century

there were in Britain some fifteen such sites. There were also two
failures while, later, local government reorganizations almost certainly
created new ones. Not all were founded at the same time, and phases of
development can be detected which equate with the pattern of military
advance. But no matter how they were founded it must be remembered
that, behind the supposed autonomy of each area, lay the hand of the
provincial governor, who could, probably after reference to the
emperor, unilaterally revoke or alter the conditions.

Fig. 19 Silchester

The functional level of administration to be observed, therefore, if a
settlement is justifiably to be called a town, is that associated, as with
the chartered towns, with a self-governing community.

The sites which fall into this category may be considered as follows:
Canterbury and Verulamium probably appeared first, together with
Chelmsford, although the Trinovantes were not attracted by their new
capital at the latter site. Caistor-by-Norwich, Chichester, Winchester
and Silchester came with the ultimate absorption of the client kingdoms of the Iceni and Atrebates into the province between AD 60 and

80. In the 80s also, and equating with the advances of Agricola in the north, Cirencester, Dorchester, Exeter, Leicester and Wroxeter appeared, while the Hadrianic troop movements following the construction of a permanent frontier produced Caerwent, Carmarthen, Brough-on-Humber and Aldborough.

These towns were essentially native in composition, although outwardly their appearance would depend on the extent to which classical architecture was adopted to suit local materials, finance and needs. But they were built largely by, and for, natives, who paid for them. Some governors, such as Agricola or Julius Frontinus, gave encouragement and may have made grants available, probably from their provincial expense account; some emperors, such as Hadrian, remitted taxes. Initially, also, help may have been given by military architects and builders, for the constructional methods then introduced would have been strange to most natives; alternatively, there was probably no lack of civil architects from neighbouring provinces.

If the plans of most of the towns are studied, it will be seen that there is some degree of conformity between them. In the early stages of their development, fortifications were seldom provided, or needed, since the protective function was exercised largely by the Roman army on the frontiers and by the concentration of people in one place. Only at Verulamium, Silchester and Winchester have fortifications dating to the first century so far been found and there are probably special reasons for their construction. The remainder were open towns, and almost every one shows evidence of intregrated planning, with a regular grid of streets laid out at right angles to one another. Planning on this scale could only have been carried out by a competent authority on a virgin site owned by the tribal rulers on behalf of the tribe, since no powers of compulsory purchase existed. The existence of a planned town therefore implies the existence of a self-governing community which, in the cases at present being considered, would be the tribal civitates. It will be noted, also, that quite a number of these towns overlay the sites of earlier forts or fortresses: Verulamium, Exeter, Cirencester, Wroxeter, Leicester and possibly Aldborough. The forts would have been originally sited on land requisitioned with, or more likely without, compensation for the evicted owners. With the evacuation of the forts and the constitution of a civil authority, the land was presumably made over *en bloc* to the latter and not returned to the original holders.

One major question to be answered involves the choice of sites. Why, for instance, did a civitas capital appear at Dorchester or Cirencester and not at Ham Hill, Badbury or Bourton-on-the-Water, all important sites in the pre-Roman period which gave rise to Romano-British settlements? The answer can best be obtained by considering a specific example of the mechanics involved.

At Cirencester, a fort was established within a year or two of the invasion. Its siting was dictated by the overall strategic requirements of the first frontier of Roman Britain and by the tactical needs of the local position. The fort itself was established at an important junction of roads from Silchester, Verulamium, Leicester and Bath, at a point where a river had to be crossed. Fords have always been favourite places for ambushes, consequently the military needs of the position are readily explained. The positioning of other forts in Dobunnian territory will have been governed by similar reasoning, but at Cirencester an additional factor was the existence, some three miles to the north, of the native oppidum at Bagendon, the seat probably of the restored Dobunnian ruler and his court.

While military administration lasted in the country of the Dobunni, any instructions relating to the natives would have been relayed from the governor to the local army commander, or directly through the procurator's men (see Ch. 5 below), who would have been required, as far as was possible, to maintain workable relations with the native rulers. In turn, the natives would have been allowed considerable freedom in managing their own affairs providing they behaved themselves.

Any body of troops, especially when stationed in a foreign country, has always acted as a magnet for local traders. Those at Cirencester were no exception, and it is probable that, to begin with, local traders made daily journeys with their wares to and from Bagendon and from other nearby sites. The inconvenience of such an arrangement soon seems to have been realized and, within a decade or so, many had actually removed, and a thriving trading centre was growing up on land immediately north-west of the fort. The reflection of this movement can be seen at Bagendon, where from the late 50s the population markedly declined before dwindling away altogether. The new settlement would have been encouraged and regulated by the Roman army and before long would probably have had the formal status of a vicus conferred upon it.

When the time came for the removal of garrisons from Dobunnian territory, for reasons already outlined in the preceding chapter, local government would have been handed over to the newly constituted *civitas Dobunnorum*. The vicus at Cirencester was thereupon chosen, with the governor's approval, to become the civitas capital, presumably for no other reason than that the principal tribal leaders, who would now be expected to run it, already lived there. The new capital was then developed in the normal manner, not only on the area of the vicus, but also on that of the abandoned fort. The trade provided by the soldiers was replaced by the sale and purchase of merchandise produced not only in the town but also in the surrounding countryside. In this respect Cirencester would have acted like a country market town and would, moreover, have attracted traders from further afield hoping to capture new markets. These traders, if from other provinces, would have brought with them more than goods for sale; they would have brought new ideas relating to improved technology and agriculture, to the standard of living, cultural advancements, religious beliefs and to more sophisticated amusements. They were to play an important part in the romanization of Britain. It is probable also that, among the native population, the more go-ahead members of society will have been attracted to the newly created towns, avid for the opportunities they offered and eagerly embracing the new way of life.

The process of urbanization just described for Cirencester was repeated elsewhere. At Dorchester, the tribal aristocracy living in the hill-fort of Maiden Castle caused the civitas capital of the Durotriges to be set up at Dorchester nearby. Sometimes, as at Canterbury, Veru- lamium or Leicester, little or no movement of people was required, since the relevant fortifications of the army were sited close to the existing native centre. Sometimes, also, where the tribe exhibited little or no centralized organization, a legionary fortress with its greater number of better paid soldiers provided the extra attraction for the tribal leaders, as at Exeter and Wroxeter.

In all cases, it is probably true to say that the foundation of these towns was a voluntary process, carried out with the encouragement and approval of the provincial administration, but not by compulsion. Even given their conformity of planning, there is too much variation from town to town for them to have been the product of a rigorous enforcement. While it is possible, as it was from time to time in Roman Britain, to compel people to do many things and push them around to a great extent, one thing that cannot be done is to force them to spend their own money on goods, buildings and services they do not want. To be effective in the face of opposition, the money has first to be taken from people in taxes and the revenue then used by government agen- cies, in which case a 'standard pattern Romano-British town' would probably have emerged to grace the province. It did not, and probably the only example of a site for a capital being foisted by the provincial administration upon a civitas was Chelmsford for the Trinovantes; it failed. Moreover, the Roman administration simply did not have the personnel for general enforcement of this nature. So few were they that it is likely that a very large number of the inhabitants of Britain would not have seen a Roman soldier or provincial administrator from one year's end to another. It was the native Britons, perhaps joined in some cases by other provincials, who had the towns built and who maintained them, and this fact cannot be emphasized enough. The Roman administration did little more than provide the initial models, approve the sites and give some spasmodic help.

So far, we have considered three classes of town, and we have still to justify fully the use of the term to describe the civitas capitals.

Their planned nature, as already observed, is a prerequisite. Although irregularities in the street systems sometimes occur, in the main, the streets were laid out at right angles to one another forming rectangular blocks of land – *insulae* – between them. Two main streets, usually carrying through flows of traffic, intersect at the centre and were referred to as the *cardo maximus* and *decumanus maximus*. In one of the four insulae beside this cross-roads was normally to be found the forum and basilica, the principal public buildings; Cirencester and Silchester are both good examples of such planning. Occasionally, when a town enlarged its boundaries, a fresh alignment was adopted for the new streets, as can be seen at Wroxeter. Occasionally, also, some elements of an earlier, unplanned street system were preserved when a new grid was laid out, as at Silchester and Caistor-by-Norwich. In most chartered towns in the Roman world it was an offence to encroach on or interrupt any public right-of-way, so special interest attaches to the few examples where a house had been built over a street, as at Gloucester. As time passed, subsidiary roads, often providing additional access to a particular building, were constructed, so effectively reducing the size of some insulae, as at Leicester and Canterbury.

The streets themselves were constructed of local materials; gravel and limestone brash were perhaps the commonest as both tend, when compacted, to cement themselves together by natural processes. The surface was frequently cambered and side drains were provided to carry away water. Whenever a surface became worn or pot-holed, as must frequently have happened, a new layer of aggregate was put down. Extensive wear also caused formidable quantities of dust, or mud if it was wet, to accumulate, and this, combined with repeated resurfacing, must have been a grave nuisance to house- and shop-holders, as it resulted in a gradual overall rise in the level of the streets. Conseqently, when a town street is excavated today, it is often found that the level has risen by as much as 3m. over 330 years, a rate of about 1 cm. per year. Over a lifetime therefore, a householder might have found that instead of walking out on to a surface level with his front door, he was having to negotiate a considerable step up. In many cases this led to floors being raised in houses and in extreme cases to complete rebuilding after the site had been relevelled. This one factor, more than

Fig. 20 Outline plans of towns at: a) Cirencester; b) Caistor; c) Lincoln; d) Wroxeter

any other, probably accounts for the great depths of deposits to be found in most Romano-British towns.

Foremost among the functions of these towns was the need to act as administrative centres for the civitates. In the chartered towns, the administration was in the hands of two pairs of magistrates, who were responsible to an appointed council of up to a hundred members. Although we have only a little evidence from Britain, it is probable that the civitates were similarly governed. In the chartered towns, the basilica or more correctly the council chamber provides the physical

Fig. 21 Forums at: a) Cirencester; b) Verulamium; c) Silchester; d) Caerwent

evidence for the existence of the council and magistrates. Likewise, the civitas capitals were provided with basilicas and we may deduce, therefore, a similar level of administration. However, a degree of caution must be exercised, as the development of the monumental, unified, forum-and-basilica complex, like those at Cirencester, Silchester or Leicester, did not occur in the western provinces much before the end of the first century. Before, less easily recognized buildings may have served the same purpose, so that, although we may argue that their presence represents a certain level of local government, an absence, especially in the years soon after the invasion or in the fourth century, does not necessarily imply that such government was nonexistent. For instance, the three early towns of Colchester, Verulamium and Canterbury have yet to produce evidence for commensurately early basilicas.

The forum and basilica of a town usually consisted of a large open space surrounded on three sides by porticoes, perhaps fronting rows of shops and offices, and with the basilica occupying the whole of the fourth side. An elaborate entrance was usually sited in the middle of the range facing the basilica, and in some cases, as at Silchester, an external portico surrounded the whole, or part of, the building.

The basilica was a long, aisled hall with at one, or more usually at both ends of the nave raised platforms, or tribunals, used by the magistrates for conducting judicial and official business. A range of rooms was attached to the hall on the side away from the forum; they were used as offices and for meetings of the council, while one room, centrally placed in the range, probably served as a shrine for statues of the emperors or local protective deities. Occasionally for reasons of economy, one of the aisles of the hall was dispensed with, as at Caerwent and Caistor-by-Norwich.

The forum, as already described, consisted primarily of an open space which could be used not only for gatherings of a political or administrative nature, but also as a place in which, on market days, stalls could be set up. If rooms were additionally provided around this area, they could be rented out as shops, or used as offices by the administration.

The plans of most of the forums and basilicas in Britain strongly resemble those of military headquarters buildings, and is one reason for supposing that army architects were seconded to towns to help in their construction. There are some exceptions, notably at Verulamium, where the plan owes more to central Italian designs, and the council chamber and tribunals are centrally placed in the range opposing the basilica and are flanked by temples.

A settlement, therefore, which had been provided with a basilica and forum, possessed the requisite level of local administration for it to be called a town. This is the main reason for supposing that London became a chartered town as, by the end of the first century, these buildings had been constructed.

Another of the principal functions which enable us to distinguish between a town and a lesser settlement was that associated with the provision of amenities. As with the administration, these can often be linked with certain specific structures. In addition to the provision of well-paved, spacious streets and covered porticoes, we may number among them running water from an aqueduct, good sewage and surface water disposal, provision for public lavatories and bath-houses, a reasonable standard of comfort in private dwellings and the availability of entertainments, amusements and educational facilities.

It can be shown that every chartered town and civitas capital in Britain was supplied with fresh water from an aqueduct, and distributed by means of wood, lead, stone or ceramic pipes or channels. Drinking basins were often provided at street corners and fed from this supply, as at York and Gloucester, but most of the water would have been channelled to the public baths, which consumed large quantities. Waste water from the baths was used to flush lavatories and the main sewers. Some private supplies were also arranged, for which the user would pay a water rate; examples can be seen of shops so served at Wroxeter and Verulamium.

The aqueduct channels which brought water to the towns of Britain were, like their military counterparts, of simple construction. The comparatively gentle undulations of the British countryside did not call for grandiose structures like those often to be seen in parts of Gaul and Spain, where steep, narrow gorges had to be crossed. The nearest, sufficiently high source of water was chosen for the supply, either by damming a stream or diverting a spring, and the flow conducted by gravity in carefully contoured channels dug in the ground, as at Dorchester and Wroxeter. Only at Lincoln is there seemingly a more sophisticated arrangement where, owing to valleys having to be crossed along the route, the water was carried in ceramic pipes, jacketed in concrete to withstand a pressure. An aqueduct of the former type was capable of carrying several million litres of water a day.

The counterpart to an aqueduct was an adequate sewer. Once an aqueduct was working, its flow could only be controlled with difficulty – there was no turning off at the main. Provisions had therefore to be made for carrying away, not only effluent, but also any surplus capacity. Major sewage systems constructed of masonry are well illustrated by examples at Lincoln and Verulamium, where they ran under or beside main streets, but sometimes, as at Cirencester or Caistor-by-Norwich, they were only lined and covered with wooden planks.

Public lavatories were occasionally provided by enterprising shop-keepers, but more normally were to be found connected to the public bath-house, where they were flushed by waste water from the baths. In Britain they seem to have consisted of wooden seats placed either directly above the main sewer, or over an inclined shoot connected to it. A shallow gutter in the floor in front of the seat carried water for rinsing the sponges tied to sticks, which were used in place of lavatory paper. Multiple capacity was the norm and no sex discrimination was apparently observed. The alternative was probably a back-yard earth-closet or the jars placed at street corners by the fullers for the convenience of passers-by; fullers used stale urine for the treatment of cloth.

The principal amenity in the Roman world was undoubtedly the bath-house (see Fig. 49). Although some rich members of society had bath-wings attached to their town houses, they were rare, and in the main, people of all classes made use of the public baths. The buildings became, therefore, more than just places for ablutions, and people gathered to exchange news and gossip, to take exercise, even to buy and sell goods, since many public baths were equipped with shops or had itinerant merchants displaying their wares.

Most public bath-houses were based on one of two standard plans. Those in Britain, as with forums and basilicas, owed much to military prototypes, and the commonest basic form consisted of a suite of rooms arranged in series with each maintained at a different temperature, so resembling the modern Turkish bath, which is, after all, derived from Roman models. Minimally there was a dressing-room, with latrine leading from it, an unheated room, a warm room and a hot room. Each might be provided with a small plunge bath maintained at an equivalent temperature, and sometimes one or more of the rooms or the plunges would be duplicated. The heated rooms were kept moist by injections of steam but there might be, additionally, one or more small rooms kept with an intense dry heat, as in the modern sauna. Most bath-houses also had either an open area, perhaps surrounded by porticoes, or a covered hall, attached to them, where the bathers could exercise or play games.

The hot rooms were kept at their required temperatures by conducting heat from external fires through stokeholes, under the floors and up ducts built in the walls and sometimes in the roofs also; the latter were normally vaulted, sometimes with a cavity construction to conserve heat. A boiler made of copper or lead sheets was placed over the stokehole to provide steam and hot water for the plunges.

The normal bathing process employed the hot rooms to open the pores of the skin and create a good sweat, after which the dirt was scraped off by means of a curved iron or bronze blade – a *strigil*. If the bather were fortunate a slave or friend did it for him; otherwise he managed as best he could by himself. Soap was known, but seems rarely to have been used. A retreat through the unheated room, and possibly a dip in the cold plunge, closed the pores, and, after drying, the oils lost from the skin in the process were replaced by anointing with suitable animal or vegetable substitutes.

The site occupied by a bath-house obviously had to be related to the provision and removal of water. No standard place in the town, unlike that occupied by the forum and basilica, can therefore be expected, although where possible they were situated near the centre.

As towns developed, so the standards of living of their inhabitants improved. By the early second century, this rise is demonstrated by the appearance of comfortable, well-appointed houses. At first, most townspeople were probably concerned with trade and lived over or in their shops. But as wealth accumulated, so separate living accommodation tended to be provided by the richer merchants for themselves, inferring that either their businesses had been sold at a profit or were being managed by a tenant or slave.

The earliest houses were frequently simple in plan, usually having no more than five or six rooms connected by an external, covered portico. Often, in areas where there was little good building stone, they were constructed with wooden frames, with the walls made of wattle and daub, and the roofs of tiles. This did not, however, prevent the walls from being plastered and painted with frescoes: one second-century example from Verulamium was decorated with imitation columns. Neither did it prevent the householder from having glazed windows or a mosaic floor laid in his dining-room, nor good concrete or wooden floors in other rooms. It meant, however, that underfloor heating on the hypocaust principle could not be employed and rooms were no doubt warmed by braziers, while lighting was provided by oil-lamps or candles. Sometimes these houses contained a further wing, usually set at right angles to the main residence and reached by an extension of the covered portico. Markedly plainer in design and execution, it probably contained the domestic offices and the quarters for slaves or servants.

The standard of upper-class housing increased rapidly, sometimes as the result of extending existing buildings, sometimes by complete reconstruction. When reconstruction occurred, wooden frames were frequently replaced by masonry walls, or by a combination of masonry and cob, or half-timbering, so enabling hypocausts to be incorporated for heating. As then planned, the houses often formed two or more wings around an enclosed courtyard, which may have been laid out as a garden. Such houses, although owing something to Mediterranean styles, were usually less compact. Land was still abundant and cheap, except in the very centre of a town, where most shops lay, and so there was no need to practise economy in layout. Such planning also provided the owner with maximum privacy and security from thieves, a very necessary precaution in the absence of a police force to apprehend criminals. The best rooms in the house would be decorated with mosaics, painted ceilings and frescoes, often of an elaborate character. One house in Leicester, obviously the residence of an important and wealthy inhabitant, had the whole of the inside wall of the portico

1. Iron Age Coins
1. *Gallo-Belgic gold stater, Allen Class B, c. 75 BC*
   These are perhaps attributable to the Veliocasses (Dieppe area); their
   British distribution centres on or near London
2. *British 'potin' coin, c. 70 BC*
   Widely scattered in south-east England from Dorset to Kent, these are
   best known from concentrations of hoards in the lower Thames valley.
   Their continental prototypes appear to be substantially pre-Caesarian
3. *Gallo-Belgic gold stater, Allen Class A, c. 70 BC*
   Attributed to the Ambiani (Amiens area), and widely imported into
   southern and eastern England. A few worn examples survived to be
   hoarded with coins of the period of Caesar's Gallic wars. It is generally
   found within the angle formed by the North Downs and Chilterns
4. *Gallo-Belgic gold stater, Allen Class C, c. 60 BC*
   A coinage of the Ambiani, it is mostly found in Kent though there is a thin
   scatter to the north of the Thames
5. *Gallo-Belgic gold stater, Allen Class E, c. 58 BC*
   The coinage of the Ambiani during Caesar's Gallic wars. They occur
   along the line of the Chilterns and North Downs and are numerous along
   the Sussex coast. Beyond this main concentration is a general scatter
   extending to Humber and Severn. Only the earlier stages of this coinage
   are regularly found in Britain
6. *British gold stater, Allen Class A, c. 60 BC*
   The type is found mainly in Surrey, Sussex, Hampshire and east Dorset,
   with a scatter along and beyond the Thames. Their distribution is
   complementary to that of Gallo-Belgic, Class C (no. 4) with which they
   should be broadly contemporary
7. *British gold stater, Allen Class L, c. 40 BC*
   This coinage is largely found north of the Thames, and its distribution
   seems to centre on the northern end of the Chilterns. There are several
   varieties, and its issue may have occurred sporadically over many years. It
   is attributed to the Catuvellauni, and is ancestral to the coinages of
   Tasciovanus and Cunobelinus
8. *British gold stater, Allen Class Q, c. 45 BC*
   This coinage of the Atrebates is a slightly older contemporary of British L.
   It is essentially found in Berkshire, Hampshire and West Surrey, though
   there are numerous others, especially along the Sussex coast
9. *Gold stater of Cunobelinus, c. AD 25*
   Cunobelinus, 'King of the Britons', came to rule most of south-east
   England from his capital at Camulodunum. He died not long before
   Claudius' invasion. His coinage shows strongly rationalizing and
   classicizing tendencies
10. *Silver coin of Cunobelinus, c. AD 25*
11. *Bronze coin of Cunobelinus, c. AD 25*
    Silver and bronze coins, increasingly frequent in the last half-century of
    independence, testify to the incipient growth of a monetary economy.
    Bronze coins in particular, seem to be concentrated on the sites of oppida
    and temples
12. *Gold stater of Tincommius, c. 10 BC*
    Tincommius, scion of a famous family, ruled the Atrebates. His coins
    showed a transition from the traditional style to one based on classical
    concepts
13. *Gold quarter-stater of Eppillus, c. AD 10*
    The brother of Tincommius ruled at Calleva (Silchester). Quarter-staters
    were particularly characteristic of the Atrebatic kingdom
14. *Cast bronze stater of the Durotriges, first century AD*
    These degenerate descendants of British Class A staters (no. 6) were cast
    in large numbers towards the end of British independence. They persisted
    in local currency well into the second century
15. *Gold stater of Bodvoc, c. AD 40*
    The gold coins of the Dobunni derived their typology from those of their
    neighbours, the Atrebates
16. *Silver coin of Antedius, c. AD 20*
    The Iceni struck few gold coins, but a very large series of silver, which is
    often found hoarded with Roman denarii down to the reign of Nero
17. *Gold stater of Dumnocoveros, first century AD*
    Coins of the Coritani are thinly distributed over a large area between
    south Yorkshire and northern Northamptonshire. They have sometimes
    been found with Roman coins, and their typology seems to be related to
    the well-known coinage of Cunobelinus (no. 9)

2. Reconstructed Iron Age round house

3. Aerial photograph of the Roman fort situated in the corner of the Iron Age hill-fort at Hod Hill

32. Aerial photograph of the town at Silchester

33. South wall of Caerwent

34. A selection of Roman coins
  1. *Gold aureus of Claudius I (AD 41-54)*
     Gold coins such as this piece, which celebrates the triumph over Britain, soon swept away the inferior British staters
  2. *Silver denarius of Mark Antony, 32 BC*
     Until after the end of the first century, more than half the Roman silver coinage consisted of old, worn, Republican denarii, many of them of this legionary issue made just before the battle of Actium
  3. *Copper as of Claudius I (AD 41-54)*
  4. *Contemporary forgery of no. 3*
     The sudden imposition of the Roman coinage and currency system led to a shortage of ready money. Combined with widespread unfamiliarity with imperial coins, this created a situation which forgers of all levels of competence were quick to exploit
  5. *Brass sestertius of Vespasian (AD 69-79)* (obv. only)
     These fine coins, generally with a laureate obverse portrait, formed the largest base metal denomination in circulation down to the 260s
  6. *Brass dupondius of Hadrian (AD 117-38)* (obv. only)
     Half the value and weight of the sestertius, this denomination was often distinguished from the very similar as by the Emperor's radiate head
  7. *Brass sestertius of Gallienus (AD 253-68)* (obv. only)
     From the later years of the second century, the Roman mint often struck sestertii on blanks with two parallel sides. Galloping inflation led to the brass and copper denominations being discontinued after 260
  8. *Base silver denarius of Sèverus (AD 193-211)*
     Inflation was also reflected in the increasing debasement of the silver coinage. This piece celebrates Severus' victories in Britain
  9. *Base silver 'antoninianus' of Caracalla (AD 211-17)* (obv. only)
     We know neither the real name nor the value of this multiple denarius denomination. In a period of rapidly rising prices, it quickly superseded the ordinary denarius in general use. Note the Emperor's radiate portrait
 10. *Base silver 'antoninianus' of Tetricus I (AD 271-4)*
 11. *Contemporary forgery of no. 10*
     The silver currency reached a nadir of style, technique and fineness with the coins of the Gallic emperors and their Roman contemporaries. Several mints now worked at full pressure to supply currency needs, and the rapidly degenerating size and style of the imperial coin made a golden opportunity for forgers
 12. *Base silver 'antoninianus' of Carausius (AD 276-93)*
     Even in Britain, the usurpers of this period required more than one mint. This coin, vainly invoking peaceful co-existence with the continental emperors, was struck at London
 13. *Base silver 'follis' of Diocletian (AD 284-305)* (obv. only)
     This fine coinage was part of a vain attempt to stabilize, or even to reverse the inflationary spiral. It was struck at Trier
 14. *Base silver centenionalis of Constantine II (AD 317-40)*
     In 318 yet another coinage reform was instituted. This piece was struck in London c. 320; the London mint closed in 325
 15. *Base silver centenionalis of Constantine I (AD 306-37)*
     These coins honouring the cities of Rome and Constantinople are among the commonest Roman coins of the mid fourth century
 16. *Bronze coins of Constantius II (337-61)* (rev. only)
 17. *Contemporary forgery of no. 16* (rev. only)
     The ineptitude of the Roman government in dealing with currency problems is well illustrated by the events of AD 354. The coinage of that year (no. 16) was intended to supersede all earlier pieces; the effect was not merely to give rise to forgery on an enormous scale, but also to provoke the hitherto unprecedented overstriking of authentic coins by false dies
 18. *Bronze coin of Honorius (AD 395-423)*
     The latest Roman bronze coins to enter Britain in quantity were these little, ill-struck pieces of c. 400. Their currency was largely restricted to southern and eastern Britain
 19. *Clipped silver 'siliqua' of Arcadius (AD 395-408)*
     After the cessation of Roman government in Britain, the surviving silver coins were severely clipped. No coinage was produced at this time, for its use depended on the Roman fiscal system, rather than the needs of internal commerce

B   Infant burial
C   Courtyard
D   Drain
Dr   Corn Drier
H   Hypocaust
L   Latrine
M   Mosaic

0   10   20   30   40   50 m

Fig. 22 Town-houses at: a) Gloucester; b) Caerwent; c) Dorchester; d) Verulamium; e) Silchester

round his courtyard painted with a continuous frieze incorporating flowers, animals, birds, human figures and architectural perspectives executed in the Pompeian manner. Another at Verulamium had a mosaic in the dining-room – the most important room in the house – illustrating a life-like portrait of a lion carrying a stag's head in its mouth, with realistic drops of blood falling to the ground.

The use of decorative features such as these, originating in the centre of the the empire, imply the presence in Britain either of copy-books containing the designs or of travelling artists employed on contract. It indicates, also, the extent to which native Britons had wholeheartedly adopted the new way of life. But the rooms in these houses would, to modern eyes, appear sparsely furnished. An assortment of couches, basket chairs, low tables, often circular with three legs, and some cupboards or presses were all that the householder required. Occasionally a small domestic shrine was included, as in a shop at Verulamium.

Less evidence, somewhat naturally, survives to represent the other end of the social scale. It is sometimes claimed that apparently vacant areas within a town were taken up by small huts, forming shanty towns. To what extent this would have been allowed by the authorities is not known, for, since the land presumably belonged to someone, any occupants would have been tenants or squatters. Indeed, we might doubt their existence, for such people, if they were not retainers or slaves and so accommodated in their masters' premises, are unlikely to have gravitated to towns. A peasant class, whether free or bound to the land, would almost certainly have remained in the country, where some sort of living could be more easily scratched. It is probable, however, that every town had its quota of beggars and itinerant pedlars, living rough and snatching sleep in porticoes and alleys if they could not afford the price of a night's lodging. Moreover, if the patronage system of Roman society extended at all to Britain, as seems probable, particularly in towns, there would have been few people in a really penurious state.

Other amenities provided in towns were entertainments or amusements, catered for by amphitheatres and theatres. The former were relatively common features in Britain, the latter are less seldom seen and when they existed were more often than not connected with temples. A third place of entertainment, the circus, where chariot- and horse-racing were carried on, has yet to be identified in Britain, although there is evidence of an interest in the sport.

Amphitheatres were large, elliptical structures, built so that the maximum number of people could view the entertainment, normally of a vulgar nature. The seating in most British amphitheatres was raised in tiers on earth banks, retained by wooden or masonry walls, and surrounding a central arena. Access to the arena was obtained by entrances at each end of the long axis, while the seats were approached from round the circumference. Probably the best surviving examples are those at Cirencester and Dorchester.

There is some evidence for gladiatorial shows. But they were expensive and since most spectacles were put on and paid for by influential townspeople, it is likely that wild-beast shows were more commonly promoted, in which various types of animal were matched against each other as in bear-baiting and cock-fighting. Executions for high treason were also carried out in the arena and were usually considered excellent entertainment. Estimates of the seating capacity of amphitheatres have shown that they could accommodate a town's inhabitants and visitors from the countryside as well. Special boxes were provided for distinguished people, and one or more shrines, usually dedicated to Nemesis, were incorporated by the arena entrances.

The few theatres attested in Britain were intended for more tasteful entertainments, although one, at Verulamium, was probably constructed to double as an amphitheatre and in any case was related to a temple behind it. The largest known example is the urban theatre at Canterbury, which was built in the early third century in the true classical manner, with a D-shaped outline, to replace an earlier structure. The tiers of seats rose round the semi-circle while the stage was placed against the diameter. In the centre of the seats and immediately fronting the stage a flat semi-circular area at ground level – the orchestra – provided seating space for distinguished members of the audience.

The association of theatres with temples in Britain has already been mentioned, and it is likely that shows of a religious or semi-religious nature were performed. But there is no reason why they should not also have been used for purely secular displays, in which case recitations, mimes, pantomimes, tragedies and farces may well have been included. Many shows of this nature were extremely topical in their content.

Education may also be considered an amenity. Certainly, Latin and civilized manners are known to have been imparted to the youth of Britain, and Tacitus records that they made excellent pupils. Schools, however, were informal affairs, and most rich parents probably employed private tutors to teach grammar and rhetoric. Plutarch records that he had conversations with a schoolmaster, Demetrius of Tarsus, recently returned from Britain; it is possible that this same Demetrius was the one who dedicated to the gods of the governor's residence at York.

The remaining functions of towns, economic and protective, tend to be shared by settlements of a lesser nature. It is as well, therefore, that some consideration should now be given to the latter.

Apart from the urban sites already described, there were in Britain a large number of nucleated settlements showing considerable variation in size and composition. Some were fortified, others were not. Some became primarily trading centres, the result, once they had been founded for one reason or another, of spontaneous economic growth to meet local requirements; others developed as mining, industrial or religious settlements, providing for the needs of the relative communities. Those which became fortified used to be referred to by

M - Mansio
B - Basilica
T - Temple

Traces of buildings
visible from the air

Roads

Fig. 23 Minor towns or villages at: a) Godmanchester; b) Thorpe; c) Chisenbury Warren; d) Catterick; e) Corbridge

archaeologists as 'small towns', but the term has proved inadequate, since some were little smaller than genuine towns, while it is now recognized that many of the sites which were apparently never fortified often covered very considerable areas. For the same reason, the term village is hardly applicable in all cases, although it might suitably be applied to some. Recently also, an attempt has been made to call them 'native' towns, but it should be resisted, since it is difficult to justify its use. Moreover, to be so claimed these sites should only exhibit archaic

Fig. 24 Minor towns or villages at: a) Braughing; b) Hacconby; c) Sapperton

forms of architecture current in the native Iron Age; they frequently do not, and employ largely Roman styles, if in a simplified manner. Consequently, they are only separated from towns proper by degree and, when all is said and done, civitas capitals were as much native towns as these sites. The use of the word 'native' in this context is as meaningless as 'small town'.

Many of them, however, began in the same way as most civitas capitals, as vici attached to forts. Thereafter, the processes of development were very different. Sometimes, the fort was replaced by a *mansio*, an inn provided for members of the imperial post, a building found in most civitas capitals as well. With the lesser sites, the presence of a mansio often acted in a similar way to a fort and attracted local natives, as at Catterick or Wanborough. The sites themselves seldom exhibit any trace of deliberate planning in their layouts, usually starting as ribbon developments of shops and houses alongside main roads. Then, as need arose, side streets or lanes were constructed in a haphazard manner to give access to more distant houses or land. Frequently, many grew to cover large areas, perhaps as much as 40–50 ha. in extent. But if fortifications were later erected, they equally frequently enclosed only a small proportion of the whole.

As a group, therefore, these sites defy easy classification, and it is likely that no one word or phrase will ever do to describe all. It is possible that some possessed the Roman legal status of vicus, but even if they did, we do not know which, and it would not serve as a meaningful distinction, since most civitas capitals ranked so. It may be that we should follow the practice of some archaeologists and call them lesser, or minor, towns. But if we are to use town to describe them, albeit in a qualified form, we must firmly remember the distinctions which separate them from towns – or cities – proper. Even so, it seems unsuitable to dignify some of these sites as towns, for by no stretch of the imagination were they any such thing. The whole subject of 'small' towns bristles with difficulties and contradictions caused by, as much as anything, a lack of sound evidence about them.

The principal distinction between these sites, whatever they are to be called, and our defined towns is their complete lack of any but the most superficial planning, their association with only the lowest grades of local administration and the lack of all but the most primitive amenities. Even if an element of planning seems to be involved, as at Alchester, Catterick, Corbridge or Godmanchester, evidence for public baths, aqueducts, theatres, amphitheatres or high-standard housing is almost entirely absent. Nevertheless, it would be a mistake to apply this prescription too rigidly, since some exceptions do exist. Catterick possessed a working aqueduct, admittedly inherited from an earlier fort, and might also have had a small bath-house, had the construction work ever been completed. The mining settlement at Charterhouse-in-Mendip appears to have had an amphitheatre; Wanborough (Wilts) had at least one dwelling-house with mosaics; Braughing (Herts) had a small bath-house, but perhaps not of a public nature; Wycomb (Glos) seems to have had a theatre, although probably connected with a religious establishment. Despite these exceptions, it is probably true to say that no site of this type contains a preponderance of structures related to amenities, as are to be found in our defined towns.

Moreover, none has yet produced evidence for a forum and basilica,

although a further caution has to be exercised in this respect, since, by
the third and fourth centuries, when many of these minor sites reached
their maximum development, the provision of a forum or basilica was
no longer considered essential for the good ordering of local government. So later promotions to the rank of civitas capital cannot be
detected by this means, and sites such Ilchester, Water Newton, Bath,
Towcester and Carlisle – all strong candidates – cannot readily be
distinguished.

But all these sites, whatever their size or reason for existence, share
two of the main functions of the higher forms of urban settlement: trade
and protection.

In all sites, large and small, of high and low status, buildings early
appeared which can be identified as shops or workshops, the two words
being largely synonymous in the present context. They can be identified soon after the establishment of great towns such as Colchester,
Verulamium, and Cirencester. They are to be found in the minor towns
such as Water Newton, Margidunum and Catterick, in the military
villages of the north, such as Housesteads, and in the less well-defined
settlements such as Camerton and Wycomb. Normally, they occupy
the frontages of main roads or principal streets in town centres, which
were the most desirable commercial sites. As today, land values were
probably higher in town centres, with the length of frontage frequently
governing the cost. Consequently, most shops of Roman Britain had
narrow frontages and jostled one another in close profusion. Enlargement of a successful business could, therefore, only take place either by
buying up neighbouring premises or by extending the building to the
rear, a process which can frequently be seen to have taken place, as at
Caerwent, or at Verulamium in the second century.

Most shops appear then as narrow strip-like buildings with the long
axis at right angles to the frontage. The front probably contained a
single wide entrance, extending across most of the width of the building, to be closed, when necessary, by wooden shutters, the emplace-
ments for which can admirably be seen in one at Catterick. The
entrance would give on to the business section, while behind it would
either be storerooms and workshops or the living-quarters of the shop-
keeper. There is good reason to suppose that many shops had an upper
storey, in which case the positions of stores and residence could be
permuted according to need. Frequently also in the better class towns,
shops were provided with covered porticoes at the front to protect
goods on open display and provide shelter for shoppers.

There is some evidence to show, occasionally, that blocks of shops
were built as an investment, either for sale or letting, as at Verulamium
and Cirencester. At the former it is difficult to say precisely which, but

Cobbled Frontage

drain

Furnace

Altar

0   5   10   15   20 m

Fig. 25 Shops at Caerwent

at the latter piecemeal redevelopment, shop by shop, with masonry gradually replacing timber-framed buildings, implies that each shop had been sold separately. Market forces were being applied, as at least two shopkeepers had bought up their respective neighbours.

These same forces also affected the quality and size of the buildings. At first, most shops were constructed with timber-frames and wattle-and-daub, or cob, walls. The floors, if not of planks raised on joists, would have been of puddled clay or chalk, gravel or sometimes concrete. Such structural methods did not always preclude refinements and an early shop at Cirencester had good quality frescoes on the walls of the living-quarters. As capital accumulated in the hands of the successful, so their premises were enlarged or improved, and as noted above, masonry replaced wood, neighbouring shops were amalgamated, standards improved. But there would always have remained, at the lower end of the scale, humbler buildings of a commercial nature. Consequently we can envisage several types of contemporary operation. Shops may have belonged to resident freeholders; they may have been let to tenants; or they may have been managed on behalf of the owner by a retainer or slave.

Apart from shops, however, there were other buildings in towns which possessed commercial functions, although they are normally to be found only in the major settlements. First among them, as briefly indicated above, was the forum. There would be provided, not only shops let out by the local authority, but also covered porticoes and a large open space for temporary market stalls, best demonstrated by evidence from Wroxeter, as, when the forum was burnt down in the later second century, stalls erected in the external portico were upset in the panic and deposited their contents of pottery and knife-sharpening stones in the nearby gutter.

But an open space, without porticoes or permanent shops, could function just as adequately as a market. When the forum at Wroxeter was burnt down a second time at the end of the third century, it was never rebuilt. Yet the levelled space seems to have remained in use and may have continued to serve as a forum. In the same way, open gravelled areas in the centres of the minor towns at Catterick and Godmanchester probably provided market-places since forums are not to be expected.

In some more prosperous towns, such as Wroxeter, Leicester, Cirencester or Verulamium, the need was felt for additional, formal market space, so extra buildings were provided, often modelled on the forums. They usually appear as open areas enclosed by one or more ranges of shops and sometimes also possessing external and internal porticoes. At Leicester, a large, basilican-style covered hall was also added; it can be distinguished from the main basilica by its lack of tribunals.

The goods and services provided by these premises covered the whole range of commercial activities, but it is not always easy to identify the trade of a particular shop, for two reasons. Shops which traded in organic materials such as bread, fruit or vegetables are unlikely to provide evidence because of the perishable nature of the goods when buried under normal soil conditions in Britain. Also, most shops, unless destroyed in a catastrophe like a volcanic eruption or a fire, will have been cleared of their goods before being rebuilt or left unoccupied. Despite these restrictions there is, nevertheless, a growing body of material, related to their commercial activities, being put together by modern methods of research. Almost every trade can now be represented by one form of evidence or another.

Pottery and glassware shops are known at Colchester having been burnt in the Boudiccan rebellion, so sealing the stock below a level of ash and building debris. Wine shops are known in Verulamium; oysters were sold in the forum at Caerwent, while a slave managed a goldsmith's at Norton in east Yorkshire; other goldsmiths worked at Verulamium and London, where some interesting remains were found below the governor's palace (see Ch. 5). Coppersmiths' workshops have been identified at Catterick and Verulamium, while individual coppersmiths are known by name at Colchester, Lincoln and in Suffolk. A silversmith operated a large establishment at Silchester, while a glassworker at Leicester indulged, as a sideline, in the illegal smelting of base, late silver coinage to recover the valuable metal. Blacksmiths, more than any other craft, must have been ubiquitous, with few towns or villages lacking a resident practitioner. Silchester, Verulamium and Great Chesterford have all produced caches of ironwork, so implying their presence, while an anonymous tombstone from York depicts a blacksmith with the tools of his trade. Dedications on altars indicate the activities of sculptors and stonemasons from other provinces in the Bath-Cirencester region. Glassware, mainly window-glass and simple vessels, was manufactured at Caistor-by-Norwich, Mancetter and Wilderspool, as well as at Leicester.

Tanners and dyers seem to have operated at Silchester, while breadmaking on a commercial, rather than on the more normal domestic, scale is indicated at Canterbury, London and Lincoln. At Cirencester, a row of shops may have provided cooked meats, while opposite them lay a butchers' market. Another butcher's shop has been claimed at Verulamium.

From other provinces come also an interesting series of monumental reliefs depicting commercial activities: a wine shop, a butcher's, a cutler's, a cobbler's, tailors' and possibly a money-lender, among others. Painted frescoes at Pompeii depict cupids dyeing and preparing cloth. All these trades were no doubt represented in the main urban centres, while many would also have been found in the minor towns and villages.

In societies which are largely based on agriculture the specialist tradesman, whether in town or village, provides a key service to the rural communities. Only the largest country estates in Roman Britain could have maintained their own technical work-forces. All other farmers would have depended on town or village craftsmen for the supply of new equipment and the repair of old. It was probably by this process, more than any other, that information about the new technology became disseminated.

In addition to the manufacturing and distributive trades carried on in towns and other minor settlements, there were some which not only required the presence of industrial raw materials but which, if carried out in normal settlements, would have caused considerable inconvenience. The mining of metal ores and coal, charcoal-burning, quarrying stone, sand, gravel and clay, lime-burning, brick, tile and pottery manufacture, salt extraction from sea-water or saline springs: all were activities which could be most easily carried out at source, and frequently, therefore, they gave rise to their own specialized communities.

Of metals occurring naturally in Britain, gold, silver, lead, copper, iron and tin were the only ones in which interest was shown in the Roman period, and the most valuable, gold and silver, were worked under direct imperial control, or under licence, for they were needed to augment supplies of coinage.

Gold, as far as we yet know, was only mined at Dolocauthi in Carmarthenshire, mainly during the second century. The scale of the workings there, together with obvious signs of well-ordered control, strongly suggests operations under imperial licence, with protection and oversight possibly being provided by an adjacent fort. The mines were large, using both open-cast and underground methods of extraction. An extensive settlement grew up to supply the needs of the community, although it is probable that here, as in other mines, much of the labour would have been provided by convicts or slaves. Unfortunately little is known in detail about the settlement, but manufacturing goldsmiths seem to have been present, so some of the produce at least must have been sold, probably by auction, on the open market.

The ores of silver and lead occur naturally together. In the Roman period, the chief areas of mining activity were the Mendips, developed within a few years of the invasion, the Peak District of Derbyshire, and the area around Shropshire and the north Welsh border, both developed by about AD 80; other districts in the north Pennines may later have provided a quota. Down to the end of the second century, many of the mines were supervised by military detachments, notably from Legio II and Legio XX, but increasingly they were transferred to concessionary hands and the names of local authorities, private individuals and at least two companies are known, from dies cast on ingots of lead, to have been involved. Little is known, however, of the settlements connected with the mines.

At Charterhouse, in the Mendips, a sizeable centre has been identified with an amphitheatre, although the latter may have been associated with a military detachment in the area than with the settlement. One of the main companies was the *Societas Lutudarensis* in Derbyshire; somewhere, perhaps close to the fort at Brough-on-Noe, must lie its headquarters.

Iron was probably the most important metal to native Britons. The ores are found widely distributed throughout the Weald of Kent, the Forest of Dean, and in a band following the oolitic ironstone from Northamptonshire through to Lincolnshire. Outlying areas occur in Yorkshire, Norfolk, Cheshire and Northumberland. Indeed, the metal occurs so commonly in Britain, that it is unlikely that any formal control was exercised over its extraction, except for certain areas run by military or naval detachments for their own use. Some rather sprawling settlements of no great size grew in Northamptonshire, east Leicestershire, Lincolnshire and Norfolk, although it is not always easy to differentiate between small settlements of this type and those where production apparently centred on a villa. Not much is known of their equivalents in Kent, Sussex or Gloucestershire, although it is probable that the wealth of the two minor towns at Kenchester and Weston-under-Penyard (Glos) depended largely on the ironworkers of the Forest of Dean.

The primary extraction of tin and copper does not seem to have spawned any great settlements, most of the work being carried out on an extremely local basis. Tin was found in Cornwall, where it was both mined and recovered from stream beds. Surprisingly, official interest only seems to have been shown in the late first and again in the fourth centuries; in between times, the British source could not compete with the rich Spanish mines, and only when the latter were exhausted did interest revive in Britain.

Secondary working of pewter, an alloy of tin and lead, took place at Camerton and at Lansdown, outside Bath, presumably using Mendips' lead. Some copper may also have been produced in Cornwall, and elsewhere it was found in Shropshire, north Wales and Anglesey. Again, quantities produced do not seem to have warranted official intervention and most was produced on an extremely local basis, especially in Anglesey. Nevertheless, as with tin, so with copper, British sources came into their own in the fourth century, when a shortage of the metal for coinage arose.

By comparison, some considerable settlements arose around the pottery industry, of which the best known is probably at Water Newton. There, a fortified nucleus of 17 ha. was surrounded by extensive areas of kilns, workshops and the houses of potters. Much of the pottery produced is of a type known to archaeologists as Castor ware, a colour-coated pottery, imitated at a number of other sites and common in many parts of Britain in the third and fourth centuries. Other major pottery-producing centres are known at Mancetter, Nuneaton, Norton (Yorks), Farnham and in the region round Oxford. Some production areas, however, seem only to have given rise to the most primitive settlements, as in the New Forest. Many of the chief potteries grew up around acknowledged towns, where they were not only assured of a local market but were also in a position to take advantage of wider connexions. At Colchester, pottery was produced which reached many distant markets, including military sites in the north, and an attempt was even made to manufacture samian ware in the last part of the second century, but it failed owing to the lack of suitable clay. Lincoln was another such site and, indeed, it is probable that most towns produced their own pottery in suburban areas. Similarly, brick and tile was normally produced close to where it was needed. Municipal brick-works existed at Gloucester and private companies operated around Cirencester.

The manufacture of pottery, brick and tile has four requirements: clay, wood, water and transport facilities. All sites in Britain possessed the first three; the fourth was not so easily come by, since the most suitable form of transport for pottery is by water, the goods being bulky, heavy and fragile. Consequently, it is often found that the most success-ful centres, with the widest markets, were situated close to suitable rivers, or within easy reach of them.

Little is known about settlements specifically associated with quarry-ing, coal-mining or salt production. As with the production of brick and tile, most quarrying operations will have been carried out in the neigh-bourhood of existing settlements to meet local needs. Huge quantities of stone, sand and gravel must have been extracted for construction work. Certain types of stone, used for specific purposes, were carried long distances: Bath stone appears as tombstones at Colchester, Bar-nack stone from Rutland at Verulamium, Lincolnshire limestone and Kentish ragstone in London. Moreover, exotic stones from abroad such as porphyry and various marbles were imported to decorate public and private buildings.

Coal was employed extensively as a fuel in Britain. It seems to have been mined from outcrop formations in a number of areas, including Northumberland, Yorkshire, Nottinghamshire and Somerset. It was carried widely and used for industrial and domestic purposes.

Salt, an important item in the diet and also necessary for preserving food and skins, was obtained by the evaporation of sea-water on coastal sites around the Wash, the Essex marshes and the Thames and Severn estuaries. The evaporation was carried out in ceramic pans supported over open fires and their situation on bleak coastal marshes did not encourage the growth of associated permanent settlements. Neverthe-less, there is some indication of Fenland sites acting as collecting and marketing points. Two inland centres, given the name of Salinae in contemporary sources, at Droitwich and Middlewich respectively, may have grown to meet the requirements of manufacturers evaporating brine from mineral springs.

There were also a number of settlements which grew up connected with religious sites, of which probably Bath and Buxton, both associated with hot springs, are the best known. Other lesser sites have been identified at several places, including Springhead, near Dartford, Wycomb, near Cheltenham and possibly Gosbecks, near Colchester. Such sites certainly attracted numerous pilgrims, whose needs had to be catered for, and who also provided a ready source of income for tradespeople. It is interesting to note that theatres were built at Gosbecks and possibly at Wycomb, so that large crowds could be accommodated.

Apart from the distinctive central temple or temples, the settlements related to them varied little from the norm, although they might be expected to contain a rather higher proportion of buildings providing accommodation. Bath is probably the best example to consider, where a great classical temple stood in the centre dedicated jointly to the local deity Sul and the Roman goddess Minerva. The hot spring rose from the ground within the temple courtyard and the water was channelled into an elaborate bathing establishment. A number of military tomb-stones are known from the area and, although there possibly was an early fort, it may have been used by the army in Britain as a curative or convalescent centre of a type known in some other provinces. In all these settlements, commerce must have provided a strong motivation for their existence.

The last main function of towns and other settlements that we have to consider is protective, and all, no matter their size or status, exer-cised it to a greater or lesser extent. Even the smallest nucleated centre offered some mutual protection to its members by virtue of their being gathered together in one place, so deterring bands of robbers or perhaps even the attentions of rapacious land-owners. Later, as the nature of the threat to communities, or to essential services accommo-dated within them, changed and became more menacing, the protec-tive function was, in many cases, supplemented by the provision of physical fortifications of ramparts, ditches and walls. Not all settle-ments were so treated, while there is also a time factor to be considered. Moreover, additional complications arise, since there was probably a strong element of official policy involved, as the central government had to protect its regional administrative and supply centres. It may be, however, that the provision of fortifications for certain sites, but not for others, will enable us in time to refine our classification of settlement types.

The erection of urban fortifications in the early empire seems to have been generally forbidden except under licence from the emperor. This was presumably the counterpart of the law which prohibited the carriage of arms by citizens except for hunting or personal defence on a journey; protection was expected to be provided by the Roman army on the frontiers. Consequently, when urban fortifications were erected, we have to look behind the act in order to seek some reason for the exercise of the imperial licence. Consequently, also, such fortifications are going to reflect imperial attitudes and policy and will only rarely be constructed for purely local reasons.

These provisions seem generally to have been observed in Britain; most towns and other settlements started as undefended sites and remained so until the end of the second century. There were, however, some exceptions. At an early date, the new towns of Verulamium and Silchester were fortified with earth banks and single ditches. It is difficult to explain why they and no other town, such as Colchester, London or Canterbury were then allowed defences, especially as the respective constitutional positions were not the same in each case. Verulamium, whether or not already a municipium, was a civitas capital within the province; Silchester almost certainly lay in the kingdom of Cogidubnus. Yet a common reason probably governed both cases, since both were uncomfortably close to the new frontier, beyond which, in the late 40s, Caratacus was still operating successfully. Even after his capture, warfare continued in south Wales, so that without a linear barrier along the frontier it would probably have been all too easy for small raiding parties to have slipped past the forts and created havoc in the province. The Celtic tribes were adept at this form of guerrilla warfare. Physical protection for the nearest towns might, therefore, have seemed essential, but it was only of a temporary nature, as within a decade or so both towns had expanded beyond these limits.

The next scare, which prompted urban fortifications, seems to have been during the civil war of AD 69–70. Attention has already been drawn in the previous chapter to the part which Cogidubnus may have played. It was probably Vespasian who conferred legatine authority on him and, perhaps as a temporary measure, gave him control over part of the province, when he was faced with an official governor of uncertain loyalty and an army on the verge of mutiny. Cogidubnus, in order to defend his kingdom and acting with full legality, fortified Winchester and Silchester and possibly also Chichester, although there is as yet no evidence from the latter site. Both the former were provided with earth

ramparts and ditches, those at Silchester adopting a different alignment from the earlier defensive circuit and enclosing a much larger
area. It is possible that the three minor sites in Sussex at Hardham,
Alfodean, and Iping, which also seem to have been fortified at an early
period, were part of this same programme.

Between AD 70 and the end of the second century, when the next
phase of major fortification occurred, some individual towns were
provided with defences. It would seem that the two coloniae at Lincoln
and Gloucester inherited the ramparts of the legionary fortresses which
they had supplanted. By then, however, the ramparts would have been
standing for a considerable time; timber lacing and breastwork would
have rotted and all would have been in a state of disrepair. Consequently, they were rapidly strengthened by the addition of masonry walls.
Following perhaps the example set by these two coloniae, Colchester
received permission to enclose itself in the Hadrianic period where,
however, the work appears to have been left incomplete, only being
finished on the west side. It is probable that all three cities took
advantage of their senior status in Britain and their semi-military
origins to petition the emperor for the rights of enclosure, as had
happened in Gallia Narbonnensis under Augustus. An element of pride
may have influenced the applications, since there was no obvious
defensive reason for fortifications at that time.

The sequence of events which surrounded the usurping of imperial
power by the governor of Britain, Clodius Albinus, in AD 193 has been
described in the previous chapter. One of the by-products of his actions
was the initiation of a programme of urban fortification greater than
ever before. Albinus no doubt soon realized that, to contest his claim
successfully against other usurpers, he would have to remove the larger
part of the army from Britain, leaving the province virtually defence-
less. Permission or orders, therefore, seem to have been given for most
major towns and some minor settlements to erect fortifications. It is
probable, also, that Albinus misjudged the time which he had at his
disposal before having to force the issue. At any rate, work appears to
have begun in a number of towns and, unlike earlier attempts at
fortification, was started in masonry. At Cirencester, Exeter, Verulamium and possibly also at Caerwent and Silchester, the construction of gates and internal towers commenced, while at Dorchester the
foundations of part of the curtain wall were laid. The whole project was
immense and would probably have involved the placing in position of
over half a million cubic metres of masonry, with all that meant in
terms of stone-quarrying and dressing, lime-burning, sand-quarrying,
mortar-mixing, employment of skilled masons and, above all, transport. It is not surprising that time ran out before the task had hardly

started. Consequently, the work had to be completed in a hurry with a return to earlier methods of earth banks and ditches. Only London, the provincial capital, appears to have had its defences completed in masonry, while among all the civitas capitals, Leicester and Canterbury, for some as yet unexplained reason, seem to have stayed aloof from the turmoil.

Somewhat naturally the area enclosed by the new fortifications was kept to a minimum so as to reduce the overall length of rampart to be erected. Consequently, isolated buildings on the perimeter were often omitted, such as houses at Cirencester, Dorchester and Leicester. This policy usually resulted in the amphitheatre being left outside, since the large area of ground it demanded would only have been available well away from the centre.

Some minor sites, also, such as Kenchester, Bath, Dorchester-on-Thames and Irchester, were then fortified. While it is possible to account for such activities in major cities and towns, it is not so easy to explain why some lesser sites were involved, especially when a large number were not.

In view of the participation of the provincial government in the programme of work, it is likely that the minor sites affected contained some key installation which had to be protected. What it was we can only guess, and a number of possibilities arise. The minor towns in Britain had probably, by the end of the second century, become important in the second level of local administration, acting as centres for country districts – *pagi* – within the framework of the civitates. It is likely that they contained buildings, either associated with local records and tax-collection, or the imperial post, and would, therefore, require protection. This may explain why, at some very large settlements, only a small area at the centre was fortified. Unfortunately such buildings are not always easy to identify, even when they have been excavated, and too little is known altogether about the internal buildings of minor towns.

Certainly the end of the second and the beginning of the third century was a period when the central administration was extending its tentacles more and more into the countryside, often by the secondment of army officers to individual regions. There lies at the centre of Godmanchester an early third-century building, not unlike a military headquarters block, which has been claimed to be a 'town hall' for a newly constituted civitas. A more likely explanation, which may also give us a clue to the functions of these minor towns, is probably provided by a contemporary inscription from a building at Combe Down, outside Bath. It refers to the restoration by a procurator's assistant of a building called a *principia*, or headquarters, either of an imperial estate or of a tax-collection area. The structure at Godman-chester is probably best viewed in the same way, and would provide a reason for the fortifications erected round the site.

One further point is worth making in connexion with the late second-century programme of urban fortifications. No physical barrier is effective unless it is properly manned. In the absence of the army from Britain, this could only have been managed by a local militia. There must, therefore, have been a degree of relaxation in the law relating to the carriage of arms if the fortifications were to be fully effective.

For reasons not yet completely understood, the urban defences erected in the late second century seem to have been retained after Severus retook Britain. Indeed, by the end of the first decade of the following century, work had been resumed on the erection of masonry fortifications. The scale of the work, coupled probably with a shortage of skilled masons, meant that the original programme was not fully completed until the later part of the century. By that time, also, some sites which had not at first been included had additionally been for-tified, such as the civitas capitals at Leicester and Canterbury and some minor towns. The latter may represent an extension of the tax-collection system, which was probably advanced yet further when, in the early fourth century, another series of sites were fortified such as Catterick and Thorpe-by-Newark. By then, also, much greater reliance was being placed on tax-collection in kind – the *annona militaris* – to feed and supply the army. Taxes of this sort, paid in grain, cattle and other produce, would have required larger areas for their collection and concentration. Apart from that more care must also be exercised in defining fortified settlements from now on, as some may have become defended road stations, as with a series between Towcester and Wrox-eter on Watling Street, or centres for detachments of the field army, as at Catterick in the late fourth century.

There are some structural distinctions which can be drawn between the earliest and latest attempts at urban fortification. For instance, the first gateways to be erected, as at Lincoln, Cirencester and Ver-ulamium were built in the monumental manner with double portals and sometimes with additional foot passages. They also incorporated massive external drum towers. Later, however, the size of gates was drastically reduced, often to a single portal surmounted by a tower, as with gates at Canterbury and Caerwent. In general, however, the fortifications consisted of a masonry wall up to 3 m. thick, backed by an earth bank which normally, but not always, incorporated the remnants of earlier ramparts. In front lay one, or at the most, two ditches. In some cases, internal masonry towers formed an integral part of the defences, while in later circuits, the earth bank tended to be omitted, in line with newly developed thoughts on military architecture.

The last major structural works on urban fortifications were carried out apparently about AD 370 and were thought to have been instituted during the military reorganization of Count Theodosius. The defences were updated by the addition of external towers, but since their foundations usually overlapped the inner lip of the existing ditch, the latter was frequently filled and a new, often wider, one cut further away. But not all towns were so treated. Some notable examples among both major and minor settlements were omitted from the programme, including Silchester. At others, distribution of towers was uneven: Caerwent, for instance, had full coverage on both north and south walls but none on the east or west.

It is usually claimed that these towers were added to deploy artillery more effectively, as in the more 'modern' Saxon Shore forts. Artillery needed trained army personnel; with the manpower shortages of the late Roman empire, there may well not have been enough to go round in all towns and minor centres. So they were apportioned where the need, or the threat, was considered greatest.

Certainly by the late fourth century, a number of towns, as well as some other sites, including villas, contained detachments of the regular Roman army, who left characteristic items of equipment behind them, such as belt buckles with animal-head decorations. We do not know in most cases if they were units of the field army, but at Catterick, about AD 370, a major reorganization took place to allow the billeting of troops within the town, in which many of the residents appear to have been evicted from their houses and shops.

We have considered the principal functions of cities, towns and other settlements, their distinctions and their foundations, and it remains to review their subsequent developments.

No matter what dictates governed the choice of site or the reasons for the establishment of a town or village, it would, once founded, have been almost entirely at the mercy of economic forces. Consequently, although many may have shared a common purpose at first, their subsequent developments were by no means always comparable. In some instances there is clear evidence for the foundation of a civitas capital, such as Caistor-by-Norwich, Wroxeter or Leicester, although the most important buildings, the forum and basilica, were not provided for another thirty years or so. This may, in part, have been due to apathy, but it could also point to a lack of money and their ultimate completion in the second century may have been brought about by massive remission of taxes by Hadrian. Silchester possessed a public bath-house well before the end of the first century, but at Leicester,

Wroxeter and Caistor-by-Norwich they were not built before the middle of the second. At Cirencester the amphitheatre was not constructed until the early second century, whereas Canterbury and Chichester were provided with buildings for public entertainment before the end of the first. The theatre at Verulamium was not built until the middle of the second century, at about the same time as one was being constructed at out-of-the-way Brough-on-Humber. Moreover, the growing need to accommodate larger numbers of spectators is evident at Canterbury, where the theatre was completely rebuilt on a more generous scale in the early third century, and at Verulamium, where an enlargement took place in the early fourth. A considerable disparity between towns often exists, therefore, in the rate at which public buildings were provided reflecting, as with forums and basilicas, the contrasting needs and the variable availability of the necessary finance.

The rate of expansion in commercial enterprise is likewise indicated by the provision of extra public markets. For instance, Verulamium was provided with one in the late first century, Cirencester and Wroxeter were catered for by the middle second century and Leicester by the early third.

The development of private housing and shops is more difficult to summarize since, with them, we are dealing with a much greater variety of personal circumstances and not with reasonably predictable, corporate communities. Something has already been said about the standard of housing and shops earlier in this chapter, but we can usefully add the example of private-housing development in the colonia at Gloucester. At first the legionary veterans were accommodated in terrace houses which, in block, much resembled a legionary barrack. Partial demolition and rebuilding of separate houses within a block rapidly occurred and by the second or third decades of the second century a block had been replaced by a number of small, detached houses. Further, by the middle of the century, a number of these small house properties had become amalgamated, incidentally extinguishing a public right-of-way, and a single house with a compact, italianate plan had been constructed. As already indicated earlier, such houses are rare in Britain, although others have been identified at Colchester and Caerwent. Their existence may point to a soldier, or trader from another province, settling permanently in Britain.

If it is true to say that the middle of the second century saw a period of maximum development in cities and towns, the same cannot be said for minor towns and other lesser settlements. In many, development lagged behind that in major towns, and it was often not until the third or even fourth century that they began to show signs of possessing less ephemeral buildings. This is particularly true of the military vici in the north where the peaceful conditions, brought about by Caracalla's settlement of the frontier problem, ushered in a new era of prosperity. Here, as elsewhere, alterations were also brought about by changing legal and social conditions. Caracalla's award of citizenship to all free-born members of the empire tended to erase the earlier distinctions between cities, towns and other settlements, and in so doing presumably removed some of the gloss from the former, possibly making it not so unfashionable to live in a minor town or village.

Despite the rising prosperity of many settlements, the third century was, nevertheless, a time of recession for most of the empire. Britain seems to have suffered less than other provinces, but must, like all, have been affected by the appalling inflation. But it should not be forgotten that, for certain classes, inflation can in the short term be a benefit. One of the causes of the inflation was the continually increasing need to give higher pay to the army. Britain had a large garrison, so that it may be that more and more of the money supply, but of ever decreasing value, was ultimately finding its way into the pockets of British shopkeepers and merchants. Large fortunes were undoubtedly made, if the size of some late third-century coin-hoards are taken as indicators, even if inflation rendered them valueless. In the major towns, however, the third century was marked by a decline in the construction of public buildings, shops and houses, a decline which may have been enhanced to some extent by the need to build masonry defences, so employing a large part of the available labour force and probably also tying up much capital. The volume of masonry erected round a town, as its fortifications, probably exceeded, by a sizeable amount, the sum of all the masonry in its public buildings.

With the return of Britain to the central government in the early fourth century, confidence was restored, which was demonstrated outwardly by a spate of building activity. Once more, attention was turned to the construction of amenities, with the restoration and enlargement of the Verulamium theatre and the erection outside it of a new triumphal arch across Watling Street. In Cirencester, considerable alterations were made to the forum and basilica, prompted perhaps by the town becoming a provincial capital; extensions were made to the market, and at least one other major building was erected where, earlier, there had been private houses. Many dwellings were enlarged and refurbished to include mosaics then being produced by a local firm of craftsmen. Comparable activity was reflected in most other towns.

Typical of the period was the formal doubling of the size of the colonia at Lincoln. A very large number of towns had generated prosperous suburbs, which sometimes tended to be abandoned when fortifications were erected. But, at Lincoln, a large suburb on the slope of the hill below the colonia was of sufficient importance to be enclosed by a wall in the early fourth century, and indeed it may earlier have been given earthworks. Unlike most suburbs, however, this area had been laid out in a regular manner with a grid of streets, and many amenities and important buildings.

Minor towns and settlements are also eloquent of the new confidence. Military vici in the north flourished as never before and some, such as Carlisle, Corbridge and Catterick, were enclosed within defences. In the centre of Corbridge lay two separate, third-century, enclosed compounds devoted to the manufacture of arms and equipment for the army. But civilian buildings, notably a group of temples, clustered round them. At Catterick, despite the fortified enclosure on the south bank of the river Swale, inside which work had also started on a small bath-house, confidence was such that a suburb developed on the north bank. Carlisle prospered equally, its importance probably being enhanced when it became the capital of a newly constituted northern civitas. In many other minor towns, such as Water Newton, Ancaster, Margidunum, Thorpe-by-Newark, Alcester and Wanborough, the picture is the same, often with masonry buildings replacing timber-framed ones.

There were, however, some exceptions. At Brough-on-Humber, local opinion seems to have opted for continuing country life and it seems likely that the town, even though a civitas capital, failed to prosper. Certainly by the fourth century its theatre was in ruins and being robbed of its masonry. Chelmsford too, although given earthwork fortifications in the late second century, suffered a disastrous fire at about the same time, from which, seemingly, it never fully recovered, for it never warranted the construction of masonry defences.

The early fourth-century influence continued for some time, but began to falter by the middle of the century. From then on it gradually but fitfully declined. First-class houses were still being constructed at Verulamium and Cirencester in the last decades of the century, but they tended to be exceptional. The public baths at Wroxeter had for some time been rendered unusable; no attempt was made to rehabilitate them. Towards the end of the century, a major fire destroyed the forum and basilica, the market-hall and many shops in the centre of Leicester; they were left in ruins. The overall impression gained is of a slow running-down process. If a major building was destroyed accidentally it was not replaced; if parts wore out they were seldom repaired. In contrast, there is evidence to show that, in a large number of towns and minor settlements, daily life continued much unchanged, even beyond the official rescript of AD 410. At Cirencester, for instance, the forum continued in use until at least 440, although the floor of the piazza had worn out, while the defences were kept in good order. At Verulamium, masonry buildings were being constructed well into the fifth century, while the flow from the aqueduct was still maintained and distributed in the town.

The active survival of towns and other settlements, after 410, was due in part to the bands of federate soldiers recruited from Germanic peoples and used as urban garrisons. This was a practice that had started during the later empire when such people, in return for military service, were given land in payment. Some at least of these soldiers were left behind after the formal withdrawal of the Roman army, or were at any rate quickly replaced by others. The presence of detachments has been shown at a number of places, such as Dorchester-on-Thames and Canterbury. At the former, a rapid degeneration of accommodation took place from good quality masonry buildings to wattle-and-daub houses with sunken floors. At the latter, a number of such sunken houses have been found, roughly lining a street, suggesting perhaps that a complete insula of the town had been given over to these confederate soldiers, and that a degree of order and discipline was being enforced.

All nucleated settlements were, however, under pressure. The general insecurity of the countryside and disrepair of the roads had severed them from their main sources of supply. Yet they managed to survive on crops grown in their own surrounding fields, even if they were now administered by 'strong men' in place of the magistrates and council.

But the new garrisons were both treacherous and unreliable. It must also be remembered that they had been engaged partly to fight against their own kin, since the number of Anglo-Saxon raiders and settlers was increasing. Before long, probably about 440, there was a mutiny and parts of eastern Britain then became permanently Saxon. It seems likely, although as yet there is no firm proof, that the Saxons were aided in their efforts by an outbreak of a serious epidemic disease, which inflicted severe mortality on the remaining inhabitants of the towns and lesser settlements. Only thus is it possible to account for the apparent abandonment of the walled town at Cirencester, with bodies left lying in ditches beside the streets, in favour of the nearby amphitheatre, which seems to have been put in a defensive state.

The evidence for what happened in the fifth century is tantalizingly slight, but it appears that after the initial Saxon successes around 450, the surviving British rallied. It is the age to which Arthur properly belongs, and the myth has probably grown around some major war leader of the late fifth century. At the battle of Mount Badon, usually put at that time, the British inflicted a defeat on the Saxons and there ensued a period of peace and prosperity, coupled with a maintained balance between the warring factions. It is probable that the dykes around Silchester were constructed during this period to act as boundaries between the surviving Romano-British town and its land on the one hand and a neighbouring Saxon enclave on the other. In other places there was a reversion to hill-forts as strongholds, probably because, with a falling population, they were more suitable than urban centres for forms of warfare then current.

In the end, towns and minor settlements slid into a slow decay, partly as their inhabitants died, were killed, or deserted them, partly as the economic system, in which they had played a central part, crumbled. It is doubtful if any became fully deserted, but they had long ceased to possess the institutions or amenities by which they could be called towns.

Finally, it is interesting to record that, as the major centres of urban civilization collapsed, they approached the condition of their humbler cousins which, perhaps, altered little. Therein lies the principal distinction which enables us to distinguish the former, but not the latter, as *towns*.

Chapter 4

Farms and Farming, Gardens and Gardening

Roman Britain, as with all countries before the Industrial Revolution, was first and foremost an agricultural community. Farming was the basic provider of wealth, and although many inhabitants might have come in time to accept town life, the larger part of the population remained in the countryside, practising husbandry in a variety of ways and at different levels.

The basic methods of farming in Roman Britain differed little from those used in the Iron Age. Consequently, any improvements, of which there were many, came about by an extension of familiar ways and by better facilities for the marketing of produce.

Farming in the Iron Age was largely a matter of subsistence agriculture. Since most people farmed and had their own produce, there was no market in which to dispose of a surplus, and therefore farmers grew only for their immediate needs. But the ability to produce a saleable surplus was probably there, waiting for the right economic climate. To some extent this came about with the expansion of the Roman empire to the Channel coast. The army consumed enormous amounts of grain and other materials which they were unable to produce themselves. It is likely that Caesar's forcible requisitions of corn, while in Britain, perhaps gave the local inhabitants the idea of selling corn to the army once he had returned to Gaul, and, by the beginning of the first century AD, Strabo lists corn as a British export. Consequently, by then, a surplus was being produced and the ear of corn, or barley, adopted as a symbol by Cunobelin on his coins is eloquent proof of where extra cultivation was being carried out.

With the arrival of the Roman army in Britain in AD 43, a large, permanent consumer of agricultural produce became established. Their basic rations were obtained by compulsory requisitions of grain and other goods from the farmers, a tax known as the *annona militaris*, for which a token payment may have been made. The amount was calculated as a percentage of the crop, so that a farmer, working only at subsistence level, had to produce that much more if he was not himself to starve. Once he was growing that increase, he probably realized that, by extending his production still further, he would have a profitable asset, in which he would have been helped by three other new factors.

The development of cities, towns and, to a lesser extent, minor settlements promoted classes of society which were no longer agriculturally self-supporting. They now had to be supplied with food. The extension of the road system, coupled with increased use of river transport, beyond the original military needs for arterial routes, linked town and countryside, enabling the goods to be more easily brought to the new consumers. Once there, the ready availability of a good currency, with ample small change for even the smallest transaction, will have smoothed the passage of goods from one hand to another.

The increase in production was brought about mainly by the cultivation of larger areas of land, since yields did not greatly alter. But the introduction of more and better quality implements such as ploughs, iron-shod spades, scythes and even 'mechanical' reaping machines will have greatly aided this expansion.

It is all too easy at this point to enter into a circular argument: towns could not have developed satisfactorily without an agricultural surplus to feed them, yet at the same time they were largely responsible for enabling a surplus to be produced. So it is difficult to say precisely where the process started.

A simple, light plough which cut, but did not turn, a furrow was known in Iron Age Britain, and undoubtedly continued in use in many places, and probably in far greater numbers, throughout the Roman period. But there were several improvements. A heavier plough, of similar type, or with the share fitted with ears, or ground-wrests, could be used to turn a furrow to one side or another, and its use could also allow denser soils to be cultivated. A further development was the plough with a heavy knife-coulter fitted to the beam to cut a vertical slice into the soil. If accompanied by an asymmetric share, there was a manifest intention to turn the furrow to one side only. Such a plough would also have possessed a wooden mould-board to complete the turning. Both coulters and shares of this type are known from Britain in the Roman period, although they are rare and we cannot say how frequent was their use. But it is worth remembering that even modern steel plough-shares wear out with great rapidity; shares and coulters of the Roman period would probably have been worn out almost beyond recognition before being discarded and returned to the blacksmith for reuse. Only seldom will they have been lost in the field. Consequently the number found cannot truly reflect the number then in use, since they will only turn up in blacksmiths' stocks, or as 'spares' kept in a

Fig. 26 Romano-British farm implements: a) plough; b) shears; c) spade; d) sickle; e) mattock; f) scythe.

farmyard – both rarely found occurrences. But an increase in the overall number of more primitive ploughs would also have led to a great improvement. Not only could land, cultivated slowly and laboriously before with spade or hoe, now be ploughed more quickly, but the time saved also allowed more to be brought into production.

The introduction of the iron-shod spade would have greatly facilitated the digging of drainage ditches, so improving the quality of both pasture and arable, and causing fens and marshes to be turned to agricultural production. Better quality iron axes, saws and mattocks meant that scrubland, and even heavier forest, could be cleared efficiently for cropping. The introduction of the two-handed scythe, with portable sharpening anvil on which notches in the blade could be beaten out, allowed a much greater quantity of hay to be cut for winter forage; moreover, since it speeded the work there was less chance of loss due to summer storms. Similarly, a properly balanced sickle ensured a quicker and less arduous grain harvest, while spring-handled shears eased the clipping of fleeces. These implements were the principal benefits conferred on British agriculture by Roman technology. Many others, such as improved stonemasons', carpenters', wheelwrights', coopers' and blacksmiths' tools added to the general betterment of husbandry.

Improvements, however, were not only confined to equipment. Spelt, a form of wheat suitable for a damp climate, had been introduced in the Iron Age as an addition to barley and emmer, and enabled winter crops to be grown as well as the normal spring sowing. In the Roman period its use seems to have increased, together with rye, oats and flax. Root crops, such as turnips, carrots and parsnips not only provided vegetables for human consumption, but were also welcomed, in addition to rape, as winter feed for stock.

The cereals which were grown still needed to be parched before storing and the simple Iron Age process was elaborated by the construction of well-designed corn-drying ovens or kilns. They were normally built of brick or stone with one or more flues, carrying hot air from an outside furnace, running beneath the floor. It is probable that the grain was spread to dry on an upper floor of wood and the whole would have been made weatherproof by a wooden shed. Considerable variations in size and shape are known.

There is also good evidence that careful breeding and the better supplies of winter fodder improved the strains of cows, sheep and horses. Goats were still raised for their hair and two British products of woven goat-hair achieved a considerable fame in the empire. Pigs continued to be fattened in increasing numbers, and geese and fowls were raised for eggs, meat and their feathers. Good timber in increasing amounts for construction must have been a valuable crop, even if regeneration took a long time. In the Diocletianic price code, a 23 m. fir tree, 60 cm. in diameter was listed at a price of 50,000 denarii, whereas the same sum could only be earned by selling the wheat from about 5 ha. of ploughed field. Felling of mature trees in an estate could therefore provide a very useful capital sum for an owner if he wished to develop. In between felling and regeneration, some annual income could have been obtained by coppicing for fuel and charcoal.

Fig. 27 a) Lullingstone barn; corn-driers at b) Great Casterton; c-e) Hambledon

Fields, however, remained much as before, but there is evidence that the number of 'Celtic' fields in use on southern downlands greatly increased in number during the Roman period. In places, however, some fields appear to be overlaid by others with less square proportions and of undoubted Roman date, and such changes to 'long' fields may have been brought about by greater use of heavier ploughs, but there is, as yet, no general agreement. In some areas, also, 'open' fields may have been employed, but are difficult to prove in the absence of visible boundaries. A form of crop-rotation was employed, allowing for a fallow period, and, since most farms would have had a mixture of pasture and arable, stock could have been run in the fallow fields to feed off the stubble and weed growth, while at the same time manuring the soil. Consequently hedges or fences, or in some places drystone walls, along boundaries would have been a necessity. Manure was also collected in farmyards and spread on the land, so accounting for the widespread scatter of heavily weathered pot-sherds to be found on such fields, for broken pots from the farm-buildings were no doubt thrown on the manure heap. Marling of light soils and liming of heavier ones were also practised.

In many areas it is possible to associate fields with settlements or farms, and we find that even villas continued to use the old type of 'Celtic' field. Contemporary agriculturalists recommended that a field should be of a size which could be conveniently ploughed by one man in a day, and, although there were variations, perhaps brought about by the larger and more efficient ploughs, this seems to have remained the basic factor governing their size throughout the Roman period. In some areas, stock enclosures replaced or were added to fields, being used no doubt for annual round-ups, for wintering cattle and sheep and possibly for lambing and calving. These frequently go hand in hand with large open spaces on moor, down, or fen, containing no fields; they are usually interpreted as ranches which, in some cases, may have continued to be delimited by Iron Age dykes, or in others by new boundaries. At Rockbourne Down (Hants) there was not only extensive evidence of large-scale grain production, but also a ditched and hedged enclosure of nearly 40 ha. for sheep or cattle.

Increased surplus brought increased profits to the farmers, which in turn brought further improvements to the farms. These can be most easily demonstrated by a study of the domestic farmhouses, which, when sufficiently romanized, are called villas.

It has been often repeated that villa, in Latin, means a farm, and so it does. But it implies the *whole* farm and not simply the residential building at the centre. Unfortunately, although in Roman law there was a narrow definition restricting use of the word to country buildings related to farming, in practice the Romans themselves were much more lax and sometimes used it to describe country-based industrial centres, and even, in one case, to describe a building within the boundaries of the City of Rome – the *Villa Publica*. In provinces like Britain, there is also the additional difficulty caused by native farmsteads continuing to exist side by side with their more romanized counterparts. At what point, therefore, does a farm become a villa?

Many attempts have been made to define the term in a Romano-British context, some more successful than others. In essence it would seem that a villa is a building with an agricultural basis, displaying

Fig. 28 Field-systems at: a) Chaldon Herring, Dorset; b) Martin Down, Hants; c) Cottenham, Cambs

some degree of romanization in its structure and plan and belonging to the social and economic system of the province; moreover it should be in the countryside. But the latter restriction poses an immediate problem. There is a good deal of evidence for the existence of farms, and farmhouses, in towns. Are they to be called villas? Opinion is still divided and no easy solution is likely to present itself, especially when the problem is still largely ignored, as it has been in the latest book to appear on Roman villas. Furthermore, it is strictly incorrect, according to our definition, to describe as villas the houses of master-potters situated around Water Newton; yet they are so called. Again there is no ready answer.

The growth of villas in Britain was somewhat naturally a slow process: Iron Age roundhouses first gave way to simple rectangular cottages, often of cob or half-timbered construction, which in turn were rebuilt in more elaborate ways. There were, nevertheless, some anomalies, to which exceptional circumstances can usually be ascribed. Few villas with any degree of sophistication developed before the second century in Britain, although the area around Verulamium seems to have seen some growth after the Boudiccan rebellion. It is probable that these early farmhouses represent the dwellings of Catuvellaunian gentry, who continued to reside on their country estates centred round villas such as Park Street, Gorhambury, Hemel Hempstead and Boxmoor. Mostly, they consisted of a single range of some half a dozen rooms, sometimes with a cellar, and with the rooms connected by an external portico.

At Boxmoor, an additional room had been included at each end of the range to provide symmetrical wings, while the whole building was surrounded by a covered verandah. This form of bungalow would have been readily recognized by any British colonial administrator in India or Africa during the early twentieth century, but in the Roman period the type of planning is more characteristic of later villas in Britain, and owes much to Gallic examples. We need have no doubt, therefore, that, in the late first century, when it was being erected, it represented the most up-to-date design in Britain, and that its owner was in touch, probably through being a decurion, or having business contacts, at Verulamium, with continental architects and craftsmen. Mainly, how-ever, villas at this time lack the refinements, such as mosaics and bath-suites, of later examples.

In another area, a villa at Eccles, near Maidstone, was more luxurious with mosaics, a bath-building and a garden courtyard containing an ornamental basin. It may have belonged to an influential nobleman of the Cantii, or equally it could have been the residence of an emigré from another province, investing his wealth in British land, or even that of a Roman official.

In the same class as Eccles is a villa at Angmering on the Sussex coastal plain below the Downs, while some miles further west, near Chichester, was an altogether more exceptional building at Fish-bourne. Here was built, in the last decades of the first century, a villa of a size, and with a magnificence, to remain unsurpassed in Britain. The building was constructed on a terrace of some 33,500 sq.m. In the middle there was a large courtyard laid out as a garden. A central walk, flanked by ornamental arbours, or parterres, crossed the garden from east to west. Water was furnished by ceramic pipes for irrigation and probably to supply fountains and pools.

The garden was surrounded on all four sides by porticoes and ranges of buildings. In the centre of the east range, an entrance hall with external portico and ornamental pool afforded access to the long walk. In the centre of the opposing range, placed at a higher level, was an apsidal room, interpreted as an audience chamber, and approached through the portico from the garden walk. The north range was made up of suites of rooms, with their own private courtyards, and terminated at the east end by an aisled hall.

The south range, owing to the presence of modern structures, cannot be fully excavated, but appears to contain the main residential quarters of the owner, with a bath-suite at its east end. To the south again there was probably a private garden commanding a wide view over the Fishbourne inlet, whose waters, in Roman times, came close to the building with a quay situated on the shore-line.

The whole structure was furnished in a most sumptuous manner. Mosaics and frescoes of a very high quality were used to decorate principal rooms, some of which were heated by hypocausts. But, in addition to these modes of decoration, neither of which is uncommon in Britain, use was also made of ornamental stucco work and thin, coloured stone veneers to embellish the walls and floors, the stones including several different kinds of imported marbles.

We have, then, a building laid out and constructed in the very latest fashion by an owner who must have commanded a considerable personal fortune. It has been estimated that to build such a place today would cost the equivalent of nearly two million pounds. Who possessed such money in Roman Britain?

It could have been built for some important official, but it is difficult to visualize anyone below the rank of governor owning such a villa. Neither is there any specific evidence by which it might be so related. Also, it was constructed at a time when governors were still actively campaigning in Britain and they would, therefore, have had little time for leisurely country life away from the army or the capital.

Consequently, it is best seen as the work of some British prince, and in view of its position, the name that immediately springs to mind is Cogidubnus, client king, imperial legate and the only Briton, known by name, to have achieved the rank of a Roman senator. If he had successfully aided Vespasian in AD 69–71, it is likely that he received a handsome reward, sufficient probably to finance the palace, for so it must be called. Certainly the date of its construction can be closely tied to these events. It would have served, in turn, as a family residence for his dynasty and centre for administration of his kingdom and, in his declining years, a place of retirement away from the crowds of nearby Chichester.

Palace probably, but it may still have been a villa, at the centre of a great estate and managed in a more elaborate way, but nevertheless still at heart linked with agriculture. Not perhaps a villa of the kind more normally to be met in Britain, where the construction, development and upkeep had largely to be financed by the sale of agricultural produce.

It is interesting to speculate further on the dozen or so villas which grew in the Verulamium region in the decades following the Boudiccan rebellion. In some cases, such as Park Street, they replaced native farmsteads which had been burnt during the revolt, and there would seem to be some link between the development and the events of AD 60. It is hardly likely that a native farmer, who had just lost all, would have been in a financial position to start replacing his burnt house with a dwelling of much more expensive design. Two possibilities arise: either the farmer himself was killed with all his family, leaving the land without an owner or heir, or, alternatively, the farm was burnt and the farmer evicted in reprisals after the rebellion. Either way, the land belonging to a number of farms became vacant, and may have been taken by, or given as compensation to, loyal survivors among the Catuvellauni. So the changes which occurred to these villas are best assigned to new owners and not simply to improving circumstances.

By the middle of the second century, increasing capital resources enabled more and more farmers to demolish existing, native-style farms and rebuild in a modern manner, while those who already possessed villas were able to enlarge them. Ditchley (Oxon) is one such example where a winged villa was built in the middle of the century, while Park Street and Lockleys (Welwyn, Herts) had wings attached to the earlier single range of rooms. But even now these villas lacked the refinements possessed by many contemporary town-houses. Few had mosaics, and, although bath-suites were becoming commoner, they were by no means always provided. It would appear that social as well as economic changes were occurring, which can be explained in a number of ways.

We have already seen in the preceding chapter that towns in the middle of the second century were at a peak of development, which must be equated with a large investment of money. Comfortable town-houses appear in considerable numbers and can only imply that, to some extent, the upper classes had now, if not before, forsaken the countryside for life in the town. There were laws in force compelling decurions to live in towns or within a short distance of them. The rising standards of town life, coupled with the discomforts of commuting, may have led many, therefore, to take up residence, where previously they had dwelt on their estates. The later first and early second centuries had also seen large financial commitments to public buildings, all supported by private funds, but with the programmes of public building largely completed, more cash was available for private developments.

To whom then did these early villas belong and who lived in them? It is often said that the modest villas of the first and second centuries are the residences of farm managers, running farms on behalf of landed gentry who were themselves forced to live in towns because of the duties there required of them. That may be so, but it would imply a fairly high standard of living for the managers, who might be no better than slaves. Alternatively, we may see the houses as country retreats of the land-owners, with deliberately modest facilities since they seldom spent much time in them.

There is a further explanation. They could be deemed to be the houses of a growing number of 'middle-class' farmers, either tenants or freeholders, who did not at first possess the property qualifications which virtually required them to become decurions, although following generations might have aspired to such wealth. Distinct from the big land-owners, they would not have been attracted by the opportunities provided by the towns, and would not have been expected to subscribe to public buildings or festivities. Instead they opted for continuing country life, putting their profits back into the land they farmed and its buildings, so that, as they prospered by slow and gradual degrees, they may have become the owners or tenants of quite respectable farms. Certainly, the probabilities are that such men existed, and it is not necessarily correct always to associate the best, or even the second best, villas with the curial classes.

One last possibility exists: that these villas were the result of other provincials, from Gaul, or Spain or Germany, investing in the new province, once it was safe to do so. There is, unfortunately, no more evidence in favour of this than in the preceding explanations; all remains as supposition.

The developments outlined above continued unabated throughout the second century. Then came the upheavals at the end of the century, followed by the Severan victory over the British contender, Clodius Albinus. There can be no doubt that many land-owners in Britain supported Albinus; they would have had difficulty not to. In the aftermath, it is likely that many estates were sequestered by the new emperor, as happened extensively in Spain, either for retention as imperial estates, or for sale to his supporters. In consequence, a number of villas, such as Ditchley and Lullingstone, show evidence for abandonment, although it need not be suggested that the farms ceased to be worked; only the residential quarters were empty.

The economic recession of the third century also affected many, although perhaps less severely in Britain than was at once thought. But, as in the towns, there was less real money about, less confidence, and less incentive to undertake new developments. Some, however, perhaps avoided the difficulties.

The villas may also have begun to feel the effects of changes which were happening in other parts of Britain. There is considerable evidence to show that increasing amounts of arable land were becoming available in the north, particularly in Wharfedale and around certain forts. Consequently, there will have been growing competition between the villas and these new sources of grain, in which the latter had the advantage, as far as military contracts were concerned, of being nearer the consumers. In a time of recession and inflation, such competition could have been serious.

However, with the recovery of Britain in the late third century, marked social and economic changes occur in the countryside. The early fourth century saw a massive increase in the number, the size, and the standards of comfort of villas. The phenomenon cannot solely be accounted for by improved conditions and restored confidence, and there were clearly new factors playing a part, which must be considered.

Something of the general changes which took place then have been catalogued in preceding chapters. It is important to remember, in this context, two in particular: the greatly increased level of taxation and the new laws which not only prevented a man from changing his job, but also made the jobs hereditary. Furthermore, there was also a provision whereby decurions, who had always been responsible for collecting and forwarding taxes, now became personally liable for the taxes of some defaulters, such as their tenants.

There can be little doubt that a man residing in the country, farming his own land, living largely on the produce and spending both his capital and his income, not on investments to bring further wealth, but on luxuries and consumer goods, has a distinct advantage over his town-based counterpart when it comes to tax avoidance, or even evasion. It is likely that many of the curial class, who, until now, had probably also been the main land-owners, found the new obligations especially heavy. Some must have faced bankruptcy, in which case, if they possessed country estates, they would have been forced to sell. Some may have been more fortunate and were able to bribe or buy themselves into a higher social class, when they were relieved of the burdens. Their residence, or frequent attendance, was then no longer required in town, so they could retire from close proximity to the tax collectors. Perchance, also, one or more neighbouring estates might have been up for sale, so leading to a consolidation of land-holdings in fewer hands and to amalgamations totalling several thousand acres. Yet, this reason, for long thought a principal one for many of the changes, and still undoubtedly valid, has perhaps been over-emphasized.

Parts of Gaul had, in the second part of the third century, suffered grievously from enemy action, rendering much of the countryside unsafe for habitation, whereas Britain had not suffered to anywhere near the same extent. It has been suggested that, when affairs returned to normal in the late third or early fourth century, there was a flight of capital from Gaul on the part of wealthy land-owners who had been shaken by their recent experiences. Certainly one of the phenomena of the period is the emergence of a hundred or so villas which can happily be ranked with continental examples, and which are generally far superior in standard to the native product. This suggestion of a Gallic migration, although largely surmise, is to some extent supported by a coincidence of designs between British and Gallic mosaic pavements and by the presence in parts of Britain of dedications to specific deities otherwise only known in Gaul.

Unfortunately, there are so many imponderables when dealing with villas that any conclusions drawn are bound to be tentative. It is as well to remember that there were about a thousand or so country buildings in Britain which can be loosely classified as villas. Each one reflects a different set of circumstances, governed only by the whims of the owner. To try to create general patterns, therefore, is an almost in-superable task, given our present evidence. Moreover, the situation must have been changing all the time. Villas could be bought and sold, rented or managed, sequestered or bankrupted; they could prosper or decline. A miserly millionaire owner could live in a humble building at the centre of a great estate, while around him his tenants or lesser neighbours enjoyed the most palatial villas. Consequently, although it is usually argued that a large villa corresponds to a large estate, it might not always be safe to do so.

Yet the fourth century was the golden age of the villa in Britain, whatever its causes. It may be apt to compare it with the spate of country-house building in eighteenth-century England. It is not improbable, therefore, that fashion may have to be considered as a supplementary cause; an element in which the lesser man aped his peers and kept up with the Julii next-door. At the very least, it can probably be said with some confidence that the villas represent a very considerable injection of capital into the countryside, while also signifying some social and economic changes which are less well understood.

A considerable number of the largest and most sumptuous villas are to be found in Gloucestershire and Somerset: Woodchester, Chedworth, Witcombe and Low Ham may be singled out. More occur in the Darenth valley of west Kent and include Lullingstone, while others are scattered over Hampshire, Wiltshire, Oxfordshire and Sussex, of which that at Bignor, near Chichester, is perhaps the most significant. A further group lies in Dorset and yet another ranges through Northamptonshire into Lincolnshire and east Yorkshire.

These buildings were a direct development of earlier villa types. We have already seen how the earliest single-range house was enlarged by the addition of wings at each end. In the buildings presently under discussion, the wings, when further extended, became ranges in their own right so completing three sides of a square, or rectangle, surrounding a central courtyard. The enclosure of the latter could then be completed, either by a wall, as in the case of Spoonley Wood (Glos), or by a covered portico, as at North Leigh (Oxon), or even by a further range of rooms, as at Woodchester or Bignor. It should, however, be noted that, in a growth which was essentially organic, additional wings were often not joined directly to the parent house, only becoming so as time passed, or, sometimes, even being left isolated, as at Brading in the Isle of Wight.

It is probable that in most cases the enclosed courtyard, which, in embryo, can usually be detected even in winged villas, served as the farmyard. Certainly at Ditchley it contained a circular threshing-floor and a well, presumably intended to supply water not only to the community but also to the stock. The addition of extra wings, or buildings, round the farmyard may, therefore, be seen as an extension to the farm as a whole and not only to the farmhouse. Granaries, machinery sheds, stock sheds and accommodation for the farm servants may all be expected. In some extreme cases, however, the latter were relegated to an outer court, giving rise to the so-called double-courtyard villa. Here, as at Bignor and Woodchester, complete separation is achieved between the farm and the residence of the owner, in which the inner court would probably be laid out as a garden.

At their peak, villas contained all the comforts and amenities of the better class town-houses. Not only were bath-suites provided, but in a number of cases multiple units are known, either catering for different tastes in bathing, as in the baths of dry and moist heat at Chedworth, or possibly providing facilities for some of the farmworkers or retainers. Even when the owner was permanently resident, a large estate like

Fig. 29 Villas at: a) North Leigh; b) Woodchester; c) Stroud; d) Hambledon;
e) Park Street in the first century; f) Little Milton; g) Spoonley Wood

North Leigh or Bignor would have required a professional manager.
Indeed, the more the owner shut himself away from farmyard
activities, the greater the need for a competent manager. Although a
retainer, or even a slave, such a man would have had some standing
and influence and might well have possessed his own private quarters
with a bath-suite. Certainly if we are to assume that simple, second-
century villas represent the houses of managers, we ought not to find
the same people less well accommodated in the fourth century.

The main reception rooms of the villa were invariably decorated with mosaics, which in the fourth century employed a much wider variety of patterns and designs, often incorporating scenes from classical mythology, such as the Dido and Aeneas portrayal at Low Ham or that of Jupiter and Europa from Lullingstone. Walls were covered with painted frescoes, a form of decoration which was often extended into the bathing establishments. Some fine paintings of fishes and other aquatic animals come from a bath at Southwell (Notts), while an underground room at Lullingstone, apparently devoted to a water cult, contained a niche painted with the figures of three water nymphs and dolphins. Often the main rooms were heated with hypocausts, and on occasion, as at Chedworth, the functions of many of them can be identified. There, the main residential wing lay on the west side of the inner court, or garden, from which it was separated by a covered verandah. At the south end, this verandah could be shut off by a door from its fellow along the south range, so isolating the domestic quarters, containing a kitchen, a latrine and the steward's, or manager's, office, from the main house. The dining-room lay at the south end of the principal wing, close to the kitchen. It was divided visually into two unequal parts by pilasters, probably once supporting an arch across the room, and both parts were floored with mosaics, made by a local firm from Cirencester; the larger mosaic contained panels illustrating Bacchic scenes.

A small ante-chamber separated the dining-room from three other rooms, two of which formed a self-contained suite and which were presumably bedrooms. The north end of the wing terminated in a bath-suite. Running water was provided by a spring which rose outside the north-west angle; it was collected in a basin surrounded by a shrine, or *nymphaeum*, and then piped to parts of the building.

Chedworth is also an excellent example to consider with regard to the topographical siting of villas, in which act great care was taken. Many occupied idyllic surroundings, but more practical considerations probably carried greater weight. A copious supply of water, either from a spring, well or aqueduct, was obviously of prime importance. Some wells were exceedingly large, such as that at Rudston (Yorks) which was 30 m. deep and 3 m. in diameter at the top; the large amount of water which it could produce (it contained a depth of 9 m. of water when excavated) together with the probability that it did not dry up in the summer, would have greatly helped the maintenance of large herds of stock. The direction of the prevailing winds was often taken into account, and Chedworth lay at the head of a small combe, surrounded by hills on north, west and south sides, but with a fine open prospect to the east, where it looked across the valley of a minor stream.

From the foregoing descriptions, it can be seen that a typological development can be traced through this form of the Romano-British villa. Nevertheless it is dangerous to attempt a correlation of the types with chronology. While it is true that the majority of large courtyard villas were a fourth-century manifestation, developing over a period of time from humble beginnings, it cannot in reverse be claimed that all simple buildings belonged to earlier periods. It has already been recorded that the growth of villas in Britain was an organic process, representing the fluctuating fortunes of thousands of individuals over many years. Therefore, no reason exists why small houses, so characteristic of first-century construction, should not equally be found in fourth-century contexts, where they would illustrate the later rise to moderate fortune of native farmers, tenants or even immigrants. The term aisled farmhouse is normally used to describe the later examples, since they differ from the modest, early houses. Primarily, each consists of a plain rectangular building, though projecting rooms are sometimes attached. The interior is divided longitudinally by two rows of posts into a central 'nave' and two narrower 'aisles'. At their simplest they could represent granaries, barns or byres. In many, however, parts of both the nave and aisles are partitioned to form separate rooms, in which hypocausts, mosaics and frescoes are not unknown. Small bath-suites also occur, so that it is clear that they provided residential accommodation of a reasonable standard for the farmer. Yet the remaining space in the buildings equally clearly continued to give shelter for farmworkers, animals and fodder, and the overall effect, if allowance is made for the greater sophistication of the living-quarters, would have been not dissimilar to the medieval long-house, shared alike by people and animals. The presence of animals is, after all, an excellent form of central heating.

Although villas of this type occur in isolation, such as those at Exning (Suffolk), Denton (Lincs), Holbury and Clanville (Hants), they are also to be found as subsidiary buildings in larger villas: Brading, Ickleton (Cambs) and Mansfield Woodhouse (Notts) are good examples. In the latter cases, it is to be assumed either that they were barns or that they provided accommodation for farmworkers of the estate, in which case some form of social distinction can probably be made. It is unlikely that all farmworkers would qualify for heated rooms and baths, and so it may be possible to differentiate between the upper and lower servants.

Another villa, which is a direct development of the rectangular native-style cottage of Roman Britain, to be seen in great numbers in the settlement at Chisenbury Warren (Wilts), is that at Iwerne in Dorset. This villa lacks the tripartite arrangement of the aisled house and contains a living-room, a hall or large kitchen, and a byre, all under

0   100   200 Km

Fig. 30 Distribution of villas

the same roof. In essence it probably represents the same class of farmer as the isolated aisled villa, but one living in less comfortable circumstances.

We have so far considered villa buildings, their types and developments. We must next review the relationship of one villa with another, and with other farming communities, and any evidence for land tenure which may arise therefrom.

If a line is drawn from the Severn estuary to the north Yorkshire moors, most villas will be found south and east of it; a few lie beyond in the Vale of York, in the west Midlands and in south Wales, but these outlying exceptions are matched by an almost total absence in Devon and Cornwall. The area which they occupy represents the greatest concentration of the best agricultural land in Britain, and this is certainly one of the reasons for their selective distribution. But first-class pasture and arable is not unknown elsewhere, if in more restricted quantities. Clearly, therefore, other reasons for their distribution must be sought, and are probably to be found in their relationships with road systems and towns, both of which were a necessary part of the so-called villa system. Where urbanization falters and then fails, so do villas: the latter could not survive without the former.

There are, however, some towns which have a marked villa-free zone about them, even though beyond the zone villas cluster thickly. Such a town is Cirencester with only one villa known in a 6½ km. radius circle; Dorchester and Silchester are similar cases. Few villas are known in east Kent, although there are many in the north-west of the county. There are also country areas, remote from towns, almost entirely devoid of villas, such as Cranbourne Chase, Salisbury Plain and the Fens, but let us consider the urban cases first.

It is highly probable, as already indicated earlier, that much land around towns was farmed from them. What we do not know, unfortunately, is how it was organized, and several possibilities arise. It may be that few or no villas simply means larger land-holdings. At Cirencester for instance, the one villa at Barton Farm on the outskirts of the town may have controlled the whole of the 6½ km. radius; similarly at Dorchester. Alternatively, the land may have been publicly owned, either as common land, following the old Celtic practice, or let out to tenants who resided in the town; or it may have been farmed directly by the civic authorities. Most civitas capitals grew in close proximity to old tribal centres, and the ground on which they stood formed but a small part of the tribal lands, effectively controlled by the chiefs, but probably not theirs to dispose of without approval. In a Romano-British context, can we see in these areas around towns, the residue of the 'common' lands, still held by the tribe (the civitas), administered by the chiefs (the decurions) and used for the public good (rents from tenants etc.)? If so, then it would seem that the tribal rulers of the Cantii were more successful in holding off private enterprise, in the area around their new capital, than were the Dobunni. We might speculate further. Was the sale of land for private development confined, to begin with, to tribal margins, and were the profits so obtained sunk in the first public buildings of the new towns? As time passed more and more land might have been disposed of until only a residue remained at the centre, the amount varying from tribe to tribe, according to their inclinations. This may be a speculative, part solution to the problem, but it is not the only possibility.

Fig. 31 Urban farms at: a) Cirencester; b) Silchester

There is increasing evidence to show that a number of towns had farms, and farmhouses, within their boundaries. Certainly, at Silchester, there is a house near the north gate which is associated with barns or byre-like buildings. Another, of the fourth century, close to the Verulamium Gate at Cirencester, is not only planned like a winged villa, but has, to its rear, ancillary buildings which can only be interpreted as workshops used by people engaged in the maintenance of buildings and machinery. Indeed, one of these structures, had it been found in open countryside, would have been called an aisled farmhouse; it seems partly to have been used as a forge. The main house does not appear large enough to warrant a permanent labour force of the kind described, but a large estate might well do so, and there is evidence that many large estates employed enough staff to be virtually self-sufficient. Beyond the buildings, in the south-east quarter of the town, there is also known to be a considerable open space, which could have served as a paddock or home pasture. Although it has never been excavated, a similarly planned house shows in aerial photographs of Wroxeter and again seems to be associated with areas that have no buildings.

A late fourth-century house in the centre of Verulamium was designed as a small courtyard house. In the early fifth century a corn-drying kiln was inserted in a room at one corner of the house, clearly indicating that the owner had grain to dry and, in those uncertain times, was anxious to bring it within the town walls as rapidly as possible. In minor towns, a typical winged corridor house is known at Great Chesterford.

There are, no doubt, many more such buildings to be identified in towns, and urban farms must have been comparatively common. What are they to be called? Strictly speaking, according to Roman law and usage, they were not villas. Yet, is it right to call the house at Barton Farm, some 400 m. beyond the walls at Cirencester, a villa while we deny the term to the buildings described above which were just within those same walls? Some authorities consider that the distinction should be preserved. But we may well ask what accident excluded one and included the other within the defences. If the plan of Cirencester is examined it will be seen as a roughly elongated oval. The Barton Farm house lay at one end of the long axis while the other lay close to the short axis. It would, therefore, have been much easier to have excluded the former if it was an isolated building on the fringes. But to have left out the latter would have required the realignment of the whole of the eastern fortifications. There is little doubt that both were farms before the town boundary was consolidated with a rampart and wall. In the circumstances we would do well to remember the Villa Publica in Rome, which did not lose its name, despite being later enclosed within the city walls.

We need not be surprised, therefore, to find farms situated in towns. Indeed it is an extension of the principles which lay behind the deliberate foundation of coloniae. It will be remembered from the preceding chapter that an army veteran would have been given a plot of land in both the town and in the territorium surrounding it. Such land would consequently have been worked from the town, perhaps in time resulting in the establishment of villas. Admittedly, though, villas are not as densely congregated in areas which may represent colonial territoria as in some others. Unfortunately, also, the extent of these territoria is not known and can only be guessed at. In many provinces the land was divided into regular plots when the colonia was founded, a process known as centuriation, in which it was divided by a grid of accommodation roads into squares with sides of 20 *actus* (710 m.). It is to be expected that at least the three military coloniae at Colchester, Lincoln and Gloucester would have been provided with centuriated territoria, although there is some reason to believe that the first foundation at Colchester was not so dealt with. Unfortunately, owing to extensive alterations in land boundaries in the Saxon and Medieval periods, little more than vestigial traces survive of earlier divisions which may not necessarily be associated with centuriation. It may be, also, that consolidation of the original holdings took place during the Roman period, leading to their obliteration. The plots granted to the veterans were not inalienable and could have been sold by themselves or their descendants.

Another form of land settlement for veterans has also been recognized in Britain. Sometimes retired auxiliaries, espccially if they were recruited from beyond the frontiers, were settled within the empire. Such a settlement is known at Ribchester (Lancs), where a garrison of Sarmatians is known and where inscriptions attest both the existence of *Bremetennacum Veteranorum* and the *Regio Bremetennacensis*. These 'regions' became a regular part of the late empire and were administered by a military officer known as *regionarius* (Ch. 5). At Ribchester, a legionary centurion had been seconded for this duty and he also commanded the auxiliary fort.

We have seen, therefore, that land around major towns, particularly where there is an absence of villas, could have been worked from the towns, where the farms lay. But this is in direct contrast to the conditions outside many minor towns or lesser settlements. It has long been recognized that such places as Bath, Ilchester and Rochester have some of the largest villa concentrations in Britain around them. Why this should be is not entirely clear, but it may be that the lesser sites did not provide enough amenities to be attractive to the major land-owners. There would consequently have been little or no incentive to reside in the minor towns. The alienation of tribal lands, discussed above, may also have a bearing on the problem. The core of every large fourth-century villa is usually a humble first-century cottage. That one could grow to the other means that it was ultimately successful as a farm, and presumably the size of land-holding had to grow with it. Many minor towns tend to lie near the boundaries of civitates, and it is possible that land was at first more easily acquired by private owners on the margins of tribal territories than in the centres. So a concentration of large estates might come about in those peripheral regions.

Great difficulties occur when attempts are made to relate one villa with another, since so many possibilities arise for which there is virtually no evidence.

It is probably true to say that a very large, residential villa such as Woodchester or Bignor lies at the centre of a great estate, but it is almost impossible to say how large it was. Attempts have been made to calculate areas by relating granary capacities, where known, to them. For instance, Ditchley, a comparatively modest villa, has a granary thought to be equivalent to about 300 ha. of arable land. Bignor, on the other hand, a major site, is estimated to have had slightly less arable at about 300 ha., but in addition some 200 sheep, which would have needed about 180 ha. of pasture, probably on the Downs, together perhaps with 100 head of cattle run on the water-meadows of the river Arun. Woodland for timber, coppicing and fattening swine will also have been part of the estate, which may in all have run to 1000 ha. or more. But if we then try to relate these figures to Woodchester or Chedworth, it is found that other villas would fall within the areas. From this it is possible to conclude that there must be some land-owner and tenant relationships, with the main villa acting as a home farm. There are, however, further complications. A large estate might be run by a manager on behalf of a permanently absent landlord, in which case only a modest house would be provided. How then are we to distinguish between the house of the manager and those of the tenants, which might well be larger and more comfortable? It cannot be done in our present state of knowledge, and such conclusions as may be drawn must in the main be restricted to the largest, residential houses. The complexities of the problem are perhaps best illustrated by Lulling-stone where there exists, not only an extremely comfortable, though modest-sized, villa, but also a barn or granary which is almost as big as the residential house. The main house is hardly the dwelling of a farm manager, neither is it really big enough to accommodate the complete family and all the retainers of a large land-owner, although it obviously belongs to a man of considerable substance. Can we deduce that it was only used for periodic visits of inspection of a large estate almost entirely let out to tenants, who would have been required to fill the barn as part of their rent? There seems no other worthwhile conclusion to draw, but it is completely speculative.

It is well known, also, that villages and minor nucleated settlements can exist on large private estates, while tenants need not always inhabit subsidiary villas. Native-style farms and villages occur frequently over many parts of Britain, and it is not always easy to relate them to the villas. A number, for instance, are known on the South Downs, not far from Bignor and some other villas on the Sussex coastal plain. At one, on Thundersbarrow Hill, outside Shoreham, a cluster of round houses lie just to the east of an Iron Age hill-fort. There is little to distinguish them from similar houses of an earlier period, except the presence of some Roman-style corn-drying kilns, pottery and other objects. The farm, or village, is associated with an extensive series of cultivated fields, while several other similar settlements exist at no great distance. Unfortunately we cannot say whether they belonged to smallholders, owning land of their own or on a communal basis, or whether the occupiers were tenants of one of the nearby villas, or were even agricultural workers billeted on outlying parts of the estate.

Marginal settlements of farmworkers do seem to occur on some estates. At Poxwell, south of Dorchester, a rudimentary half-timbered, rectangular building was constructed in the lee of a field terrace in the third or early fourth century. It contained corn-drying kilns and also a furnace for roasting iron-ore. A good deal of pottery was found, indicating that people lived there. Although the parent villa is not known, the buildings probably provided accommodation and working space in one of the more distant parts of an estate.

A further puzzle is provided by the detached bath-houses known to exist in some places apparently in isolation from other buildings. The largest number are known in Kent, where three at least occur in areas not noted for the abundance of villas. It used to be claimed that they belonged to timber-framed or cob buildings which had left no trace of their existence: a not altogether satisfactory explanation. They may have been provided for the top estate workers who lived elsewhere, as were certainly provided in some villas. But the full explanation is probably still to be sought.

Although they are much larger, the settlements or villages typified by Chisenbury Warren in Wiltshire or Meriden Down in Dorset provide similar problems. The former had over eighty rectangular house-platforms as well as a system of lanes, although it is not known if all the houses were occupied simultaneously. Both are surrounded by tracts of Celtic fields. But where do they fit into the hierarchy? Are they again villages of farmworkers on a large estate, or tenants, or are they freeholders farming their own land, either on a personal or a community basis? It has been claimed that a number of nucleated sites provided reservoirs of farmworkers, such as the walled, minor towns of Margidunum and Godmanchester. It is indeed likely that this was at least partly so, in which case the urgent question to be asked is: what was the essential difference between, for example, Chisenbury Warren and Godmanchester? Reduced to this level there appears a strong resemblance between them, yet differences in organization clearly did exist, but precisely what they were and why, we cannot say.

The case of Chisenbury Warren has been deliberately cited, as it lies on the north-east edge of Salisbury Plain, an area which, together with adjacent Cranbourne Chase, has a marked lack of villas.

Throughout the empire there were areas of land which became the personal property of the emperor, either by conquest, or by sequestration, or by deed of gift. Some of the areas were concerned with mineral extraction, such as the silver and gold mines of Britain. But in the main they will have comprised holdings of agricultural land. Two areas command attention in this context. One is that referred to above around Salisbury Plain. It was a region which, with its multitude of hill-forts, had bitterly resisted the advance of the Roman army in AD 43. Although there were a few villas, which were generally modest and of late development, there were many native settlements which continued almost unchanged from the Iron Age well into the Roman period, and show little sign of romanization. Yet an assessment of the capacities of their grain storage pits has indicated that, when compared with similar sites elsewhere, between a half and a third of their production was taken away, in place of the normal tax of about a tenth or twelfth. This has led to suggestions that the area, in response to its initial hostility, was reduced to an imperial estate, in which the inhabitants were deliberately kept at a low subsistence level in order to provide grain for the Roman army. Later changes support the view that there was an alteration from arable to pasture, as stock enclosures tend to replace, or are added to, the earlier settlements, as at Woodcuts, Rotherley and Tollard Royal. Since these changes went hand in hand with the emergence of two or three small villas, such as Iwerne, it is probable that, if it was an imperial estate, a different method of working had been introduced, perhaps involving tenancies.

Imperial estates were managed, on behalf of the emperor, by the provincial procurator. He would have a number of assistants to run individual holdings, each of which would be provided with a headquarters. One such building, usually called a villa, is known at Combe Down, outside Bath; it produced an inscription, already referred to in the preceding chapter, which mentions the restoration of a principia by a procurator's assistant in the early third century. We do not know what estate he managed. It may have been connected with the silver mines of the Mendips, or quarries in the Bath region. Alternatively, it may represent an agricultural estate perhaps sequestered after the Albinus fiasco. But the inability to differentiate between this building and an ordinary villa adds yet another dimension to our problems. Who is to say, in the absence of other evidence, which villas acted as centres for imperial estates?

The will of Prasutagus and the Boudiccan rebellion between them provided Nero with large tracts of land. In the Antonine Itinerary only one villa in Britain is listed, the Villa Faustina at Scole on the Norfolk-Suffolk borders. Why should it have been included as a place to visit on a supposed imperial journey? Presumably because it acted as a centre for a very large imperial estate, derived probably from the aftermath of the rebellion.

Another region often assigned the same status is the Fenlands of Lincolnshire, Cambridgeshire and Norfolk. This was an area which, during the Iron Age, was predominantly under water, peat or salt-marsh and consequently only inhabited along its margins. During the early part of the Roman period some of these settlements continued to extract salt from sea-water. But during the principate of Hadrian, perhaps as the result of his visit to Britain, large-scale development took place, coupled with a major scheme of land drainage. Hadrian was personally interested in land reclamation, having previously instituted schemes in Africa. Moreover it was he who liberalized the Mancian Law by introducing two important concessions for tenants who took occupancy of waste land on imperial estates. Providing they created a domicile, did not try to sell the holding and kept the land productive, they paid no rent for the first five or ten years, and became virtual owners of the property. Even if, therefore, the Fens were not part of Prasutagus' domains inherited by Nero, we can still make out a strong case on these grounds for them to have been an imperial estate. In support we might cite the scale of the works, which appear too great for private enterprise to have been responsible; only the central government could have provided the necessary organization and capital expenditure. And there is also the nature of the settlements, usually consisting at first of solitary farms, fairly closely placed to one another, each of which then appears to*proliferate to about a dozen or so main buildings. These farms look remarkably like the original domiciles of the first settlers, followed by fragmentation of the holdings in the hands of their descendants, so that in time they came to resemble loose nucleations. Villas are unknown in the Fens, although a number occur on the higher ground of the Fen edge. Their absence is often considered to be supporting evidence for an imperial estate, which may or may not be so. But it is highly unlikely that a man who aspired to a villa would have placed his house on low-lying, insalubrious land, swarming with mosquitoes and other disease-carrying insects.

There is, furthermore, the principia-like building constructed at Godmanchester in the early third century. Godmanchester lies on the southern edge of the Fens and on main roads running both north-south and east-west, so it would have been an ideal site for an administrative headquarters. It was built at a time when a general tightening up of imperial administration was taking place, and the more liberal approach of Hadrian towards his tenants had probably long been forgotten.

The method of drainage introduced in the area appears to resemble that used in some places today: blocks of land are successively surrounded by large dykes into which minor drainage channels discharge. Since the main rivers of the area run north-east-by-east into the Wash, the two principal dykes, the Car Dyke and the Midfendic were constructed to run roughly north-south, so that water flowing from the higher ground to the west could, as necessary, be transferred from one river to another. For a long time, the Car Dyke was considered to be a continuous channel, stretching from near Cambridge almost to Lincoln, and intended for navigation as well as drainage. More recent work has shown that it is made up of discrete sections, and could not have been used as a continuous canal. Navigation and drainage have, in fact, conflicting requirements, the maintenance of deep water being inimical to that of good drainage.

As briefly noted above, there are in the Fens many farms and villages associated with extensive areas of field-systems. They lie almost entirely on the silt Fens and none are yet known on the peats. They vary from single farmsteads through all gradations of nucleation to large settlements covering several hectares and sometimes extending up to fifty. One of the best known of the nucleated sites is that at Cottenham in Cambridgeshire. There, both banks of the Car Dyke are flanked by farmsteads surrounded by a complicated pattern of fields, droveways, access lanes and paddocks. Some of the fields are arranged in blocks of narrow strips, for long identified as 'granaries', thought to have been used for storing grain from the imperial estate before it was shipped to northern garrisons along the canal. It seems more likely that they are to be associated with horticulture or, alternatively, they may have been stock pens for the corralling of sheep and cattle during annual round-ups. Certainly recent investigations tend to show that, while grain production was important, the economic strength lay in stock-raising, and many of the areas between settlements, where few visible field boundaries exist, may have been used as ranches for cattle and sheep.

As in Cranbourne Chase, there is little sign of regular land-divisions, probably owing to the tortuous nature of many of the natural water-courses. There are some rectilinear field-systems, such as that near Upwell, Cambridgeshire, but they tend to be rare. Yet some authorities have detected a sense of order in the main arrangements.

Despite a concentration on agricultural activities, it must not be forgotten that the Fenland region also continued to produce large quantities of salt, which may also have been an imperial monopoly. It is likely that shellfish from the estuaries of the wash provided another source of income; oysters are found in prodigious quantities on most Romano-British sites, while in addition mussels, whelks, cockles and winkles were collected.

Some further sites may also be considered as imperial estates. The villa at Hambledon (Bucks) was modest in size, but contained in its farmyard a considerable number of corn-drying kilns, suggesting large-scale grain production. In addition, the large number of infant burials would imply a high slave population, while seventy *styli*, instruments for writing on waxed tablets, would point to considerable bureaucratic control. If not an imperial estate, it probably formed the centre of a large, private holding, run by a manager on behalf of an absentee land-owner. A rather similar villa exists at Rockbourne (Hants), while an imperial dedication at another at Clanville also carries connotations of imperial ownership.

In considering villas, we have also been able to take in much of the related pattern of farming in lowland Britain. There remains one last aspect to be described before we can turn elsewhere.

Villas in Britain were not normally fortified. When they were founded, there was no need; warfare was far away. By the time the real need arrived, the system was already in decline and, although there is ample evidence to show not only the continuance of villas, but also new construction, beyond the barbarian conspiracy of AD 367, it was altogether more modest and lacked the flamboyance of the early fourth century. At best, they were sometimes equipped with a ditch and bank, perhaps topped with a hedge, as at Ely, near Cardiff, or with bank, wall and ditch as at Ditchley; in neither case were they of defensive character. Such structures were intended to afford protection from vagrants, petty thieves and marauding animals, to keep stock in and to provide drainage.

Large, fortified villas are, however, known on the continent, where the idiosyncrasies of wealthy owners were given realism in the form of defensive walls. Such a villa at Anthée, in Belgium, covers some 12 ha. Recently, a site at Gatcombe, a few kilometres south-west of Bath, has been investigated. It was at first thought to be a minor walled town, but there are features which cannot readily be explained by that interpretation. The area enclosed within the wall is about 6.5 ha., and the wall itself is massive, being 4.5 m. thick. The angles are not curved as in most urban defences, neither is there evidence for bastions, rampart or ditch. It would appear to have been constructed sometime in the third or fourth centuries. Within the enclosure, a number of buildings lie on terraces on the hillside. At least two resemble aisled farmhouses or barns, while there are also traces of iron and lead working. Somewhere, also, is suspected the site of a better class building with mosaics.

If a villa, a conclusion by no means proved, it represents an owner asserting his own individuality, in a manner more frequently to be observed on the continent, perhaps in the face of the growing insecurity of the region in the later fourth century. Perhaps too it may denote an emigrant owner from Gaul, for if we are to suppose that Gallic landowners came to Britain for refuge after the third century convulsions, there is more supporting evidence for the suggestion in the region around Bath than elsewhere.

The general distribution of villas in Britain has already been considered. Although they are to be associated with alterations in the type of agricultural economy, we cannot be sure that the pattern did not also change elsewhere. The scale of working may well be assumed to have been greater in regions dominated by villas, but general farming practices probably remained much the same everywhere and a large land-owner could just as easily inhabit a mud hut as a villa; only his life-style would be different.

Some dozen or so villas occur outside the main area of distribution. One is known at Illogan near Cambourne in Cornwall, but its complete isolation in an area displaying a vastly different kind of settlement and farm may mean that it was associated more with tin-mining than with agriculture. A number are also known in south Wales and in the Welsh Marches, but neither the Demetae, the Silures or the Cornovii were greatly attracted by this type of farm. Some are also placed to take advantage of the rich land of the Vale of York, while one at least occurs in Upper Airedale, in the Pennines. The most northerly of all is at Old Durham.

These were, however, the exceptions, representing a fringe to a particular way of life. For the remainder, farms and settlements tended to continue much as they had in the Iron Age. Regional differences do, nevertheless, exist but they often owe more to Iron Age antecedents than to any Roman influence. But we must be cautious in some of our assessments as all is not always as it seems.

In the south-west, the predominant form of single farm is one called a round. Their origin seems to lie in the first century BC, and it has been estimated that up to a thousand existed in Cornwall and Devon, often surviving through the Roman period. Despite their name, they appear in a variety of different shapes and sizes, from 0.2 ha.–1.2 ha. They are invariably surrounded by a single bank and ditch, frequently of some size. It seems quite likely that hedges were planted on the tops of the banks to give increased protection, and so would appear not dissimilar to modern Cornish 'hedges', which are a combination of hedge and thick boundary wall. These banks were not defensive except insofar as they were intended to keep out thieves and wild animals. Their prime purpose was probably to give protection to the inhabitants and stock from driving rain and wind, while at the same time keeping the latter from straying. The ditch, therefore, may be seen simply as a quarry for bank material. Access was gained by a single entrance, and one or more circular houses lay within the enclosure, usually sheltering in the lee of the bank. It is not possible to say, however, how many family groups might be represented by one round. They are usually situated between the 60 m. and 120 m. contours and never lie on hill-tops or valley bottoms. In some, where evidence has survived, they are related to adjacent field-systems, in which the individual plots are not unlike Celtic fields in size and shape.

Rounds, therefore, seem to represent the class of independent farmer, who, while operating a mixed arable and pastoral system, would, further east, have ultimately erected a villa. But a combination of conservatism and a lack of urban markets and influence acted against it. It is worth emphasizing, however, that the existence of the civitas capital at Exeter did not promote any growth of villas even in its immediate neighbourhood, where there was admirable farmland. So we may conclude that the Dumnonii set their faces against the new villa development, and the way of life which it represented, in favour of traditional and well-established forms of dwellings.

That is not to say, however, that no innovations took place. A structure characteristic of the Roman period in West Penwith is the courtyard house. They are usually grouped in small villages on the moorlands, containing perhaps up to a dozen such dwellings. They are roughly oval in outline and constructed of earth and rubble banks kept in place by drystone walling. The rooms, up to six in number, were built within the thickness of the walls and opened on to a central courtyard, from which a single entrance gave access to the exterior. The rooms were probably roofed with turf, as being less likely to be blown away in south-westerly gales.

In structural respects, therefore, they seem to have developed directly from the rounds, each 'house', or 'room', in the latter having been absorbed, as it were, by a massive, internal thickening of the perimeter wall. We might, therefore, wonder if multiple 'huts' inside a round indeed represent, not individual dwellings, but 'rooms' of one 'house'. If we are right in this assumption, then these villages represent much the same class of people as inhabited the rounds, but gathered together in a community in order to share some of its assets and possibly practising a slightly different type of farming.

At Chysauster, eight of these houses were arranged on both sides of a meandering central lane, with possibly more a short distance away. Each dwelling had its own paddock or garden, while the whole community shared a large underground storage chamber, or *fogou*. The latter are, like the courtyard house, characteristic of the Land's End peninsula in the Iron Age and Roman periods. They consisted of wide, usually curving, excavations in the ground, the sides of which were revetted by large upright slabs of stone and the whole roofed with similar slabs. Entrances normally existed at both ends, from which ramps led down to the bottom; occasionally there were branching side passages. It is probable that they were used for storing meat, since the through circulation of air would aid its drying and preservation, while an even temperature would be maintained by the surrounding earth.

Each village was also directly connected to large areas of field-systems, suggesting again that they practised a mixed farming economy. In some cases larger rectangular fields replaced the smaller, earlier plots, implying improvements in agricultural methods.

In addition to rounds and courtyard houses, a considerable number of unenclosed round huts, or houses, also existed. Like the two former types they tend to be associated with fields, and probably represent the dwellings of peasant farmers, or smallholders. But as with the relationship between villas and native farms elsewhere, it is impossible to connect them with the more developed forms of settlement. But, if the villa at Illogan represents a romanized manifestation of a round, it is difficult not to imagine that some relationship existed between it and the open hut site at nearby Porth Godrevy.

Despite the general absence of romanized housing in the south-west, there was no lack of other material goods, and even the Porth Godrevy hut produced coins, a samian dish, an amphora and iron nails. Bronze *fibulae*, brooches of Romano-British form, have been found in numbers in the Scilly Isles, and it is probable that local blacksmiths, in time, became familiar with the manufacture of better class agricultural implements. Neither must it be forgotten that, from the early third century onwards, the inhabitants of even a simple round hut may have been Roman citizens, although we might quite rightly suspect that it made little difference to them.

On considering Wales, we find that regional differences can again be detected in settlement types and patterns. We have already noted above that southern Wales tended to be within the orbit of villas, although it must be admitted that in the south-west the link is extremely tenuous. There, the buildings, which are essentially simple in plan, are often enclosed within a ring-work, possibly belonging to an earlier period. A typical example is known at Cwmbrwyn, not far from the civitas capital of the Demetae at Carmarthen. A rectangular masonry building, approximately 33 m. by 7.5 m., was situated inside a roughly trapezoid enclosure, with a bank and ditch, measuring about 42 m. across; smaller, wooden sheds were also indicated in the interior. A similar site has been identified not far away at Trelissey. In neither case has it been proved that the defences are contemporary with the buildings, but if the latter were erected within an earlier enclosure, it is difficult to avoid the conclusion that it was done deliberately to take advantage of a fortified site; it is therefore possible that they were replacing earlier wooden buildings. Unlike the Cornish rounds, the bank and ditch are of a scale great enough to warrant the assumption that they were defensive in character.

Elsewhere in south-west Wales, small fortified enclosures of the type just described continued to be used and a number have produced Roman pottery. Exceptional, however, are two sites on the coast, at Gateholm and Sheep Island, where there were clusters of rectangular wooden buildings, probably dating from the Roman period. Their positions would suggest fishing villages, allied to primitive agriculture.

In the west-central part of Wales, bordering Cardigan Bay, no settlements or farms have yet been identified for the Roman period. There are many hill-forts in the area, but none have so far been shown to have been occupied after the Iron Age, and indeed casual finds of Roman pottery or metalwork are rare in the region as a whole.

In the north-east, a few enclosed native farms are known containing round wooden-framed houses. Some are related to field-systems. The best-known site is that at Dinorben, where, about the middle of the third century, a land-owner built himself a large round house, 20 m. in diameter, inside a disused hill-fort. Although the house was supplied with a wide range of Roman pottery, metalwork and ornaments, its archaic plan indicates the innate conservatism of even the wealthiest land-owners in the highland areas. The large amount of agricultural equipment found on the site indicates the main activity of the inhabitants, and among the latter was an asymmetrical, winged plough-share, of a type which can only have come from a plough with coulter and mould-board. As noted above, such ploughs were a benefit conferred by Roman technology; a balanced sickle of Romano-British pattern was also found. But surprisingly no visible field-boundaries have been recorded in the area, in contrast to this evidence for the existence of arable land. At Dinorben, there are strong indications, therefore, that a land-owning farmer was using the most up-to-date agricultural techniques available, even though he was living in the traditional native manner. This should not be forgotten when comparing other native farms with villas.

Strong contrasts with the foregoing can be seen in the north-western area, which also includes Anglesey. A large number of farms and settlements are known, and it appears that some fairly intensive re-occupation of hill-forts took place during the late Roman period. The farms are normally enclosed by a stone wall, and, within each enclosure, there may have been three or four stone buildings, mostly circular, as at Llain-Llan, but occasionally rectangular as at Cefngraeanog. The enclosures themselves vary from roughly oval to polygonal in shape, and are almost always associated with strongly marked terraced fields, the holdings ranging from 1.6–8 ha. They were normally situated on reasonably high ground, so that each farm had access to unlimited hill pasture in addition to its cultivated fields. Occasionally, isolated huts are situated in the fields, while sometimes all the huts of one farm are so distributed.

The density of these farms and settlements has led to the suggestion that they represent official Roman encouragement of new inhabitants during the third century in an area which had been depopulated by

Fig. 32 Native farmstead at Dinas Powys

punitive action in early Roman campaigns. Certainly the polygonal enclosures and their rectangular buildings might imply Roman architectural influence. But the area is also one where hill-forts of the pre-Roman period contained a high proportion of stone-built huts, and a degree of continuity might possibly be expected. Yet, in some cases these enclosed farms overlie earlier settlements of different plan and type, so that rebuilding in the new manner would probably imply a change of ownership, even if there was no change in land-holding or redistribution of land.

One of the best examples of a polygonal farmstead is that at Din Lligwy. The enclosure was formed of five straight-sided walls with a single narrow entrance on the east, leading through a rectangular 'porch' or lodge. A circular house stood in the western angle, while three more rectangular buildings were placed against different lengths of the enclosure walls. The masonry was good, and plentiful pottery and coins were recovered. There was also evidence of metalworking. Outside the enclosure are some massive field-walls, still in use today, which may or may not represent earlier field-boundaries.

Socially and economically these enclosed farms seem to represent the same class of farmer as the rounds and courtyard houses of Cornwall: independent land-owners or high-grade tenants. We shall see shortly that comparable systems occur in the north, and if the villa is taken to describe the basic agricultural 'unit' of the lowland zone, so do these farms act in the highland areas.

As in Wales, so in the north, regional distinctions can be seen in the types of settlement, depending on the nature of the earlier Iron Age occupation. For our present purpose it is sufficient to distinguish between the Pennines, the Tyne-Forth area and the Solway-Clyde area. It must also be remembered that, as in other regions where native-style farms remained unaltered, there is a strong element of continuity into the Roman period and that it is not always easy to differentiate between pre-Roman and Roman period sites.

During the Iron Age in the Pennines and the Lake District, there were few hill-forts; Ingleborough, Mam Tor and Aldmondbury, to cite those apparently most important, may not have been constructed until after AD 43 in response to the Roman presence in the south. They provide evidence in the form of hut-platforms for permanent occupation, but the greater part of the population was gathered into a large number of primitive farms and settlements, many of which were not enclosed. The principal activity seems to have been pastoralism, with the breeding of cattle, horses and possibly sheep. The great oppidum at Stanwick, with its banks and ditches enclosing an area of 300 ha. in the final phase, seems to have been built in response to the need to provide sufficient pasture within the enclosure for large herds and flocks. Some settlements have small areas of fields attached to them, but they cannot always be equated with the pre-Roman period. Nevertheless, a little cultivation of nearby fields probably took place in more favoured places in the dales.

Beyond the line of the Tyne and Solway the main difference to be detected is the greatly increased number of fortified or enclosed sites. North of the Tyne these frequently began as palisaded enclosures on hill-tops, with either one or two rows of posts round the perimeter.

More often than not the palisades were later replaced by a combination of ditch and mound or ditch and wall, giving rise to what are, in effect, small hill-forts, sometimes with multivallate defences. Circular houses found within the forts or enclosures are normally constructed of timber, such as one, 18 m. in diameter at West Brandon (Co. Durham) which was not unlike similar houses further south.

Another type of enclosure has also been recognized, usually known as 'scooped' enclosures. They are situated on hillsides in non-defensive positions and lie within a mound or stone wall. Scoops in the hillside accommodate circular houses and other features.

To the west, in Galloway, settlements are more reminiscent of north and west Scotland, with duns, crannogs and even some brochs, interspersed with fortified settlements. Duns and brochs are normally held to represent single-family occupancy, in contrast to the community settlements, and clearly point to different social origins for the people concerned.

In most of these areas, the one marked development during the Roman period is probably the emergence of circular stone houses to replace timber prototypes; they usually appear in compact groups within stone-walled or embanked enclosures and sometimes overlie earlier hill-fort defences. Both single-house and multiple-house types are known. Occasionally such settlements occur in the vicinity of abandoned hill-forts, such as that at Jenny's Lantern, Bolton (Northumb), and clearly point to the non-defensive nature of the enclosure. But by far the largest number have no connexion whatever with earlier hill-forts, and seem to date generally from the second to the fourth century AD, or even later. In the single holdings, one, or at most two, round stone houses were built within, or tangentially to, the enclosed courtyard, which is often terraced or scooped from the hillside, as at Ells Knowe or Elsdon Burn. In many ways, they are reminiscent of similarly planned dwellings in Wales and the south-west. In the multiple holdings, which are far commoner, upwards of four or five round houses occupy the roughly oval enclosure, which may have a walled paddock within it, such as Knock Hill. The largest known group, containing upwards of thirty buildings, is at Greaves Ash, where piecemeal additions had probably been made to the original nucleus. Sometimes also, loose collections of settlements, perhaps totalling more than a hundred houses, are found in close proximity. In areas nearer and to the south of Hadrian's Wall there is also a tendency for round or oval enclosures to be replaced by rectilinear ones, as at Riding Wood, where four houses inhabit a roughly trapezoidal enclosure with cobbled yards and paved entrance passages. Such settlements are prolific in parts of Cumberland and Westmorland, particularly in the area of the Cumberland plain, south of Carlisle, where, also, probably as the result of Roman influence, rectangular buildings and enclosures are more common; a typical site can be seen at Thursby.

While there is evidence during the Roman period that cultivation of cereals took place in the north, since rotary querns, a Roman introduction, are common finds on such farms, it is often difficult to identify the fields associated with them. Some areas are, of course, exceptional in this respect, such as Ribblesdale, Upper Wharfedale, and parts of Cumberland and Westmorland, where many hectares of continuous, enclosed or terraced fields were opened up in the Roman period, to increase quite markedly the amount of cereals produced. Yet the impression remains of a predominantly pastoral economy, linked with the unlimited upland grazing, good pastures for wintering in the valleys and in the small stock-yards of the farms and settlements.

Ultimately the northern farmer was probably better placed than his north Welsh or Cornish opposite number to take advantage of the growth of towns and vici. Carlisle and Corbridge must have commanded considerable markets, while both, together with the numerous vici, would presumably have contained resident farmers and farm-workers who went out each day to their work, acting as the counter-parts to the many workers from towns and minor settlements much further south. Some of these sites may have even contained farms. Certainly the reason for the growth of so many agricultural establishments in the Cumberland plain might be explained by the presence of nearby Carlisle.

Nor must we forget that, in the third and fourth centuries, soldiers could become farmers and cultivate land around forts. We might, therefore, expect some sign of fields in their vicinities; one such fairly extensive system is known at Housesteads, but it is usually ascribed to later periods. Nevertheless, their activities must have had some effect on the overall farming pattern.

Having considered farming and its various ancillary aspects in different parts of Britain, it requires no great extension to take in horti-culture.

It is probable that Iron Age man, when desirous of fruit, vegetables or herbs, collected them from the wild, and there is little evidence for any cultivation. Indeed, there was little need, since most vegetables were probably valued for their medicinal qualities and not as foodstuff. The Roman period saw not only the practice of horticulture being introduced, but also many new varieties of fruit and vegetable. Unfortunately the evidence for botanical material is not easy to find, surviving in Britain mainly in water-logged deposits, while evidence for the actual borders or flower-beds are even more difficult to trace in the course of excavation.

In other respects we are more fortunate in having excellent contemporary pictorial representations on wall-paintings in Italy, and also good accounts of horticultural practices written down by authors such as Columella in the late first century, not that it is necessarily valid to relate such evidence directly to Britain.

It is difficult to estimate, even within the widest limits, the place of vegetables in the Romano-British diet, but it is probable that most horticultural work will have aimed at producing vegetables or fruit. Ornamental gardens were well known in the Roman world, but it is likely that only the very rich could afford, or even be bothered with, such layouts, and the great central garden at the Fishbourne palace is an excellent example to consider. Its general plan has already been described earlier in this chapter; as with the building, it was probably laid out in the most fashionable manner available, and it is interesting to compare what we know of it with the almost contemporary works of Columella and Pliny. It seems to have combined excessive formality with areas of wild garden, a favourite association in the classical world, which can be seen illustrated on wall-paintings. The middle walk was flanked by arbours or parterres, alternately semi-circular and rectangular, backed by hedges, which may have been of box. The bedding-trenches provided for the latter can be closely matched in Columella's descriptions, where he advocates that, to sow a hedge, the seeds should be fastened, at the correct intervals, to a piece of rope, which is then laid in a trench and covered with soil. Further walks surrounded the whole garden, but in the two central areas so formed, no formal layouts seem to have been made, except for some pergolas flanking the paths, and we might suppose that they contained a variety of ornamental shrubs or fruit-trees; Pliny mentions roses growing on pergolas. Unfortunately, the evidence for the plants grown, apart from weeds, was restricted to one species; some seeds of Lathyrus, an everlasting pea, were found in one room. But it should not be forgotten that, in addition to various native species which might have been naturalized in a garden, such as the crab-apple, bullace, sloe, elder, or possibly the vine, several new forms were possibly introduced during the Roman period: a black plum, not unlike the Carlsbad variety, the cherry, medlar, walnut, mulberry, rose and the flowers, lily, violet and pansy. Greater emphasis than today was probably placed on pot-herbs for seasoning and medicinal purposes, and native species again could have been introduced into gardens to save the trouble of collection from the wild: parsley, fennel and coriander. Introductions apparently included dill, alexanders, chervil and the opium poppy. Many other varieties of native plants would also have been worthy of a place, such as mallow, foxglove (also useful for a drug), St John's wort, marjoram or thyme.

Apart from Fishbourne, and although a garden court may be suggested for the governor's residence in London (Ch. 5), the only other evidence for formal flower-beds comes from the villa at Frocester, near Stroud. But it seems inconceivable that the open spaces, often walled, which were associated with town-houses and villas were not put to similar use, although the accent will probably have been strongly utilitarian, rather than on visual effect. Nevertheless, box clippings as well as the seeds of many ornamental plants were found at Silchester, and it is as well to remember that many plants normally grown as food can make quite attractive displays when interspersed with other types. Neither should we forget that bee-keeping was a supplementary activity, probably practised by many households, as honey provided the main sweetening agent in the diet. The growing of suitable flowers for the bees would have been a logical extension, while almost all dyes for cloth were obtained from vegetable matter, of which we might mention dyers' bugloss and madder, both suitable for cultivation.

There are upwards of three hundred wild food products, including fungi, growing in Britain today. Not all were available to the inhabitants of Roman Britain and some, such as cabbage, broad bean, pea, parsnip, celery, mustard and possibly turnip were introduced during that period. The Celtic bean had of course been grown before, while such fruits as hazelnut, strawberry, raspberry and blackberry were abundant in most areas, and suitable for transplanting to gardens. It is not always possible, when presented with the evidence of seeds or pollen from an excavation, to say if they represent the wild or cultivated varieties; indeed both probably continued to be used. But it is worth mentioning that, during the nineteenth century, good-sized parsnip roots were obtained from wild stock inside ten years, simply by selecting seeds from the best-developed plants each year and sowing in well-prepared ground. So some form of plant improvement was well within the compass of experienced gardeners in the Roman period, and was probably recognized as one of the benefits of cultivation, the other being easy availability. Yet most vegetables would have been both tougher and stringier than modern day varieties, and a preliminary pulping or crushing to break down the coarser fibres would have made them more tender. Perhaps this is the reason why so many *mortaria* – shallow, fairly heavy, bowls with gritted inside surfaces – are such common site finds; they would have been ideal for the preparation.

What then of the small rectangular plots attached to Fenland settlements and mentioned above? They could well be plots for roots or greens, either or both for human or stock consumption, and the Fens today are, after all, noted for their excellent vegetables.

Fig. 33 Horticultural enclosures at North Thoresby, Lincs

Not far from the Fens at North Thoresby in Lincolnshire, another site of interest in the present context has been discovered. There, an area of some 5 ha., overlying a clay subsoil, was covered with a network of ditches, about 1.5 m. wide by about 1 m. deep, and placed about 7.5 m. apart. The fill of the ditches had been highly organic and incorporated large quantities of pottery, bones, chalk and stones. The area was suggested by the excavator to have been an experimental vineyard, with the ditches representing prepared trenches for the vines, but the spacing between rows is rather large, and instead we might propose an orchard for the cultivation of some variety of fruit tree.

We have looked then at the development and improvement of agriculture and horticulture during the Roman period, and must now consider its decline.

In any period of agricultural recession, it is likely to be the most advanced and sophisticated systems which slip first. The more basic the requirements of a community, the better are its chances of survival. We have already seen how villas, despite setbacks, outlasted the ordeals of the third century, which seriously affected the standard of living of many households. As then, so in the later fourth century, it was the villas which probably first felt the onset of depression. But it was a by-no-means uniform process; some proved more resilient than others in resisting the changes, which were many and various.

The beginning of the end for the villas as an agricultural system is probably to be seen in the barbarian conspiracy of the late 360s. Villas were easy prey for wandering bands of raiders, while desertion of slaves or tenants, hitherto bound to the land, in the general confusion would have had much the same effect. A number of villas in Somerset, Hampshire, Hertfordshire and Yorkshire seem to have been sacked and burnt, but this form of violent destruction was not as widespread as is sometimes made out. Nevertheless, the experience must have been demoralizing for many villa-owners, even if not actually destructive. Some of the burnt houses, such as Langton (Yorks) were rebuilt immediately afterwards, but a number of others not apparently affected by the hostilities seem to have been abandoned, their owners presumably seeking safety in the nearest towns. However, by far the larger number continued as before, and the fairly strong measures taken by Theodosius for the safety of the provinces seem to have reassured many owners, who, for the time being, remained on their estates. Moreover, we must not conclude that those which had been abandoned necessarily ceased to act as farms, although we might suggest that a reduction in the overall number of profitable farms will at first have strengthened the position of the survivors.

From then on, however, the growing insecurity of the countryside will have had its sequel in the gradual running-down of establishments, as markets became more difficult of access and profits declined. If we could detect the changes, we might find shrinkages, in that less land was being cultivated, or that fewer stock were being kept. Outlying bands of farmworkers on large estates may have been brought further in, so saving on building maintenance; certainly the workshed at Poxwell seems to have been abandoned at this time, with a new corn-dryer left unused, and it might indicate that the ploughing of marginal lands was discontinued.

Many villas, however, did survive until well into the fifth century, although we may suspect continuous contraction in most, showing perceptibly as a decline in the standard of living: corn-drying kilns being inserted into bath-wings or through mosaic floors. Some certainly ended abruptly in flames in the early fifth century, such as North Wraxall or Lullingstone, but for most it was decay following abandonment. We should also remember that the burning of standing crops – a recommended method of Saxon warfare – could be highly destructive to a large estate, even if the farm itself could be defended against attack.

Finally, it was probably the complete breakdown of the economic system, of which villas had been a part, and on which they had depended, that caused their end. Lack of maintenance of roads and the general insecurity of the countryside will have made it increasingly difficult to get even the surviving produce to markets in towns or to country fairs. We should suspect, therefore, that villas more distant from towns would be the first to be affected, but this was not always so. Other factors are consequently involved. It is probable that the markets themselves were dwindling and the number of people relying entirely on farm-produced food may have been reduced also. Moreover, as we have already noted, towns were becoming more self-reliant with regard to food production in circumstances which must have been partly forced upon them by the villas' increasing inability to deliver the goods. One factor acted on another and produced a chain effect.

Some of the richer land-owners seem to have tried to protect their estates by the introduction of small bodies of troops, or, after 408, by federate Germanic soldiers, for no less than nine villas have produced the bronze buckles characteristic of these people. But the aim may have been self-defeating and have merely attracted a more vicious attack, for two out of the nine houses so defended were burnt to the ground. If, however, reliance was being placed on mercenaries to protect villas, it may be that they were given land in exchange for their services, as happened in Gaul. Attempts have sometimes been made to show continuity between villas and Anglo-Saxon villages. There is certainly, sometimes, a remarkable coincidence between the site of a villa and that of a parish church, such as Lullingstone and Woodchester. Early settlements of Germanic mercenaries on villa estates might well provide an element for continuity, the death of the villa carrying with it the birth of the village. But, in general, the evidence is far too ephemeral to draw any but the most speculative conclusions, and, as with the relationship between Romano-British and Anglo-Saxon towns, accident of geography may have had more to do with it. Indeed it might be taken to show how well sited villas were in the first place to take advantage of the best facilities and land.

St Patrick, in the account of his life in Britain, before being captured by the Irish, gives details of villas still inhabited by their owners as late as 430, sometimes in insecure positions. Gildas, writing a century later, knew nothing of them; not even a tradition had survived. What happened in those intervening years we cannot say, but the dilapidation of the buildings themselves cannot have been long deferred after the collapse of the economy on which they had depended for their livelihood.

A contrast, however, exists in the south-west, Wales and the north. Admittedly the farmers were less troubled by Saxon immigrants, but there were still raiders from beyond the Wall and Ireland to be dealt with. Yet one suspects that, being nearer to the soil and to a subsistence level of agriculture, and with less to lose, they would have adopted a more philosophical attitude. It is possible that they would have been more troubled by refugees from the east, causing an increase in population and resulting land-hunger, which ultimately generated a migration to Brittany. But there is ample evidence to show that many farms in all three areas continued without any perceptible change into the fifth century and beyond. There was, however, one major change, mainly in Wales and the west, pointing to the growing lawlessness of the times. A considerable movement back to the hill-forts occurred, some of which were refortified for protection. To what extent this reflects the transfer of Cunedda and a large body of Votadini from southern Scotland to north Wales in order to drive out Irish settlers, is not known. But in the preceding decades, pressure from Ireland possibly forced the abandonment of unfortified farms and homesteads, which may have been taken over by the new arrivals, in favour of the better placed hill-forts.

Chapter 5

Organization and Management

The Roman empire was broadly divided between senatorial and imperial provinces. Since the emperor paid the army, those provinces containing garrisons, and which were often the latest acquisitions, tended to fall into the latter category. Britain was so treated and consequently, in law, the emperor was the governor of the province. But, for obvious practical reasons, he appointed a personal representative, an imperial legate, to act for him as a kind of viceroy.

Most provincial governors were drawn from the senatorial order, the highest social class in Rome. By means of a carefully graded career structure, a young man might aspire in time to the highest office of consul, having first held other ranks such as the command of a legion and the praetorship. The governorship of a province was an accepted part of his promotion, and he may, at first, having served as praetor, have been sent to a province with a small army containing no more than one legion at his disposal. Thereafter, having in the meantime returned to Rome for his consulship, he might have been appointed to one of a whole range of imperial provinces, containing larger garrisons, and ultimately, if he continued to prosper, to the governorship of the senatorial province of Africa or Asia, which was considered the peak of achievement, and certainly the best paid.

The governor of Britain, therefore, down to the late second century, in view of the presence in the island of never less than three legions, was an ex-consul. But if he had retained this status in an imperial province, difficulties of protocol would have arisen if the emperor visited the province in person, for the emperor himself might have held the consulship more recently and so be 'junior' to the governor in the supreme senatorial position. This factor serves well to illustrate the peculiar dichotomy which existed between the emperor and the Roman senate. To overcome this difficulty a consular governor serving in an imperial province invariably took the next lower title and was officially referred to as *legatus Augusti pro praetore*.

The governor of a province, until the early fourth century, was both general officer commanding the army and also chief justice. A high degree of versatility was therefore expected and the stages in his career were constructed with this in mind. We know the careers of several British governors, and they almost invariably included the governorship of some lesser provinces which would provide related experience. Britain was perhaps considered a difficult province, since a succession of some of the ablest men in the empire became governor, and a large proportion went on to take plum jobs in the imperial service. Quite frequently, also, some had served earlier in Britain as military tribunes or legionary commanders, so were not unfamiliar with the problems presented. This system, whereby more was expected from a man than might be thought humanly possible, tended to weed out the ordinary, leaving only those with an extraordinary and varied capacity. It has been said that a provincial governor was either a wonderful success or a gigantic failure, and both types served in Britain.

An imperial governor was usually appointed for a term of not less than three years, and some were known to have remained at their posts for much longer; Agricola in Britain served twice the normal term. On appointment, he would subscribe to the *lex provinciae*, a form of written constitution for the province containing details of boundaries, and probably taxes, put together when the province was inaugurated. He was allowed to nominate from among his friends or relations an unofficial staff to assist him in his duties. In addition to them, he would also be able to call for advice from a number of other officers, of whom the legionary legates – or commanders – were the most important. Also attached to his headquarters was a permanent administrative staff, mainly clerical and sub-clerical, who were frequently centurions or soldiers seconded from legions, whose duties might take them anywhere in the province. On appointment, also, he would have been given his instructions for the management of the province by the emperor and also a large cash float to pay for the administrative expenses. Strictly speaking he was not bound by any of the decisions of his predecessor, but a man would have been unwise to ignore them altogether or reverse them except for very sound reasons.

In a province such as Britain, with its exposed frontiers and long history of frontier wars, the military duties of a governor will obviously have been important. In major campaigns he would have led the army in person, conducting the battles and, with his staff officers, laying down general strategy and tactics for the regulation of the frontiers and the control of military areas. During much of the first century, the British governors were so actively engaged in this way that no permanent headquarters seem to have been provided and it is difficult to say either where his administrative staff was housed, or where the more static processes of government, such as record-keeping and report-writing, were carried out. For the governor was expected to keep the emperor informed in all matters by dispatches carried by the imperial postal service.

But, as already noted above, in addition to his military duties the governor was also required to carry out a variety of judicial functions. To him fell the task of making the circuit of assize centres in the province. Apart from acting as a court of appeal, all cases, both civil and criminal, involving either large sums of money or the death penalty were referred directly to him by local courts in the towns. Additionally, Roman citizens could appeal to the emperor for relief from the governor's verdict, but the expenses of doing so were probably so great as to deter most litigants except in the gravest cases. Non-citizens, however, had to abide by his decisions, from which there was no appeal. When it is remembered that the cases he tried might well involve disputes of Celtic Law as well as Roman, or conflicts between the two, the difficulties of the governor are seen to be manifest. In the circumstances, assessors might be appointed to help try the cases and, in extreme instances, points of law were even referred to Rome for decisions or guidance.

As the complexities of empire grew, intolerable burdens were, therefore, being placed on single men. Some relief, however, was to come under Vespasian, for he instituted a new post, *legatus iuridicus*, to aid a governor in his legal duties. As with the position of governor, that of law officer was a personal appointment of the emperor, although the man nominated was subordinate to the governor, and did not relieve the latter of his final responsibility. But the iuridicus would have carried much of the routine, day-to-day administration. At least two of the officers first appointed in Britain were eminent lawyers, at a time when, under the governor Agricola, attempts were being made to work out a final solution to the British problem and when many thorny legal questions had probably to be resolved.

The main reservoir of Roman citizens in Britain at first lay at Colchester, so that the principal and, probably, only assize centre at first lay there too. But it seems likely that the number of citizens living in London rapidly passed the population of Colchester, leading perhaps to a change in venue for the assize or to the creation of another centre. Certainly it was in London that the provincial administration had ultimately settled by the end of the first century, although the financial offices were earlier centred there.

A large building has been identified in the area of Cannon Street station, London, and has been interpreted as the governor's *praetorium*. As with the almost contemporary palace at Fishbourne (see Ch. 4) it was constructed round a large open court, or garden, containing pools and probably fountains. North of the court was a range of monumental

Fig. 34 Governor's palace in London

structures, at the centre of which was a massive hall, approximately 13 m. by 24 m., possibly flanked at either end of the range by a near-circular exedra to provide an imposing architectural facade. The east range of the building was made up of a wing containing groups of small rooms, perhaps providing offices or living accommodation for higher members of the administrative staff. The south range appears to have contained rather larger rooms. Unfortunately, modern buildings preclude the excavation of any more than this small sample. It is likely, however, that the palace extended southwards to the river and was provided with an impressive waterfront, perhaps incorporating a continuous colonnade. The north range seems to have been the most sumptuous, but mosaics and painted wall-plaster have also come from the west wing.

London has produced other evidence from which can be inferred the seat of the governor. A tombstone erected in memory of a man named Celsus, records that he was a *speculator*, an officer attached to the governor's staff. There were usually thirty seconded for service from the legions and their duties consisted of the apprehension, the custody and, where necessary, the punishment, of state prisoners. Another tombstone depicts a centurion, Vivius Marcianus, carrying a scroll; he has been identified as a centurion in charge of the clerical staff in government house, the *princeps praetorii*.

During the Hadrianic period, a fort of exceptional size was erected on the north-western outskirts of London. It occupied nearly 5 ha. of ground and was ultimately incorporated in the town when the civil fortifications were built. Its presence helps further to illustrate the special arrangements made at London; no other town in Britain, with the exclusion of York, was so closely associated with a garrison, and the fort was probably intended to house the military detachments required for special duties in the capital, although where these people were accommodated before its construction is not known.

The only sphere over which the governor had no legal control was that connected with provincial finance, which was managed by the *procurator Augusti*. He was appointed by the emperor from the ranks of the equestrian order of Roman society, which was below the senatorial order. The equestrian order also had its own career structure, by which a man might rise from prefect to tribune of an auxiliary infantry regiment, then to be prefect of a cavalry regiment, after which he might be promoted to the procuratorial service, so, as with the governors, gaining wide experience of both civil and military matters.

The procurator, as a nominee of the emperor and probably dependent to a greater extent than the governor on the whims of his imperial master, was given increasingly wide powers as time went on. Sometimes procurator and governor quarrelled, and he was a wise governor not to meddle in matters of the imperial treasury. In Britain, the rapacity of the procurator, Catus Decianus, played a large part in promoting the Boudiccan rebellion, while, after its suppression, Suetonius Paullinus, the legate, disagreed so radically with the new procurator, Julius Classicianus, over the punitive measures to be adopted, that Nero arranged for an inquiry, as the result of which Paullinus, not Classicianus, was recalled. On the other hand Agricola was praised by Tacitus for not interfering with procuratorial matters when he was legate of Aquitania; yet Agricola, so we are told, also corrected many matters relating to unfair tax extortions in Britain, and cannot have remained as aloof on his arrival here.

The procurator could hold his own courts and hear cases related to

1	Tower Hill
2	Aldgate
3	Bishopsgate
4	Cripplegate
5	Aldergate
6	Newgate
7	Ludgate
F	Basilica and Forum
P	Palace
M	Mithraeum
B	Baths
H	Hypocaust
━•━	Bastion
━▼━	Turret
----	Line of River Wall
~~	Roman Wharf
──	Modern Waterfront

0   500 m

Fig. 35 London

tax-collection or other sources of imperial revenues and he also commanded soldiers to assist him in his duties. Again at the time of the
Boudiccan rebellion Decianus sent 200 men to the aid of the colonia at
Colchester. Procurators could also be governors of minor provinces and
it has been suggested that, when Britain was divided into two provinces
early in the third century (see Ch. 2) one of them was, to begin with,
governed by a procurator. Certainly by the third century the chances of
a procurator being so promoted were much greater than earlier.

Imperial estates also came within the competence of the procurator
and he would have a number of junior assistants to act as managers.

Through these assistants, he was responsible for leasing mining concessions and for all the myriad activities which went on in the settlements
attached to the mines: renting shops, running bath-houses, or places of
amusement. The recruitment and training of gladiators was yet
another duty.

The principal task of the procurator, however, was to assess the level
of, and to collect, taxes, of which there were several kinds. In a newly
occupied province they were calculated by carrying out a detailed
census, not only of all land-holdings and its status, but also of the
productivity, in which the procurator would have been assisted by the
tribal leaders. Every so often a complete new census was ordered, for
which special commissioners were sometimes appointed, while in between the records were kept up to date by the tribal leaders, or local
magistrates, as they later became. There were two main types of
revenue, a land tax based on a percentage of yield of crops or animals
and a poll tax, which was more generally applied to movable property
and trades, and which was in effect a tax on income or wealth. Roman
citizens were sometimes exempt from these taxes but they were subject
to death duties, which yielded increasing amounts as more natives were
given the franchise. But all alike had to pay customs duties, as a
percentage of the value, on goods passing the frontiers and sometimes
also crossing provincial boundaries. For the latter purpose some provinces were grouped together in what were in effect customs unions.
Finally there was the *annona*, the compulsory requisition, probably at a
controlled price, of corn or other appropriate goods for army use; this
tax was not, however, evenly applied throughout the imperial period.
Each branch of revenue-raising was probably supervised by an assistant procurator, and there would have been, also, a permanent staff of
clerks and orderlies.

London early became the financial centre of the province, acting so
possibly before the Boudiccan rebellion. Julius Classicianus, procurator after the rebellion, died in office and his fine tombstone was
found to have been later incorporated in the city fortifications. In
addition, an unused writing tablet, branded with the procurator's
stamp, and also an iron stamp for marking soft metals with the legend
M.P.BR – *Metalla Provinciae Britanniae* – are hardly likely to have been
lost far from the main office. Moreover, there seems in addition to have
been a government brickworks, managed by the procurator's department, situated near London, with its output devoted to official buildings. An interesting structure beneath the later municipal forum has
been tentatively interpreted as the principal treasury building. It contained an open court, numerous offices, a hall and apparently a deep
cellar, or strongroom.

N

Fig. 36 Pre-forum building in London

It can be seen, therefore, that the total personnel employed to administer the British province was not large and at first probably did not exceed a few hundred people; lack of numbers was largely made up by their versatility. Today we are so used to everyone having their own rigid, small specialities, that it is difficult to grasp the wide range of experience which was available to the governor and procurator among so few people.

At regional or local levels, the affairs of the central government were superintended by various officials stationed in the places concerned. Among their duties will have been running the imperial postal service, the *cursus publicus*, collection of the *annona* and the security and transport of other supplies for military areas. The officials were normally called *beneficiarii consularis*, but were seldom above the rank of legionary soldier. We know of such men stationed at Winchester, Dorchester (Oxon), Wroxeter and Catterick, as well as at many northern military sites. At Catterick, the only site where two such men have been attested, there was a large *mansio*, or official inn, for members of the imperial post.

This service, largely organized by Augustus, covered the whole empire with a network of land and sea-routes, primarily for the transport of military dispatches, but it was soon adapted for the carriage of any official messages, persons or goods. Nevertheless, licences to use it were not freely given and even governors of provinces had to justify its employment, perhaps because the cost of the service, which was heavy, had to be borne by local civitates and municipalities; but abuses were apparently common and difficult to prevent. Couriers were known to travel, on average, some 80 km. a day, although in emergency this might have been increased threefold.

Mansiones and the lesser *mutationes* were placed in major towns and minor centres. The latter consisted simply of stations where changes of horse could be obtained by the messengers or wagoners, while the former contained overnight accommodation, secure parking, storage areas and stabling. Several mansiones are known in Britain, although they are not easy buildings to identify, often appearing in plan like any other large domestic residence. Yet the well-known example near the south gate at Silchester contains features which help to distinguish it from a private house: it has a large bath-house, far larger than would be required for even a substantial household, and numerous suites of three rooms, arranged in groups in the north and south wings, which flank a central court. The west wing contained larger rooms probably for receptions. The overall size of the building also tends to distinguish it from the other houses in the town. Since Silchester lay on several routes of the postal service, the mansio would have had to be large to accommodate the relays of messengers, and it would have been permanently busy.

The mansio at Catterick was somewhat smaller in size, but still had a large bath-wing and two main suites of rooms, as well as piped water. It had been built in the second century by a ninth cohort, probably of Legio VI from York, in contrast perhaps to the Silchester building, which is more likely to have been erected by the civitas Atrebatum. It is possible that the two beneficiarii mentioned above as being stationed at Catterick successively managed the mansio, or were otherwise connected with its running.

It is fortunate that a large part of the postal routes of the early third century seem to have been represented in a document known as the Antonine Itinerary, while an earlier version is recorded in a much more fragmentary state in the Ravenna Cosmography. These two sources give the names of towns, forts and villages which lie on routes, the distances between them and usually the total distance between the terminals. For instance the so-called Iter II for Britain gives the distance from Hadrian's Wall at Carlisle to the port at Richborough in Kent as 481 Roman miles, but the road taken goes via York, Chester, Wroxeter and London, by no means the most direct route. The latter fact has led some authorities to doubt its value as a true representation of the postal service. Nevertheless, it indicates where mansiones and mutationes are likely to be found and also provides useful corroborative detail for the equation of Roman and modern sites.

The identification of mutationes is more difficult than that of mansiones, but a comparatively small, rectangular masonry building with massive walls, lying just within the north gate at Thorpe-by-Newark might be so interpreted.

One last aspect of imperial management must be considered: the supply of coin. Roman coins reached Britain in three ways: in the hands of immigrant traders and settlers; sale of British goods in other provinces; and, by far the largest quantity, in the pay-chests of the army and civil service.

The coinage consisted of issues in three main metals or their alloys, gold, silver and copper. The coinage therefore had the inbuilt weakness of all trimetallic systems. A variation in the actual value of one of the metals immediately imposed an artificial value on the others, and although the values of the earliest Roman coins were related to the amount of metal they contained, being issued at so many pieces to the pound weight of metal, this soon came to be meaningless and individual coins simply became valuable tokens with their 'price' governed by the proportionate amounts of goods they bought. Nero was responsible for starting the steady devaluation of the coinage which continued slowly until the early third century, when the monetary reforms of Caracalla increased the rate of depreciation. The third century was also a time of extreme inflation which in itself was exacerbated by the rapid decline in the standards of coinage. During the reigns of Gallienus and the rulers of the independent Gallic empire, the base 'silver' coins became virtually valueless.

Diocletian again reformed the coinage, reissuing good gold and silver, but thereafter the lack of standards, particularly in the copper coinage, constantly affected values and it may be that coins came to be treated largely as bullion. One of the remarkable manifestations of the late fourth century is the number of silver coins of good quality in circulation in Britain, no doubt due to revival of interest in silver deposits there.

During the early empire the principal coins were the gold *aureus*, the silver *denarius*, the brass *sestertius* and the copper *as*, with equivalent half-value coins in each metal and an additional quarter-value copper. Caracalla introduced a new silver coin, usually called an *antoninianus* by numismatists. Its original weight was 5.75 g. as against 3.0 g. for the denarius, but its weight and fineness fell rapidly, so that by AD 270 it only weighed 3 g. with a silver content as low as 3 per cent, yet its value then was supposedly worth 5 denarii. Such was the measure of inflation. In the fourth century the aureus was replaced by the *solidus*, of lesser weight, and the denarius was revived. Copper coins also appear with a silver wash on their surfaces, but the rapidly changing standards caused a good deal of variation in type and size.

In the early period, the emperor was chiefly responsible for minting gold and silver, while the senate continued to mint brass and copper; the latter coins therefore carry the letters SC (*senatus consulto*) on the reverse side. Various mints were used for the manufacture of coins, but it was not until the late empire that they were each distinguished by a code of letters included on the coin. From Britain, an interesting find at Verulamium was the hard bronze die for stamping Hadrianic denarii. How this came to be in Britain is not known as no official mint is thought to have existed; it cannot have been incidental to Hadrian's visit to the province since the type of reverse is much later in date than the visit. In the third century, however, mints were established at London and possibly Colchester under Carausius, but were closed by Constantine about AD 326.

Coins of the Roman period were extensively used for conveying propaganda to the people, either by depicting imperial works in artistic form with an appropriate legend, or by straightforward invocations of an abstract concept, such as *Gloria Exercitus* (our glorious army) or *Fel Temp Reparatio* (a return to happier times) on fourth-century issues.

Needless to say, imperial victories were often commemorated, and an extensive series is known referring to British campaigns. Indeed one of the commonest coins of Antoninus Pius is the Britannia issue. It is of interest that Britannia as an emblem on coins first appeared on an issue of Hadrian's dated to AD 119–22.

Few coins reached Britain after the closure of the Gallic mints at the beginning of the fifth century, so that the number of coins in circulation rapidly declined, ceasing finally, so it is thought, about AD 440.

The Roman side of the provincial administration was matched by the native provincial council. This council was formed by delegates from the constituent municipalities or civitates of the province. One of its principal duties was the care and promotion of the imperial cult (see Ch. 7), and the president of the council was also chief priest. The council in Britain was centred at Colchester, where was also the main temple of the cult, the Temple of Claudius, founder of the province. The temple may not at first have been inside the colonia, although it later became enclosed within the walls. South of the temple and its precinct lay a number of buildings which were probably connected with the council. It has been argued, partly on the evidence of a dedication to the emperors on behalf of the British province, and partly because of a tombstone of the wife of a provincial slave, that London superseded Colchester as headquarters of the cult. While it is possible that the administrative buildings were moved to the provincial capital, we need not doubt the continuance of the Colchester temple as the most important in the country. Moreover, it was not unknown for the provincial council to be based elsewhere than in the cult centre.

The other functions of the council varied from province to province, and unfortunately we have no specific information regarding Britain. It would certainly have had to raise money and promote annual games and festivities in connexion with the cult; more often than not the money came out of the members' own pockets, as they never obtained the power to raise taxes or legislate. They were, however, allowed to communicate directly with the emperor, so that, in law, at least, excesses or injustice in the provincial administration could be reported, but we know of no such cases from Britain and it is more likely that the council remained a largely ceremonial body. They could, however, select a patron, usually an influential man holding high office in Rome, who, in return for various honours, could plead British affairs in the right quarter.

For the exercise of local administration, Britain must be considered in two parts: those which remained under military government and those which achieved a measure of civilian self-government. When taken over the whole Roman period, it can be seen that considerable changes in these respective areas took place.

At first, when the frontier cut across the midlands, most of the province would have been under military rule. Exceptions, of course, were the two client kingdoms of the Atrebates and Iceni, where the ruling princes were expected to maintain law and order, possibly with the help of army detachments, to collect taxes and raise recruits. From about AD 50, there was also a chartered, self-governing city at Colchester as well as three civitates. By AD 90, the two client kingdoms had been absorbed and further civitates and chartered cities had been established; the numbers were added to yet again under Hadrian. But a return to military control of some of the latter areas took place before the end of the second century, and the arrangements then recorded represent about the maximum area given over to civil administration, until its complete separation from military government in the early fourth century.

Within areas of military government it seems likely that regions were allotted to each legionary commander, who as a member of the governor's staff, will have been intimately concerned with the formulation of plans. So we can see, in the final and permanent phase of legionary distribution, much of south and central Wales being allocated to the legate at Caerleon, while the remainder of Wales and also some areas to the west of the Pennines came under the Chester command; east of the Pennines and the whole northern frontier region were probably controlled from York.

Each legionary command contained numbers of auxiliary forts, whose commanders will have been of varying rank and seniority. To what extent the latter interacted is not known, but each local commander probably had responsibility for his own area, and it will have been he, or his men, who were in closest touch with native Britons, passing on regulations originating from the governor. Where a compact tribal organization existed before the conquest, it is probable that such instructions would have been relayed through the tribal leaders, in which case it is not surprising, for instance, that we find a fairly senior officer, the prefect of a cavalry ala, ultimately stationed at Cirencester, close to the main Dobunnic centre. He would have ranked above any neighbouring infantry commanders. Some degree of tribal autonomy must, therefore, have been respected.

In regions, however, where no such united tribal structure existed, greater responsibility must have rested with each auxiliary commander to run his own area. We know, from several sources, the wide range of duties which might be expected of such a man with relation to the civilian population. He would be expected to settle disputes, keep the peace, take censuses and collect taxes, and, subject to overriding orders

35. Mosaic with a cupid riding a dolphin, from the palace at Fishbourne

36. Garden bedding trenches at Fishbourne

37. Aerial photograph of the villa at Ditchley

38. The situation of the villa at Chedworth, in a small east-facing combe opening on to the valley of the river Coln. The modern house stands in the centre of the villa

67. The Mithraeum, Carrawburgh

68. Acrostic, suggestive of Christianity, scratched on wall-plaster from Cirencester

69. Curse, inscribed on both sides of a lead sheet, against T. Egnatius Tyrannus and P. Cicereius Felix: from London

70. Glass gaming pieces from the temple mausoleum at the Lullingstone villa

71. Altar to Silvanus from Bollihope Common, Co. Durham, recording the killing of a wild boar

72. Zoomorphic bronze buckles from Catterick

from a superior officer, he would have had the last word in many matters.

But the natives were encouraged to play an increasing part in the management of affairs. Where vici had grown outside forts, the people were allowed to run their own petty affairs through two elected magistrates and possibly a council of villagers in a properly constituted manner, although we do not know in Britain the precise boundaries which must have existed between the civilian and military jurisdictions. Certainly the latter retained responsibility for all roads, and possibly the placing of buildings within a vicus, but the former could most probably have settled internal disputes between villagers and made corporate dedications to deities. But as with most matters of this kind in the empire, a good deal of flexibility will have existed and much would have depended on the character of a particular military commander and the amenability, or otherwise, of the local population. So the native inhabitants would have been introduced to the Roman way of doing things and given valuable experience for the time when full self-government might be conferred.

We have already seen, in the midlands and south, how many vici associated with forts of the Claudio-Neronian period formed the kernels of later towns and villages, and the implications which this development had in the sphere of local government. The communities so formed joined the ranks of self-governing organizations of which there were, as already noted in Chapter 3, several different kinds.

At the head were the chartered cities of varying grades: the coloniae and municipia, each of which would have had either full Roman, or only Latin, rights. Full Roman rights were normally only conferred on communities containing a predominance of citizens, and the charter of constitution enforced the practice of the Roman legal code. Latin rights could be earned by a city composed almost entirely of non-citizen inhabitants, who may have been permitted to retain many of their native laws. Promotion could, however, take place from one grade to another.

The charters, by which these cities were founded or constituted, were once considered to be conferred by the imperial government, and modelled on the constitution of Rome, but it now appears that most were concocted locally, although leaning heavily on established precedent. These charters were written constitutions for the regulation of the communities and seem to have incorporated many common features. Consequently, though we knew nothing of those which applied to the British coloniae or municipia, we can, by analogy, make some general deductions of the ways in which they were managed.

The ruling body was the *ordo*, a council of up to about a hundred

members, *decuriones*, which, certainly by the second century, was virtually a self-perpetuating oligarchy, when there was a shortage of candidates for election and nominations were made by the magistrates.
Membership of the ordo was restricted by both age and wealth, and
moreover a man had to be free-born. No ex-slave was, therefore,
eligible, no matter how wealthy, but his sons were.

From four to six executive officers carried out the day-to-day affairs.
At first they were elected by the popular assembly of the town's people,
but increasingly appointed by the ordo. They were grouped in pairs:
duoviri iuricundo, aediles and sometimes, but not always, *quaestors*. The
former pair were the most senior and had charge of the law courts,
trying petty criminal cases and civil cases below a certain value. When
remitting more serious cases to the governor's court, they would have
provided transcripts of the evidence and a summary. One or other
acted as chairman to the ordo, or if both were unavoidably absent, a
prefect could be appointed. They also had charge of the imperial cult,
the local militia and the junior officers. Although they were nominally
subservient to the ordo, there seem to have been occasions when they
could rule contrary to the ordo's instructions and the system appears to
have been constructed to include some degree of cross-checking between the parties. Every fifth year, two especially distinguished men
were appointed as duoviri. This year saw vacancies in the ordo filled,
public contracts renewed and new levels of tax assessed.

Duoviri would almost certainly have been members of the ordo
before appointment, but the aediles not necessarily so, since their age of
appointment was below that required for the council. Aediles were
responsible for the upkeep of public buildings and roads, the aqueducts
and water distribution systems and sewers. They could also, it seems,
act in place of the duoviri in the courts.

Not all cities had quaestors, but, where they existed, they were
responsible to the magistrates for the financial arrangements. None are
attested in Britain, but then neither is there evidence for duoviri; yet
they must have existed. Inscriptions do, however, record decurions.

Other important people in the municipal hierarchy were the six
men – *seviri Augustales* – charged with the ceremonies connected with the
imperial cult. These positions were open to manumitted slaves, freedmen of considerable wealth, for they personally had to underwrite the
cost of the rituals.

The municipal exchequer was financed from a variety of sources.
Chief among them were probably the fees exacted on election to public
office; moreover, the people appointed were also expected to make
some valuable gift to the town, such as a public building, or to stage an
entertainment in the theatre or amphitheatre. Rents from public land,

money from its sale, rates on water supplied to private users from the aqueduct, fines in the courts, and dues exacted on goods entering or leaving the town, all contributed; but it remained a fact that many cities and towns were always chronically short of money, and on certain occasions, the emperor remitted taxes due to the imperial treasury. Hadrian was noted for doing so, and it may be that remission of taxes to some poorer towns in Britain during his visit enabled work to be resumed or commenced on a variety of public buildings.

Many of the larger and more important cities were subdivided into constituent quarters, or vici. Indeed the normal definition of vicus is the smallest unit of built-up area having its own administration; consequently use of the word was not always restricted to villages or settlements outside forts, and constituent vici are known at Lincoln. They were probably allowed a pair of elected officers, but their duties would have been largely ceremonial, and the full administration devolved upon the parent organization of which they were a part.

The methods of local government so far described would, in Britain, have been appropriate to the four coloniae at Colchester, Lincoln, Gloucester and York with their associated territoria; the municipium at Verulamium; and almost certainly London.

In the tribal territories a similar system was adapted to the differing circumstances, and it is here that we see, most adequately demonstrated, the Roman flexibility to problems of local government in the provinces.

Britain, like much of Gaul before its conquest, possessed a clearly defined tribal structure, and these areas became the basic units in local government, each one being given, as in Gaul, the title of *civitas*. In some cases where the units were too small to be viable on their own, as in Kent and Wessex, amalgamations took place; or where a reduced client kingdom was too large, as was that of Cogidubnus, it was split.

Civitas in Latin strictly means citizenship, but an extension of the meaning embraced communities of citizens also, so that *civitates peregrinae* came to mean communities of citizens of foreign, i.e. non-Roman, origin. In many places where the term was used to describe such communities, it became synonymous with town or city. But in the four western provinces of Gaul and Britain its meaning was once more adapted to apply to whole tribal communities or their equivalents. There has, however, been much argument over this definition and there are authorities who still maintain that, in Britain, civitas equals town and that the tribal land around it was attributed to it as a territorium, as in the case of coloniae and municipia. Certainly down to the early third century, the weight of evidence is against such suggestions; thereafter changes occur which will be considered below.

In Britain, therefore, as in Gaul, a civitas was basically the whole tribal territory constituted after the Roman manner, with closely prescribed rights and duties, within the framework of the provincial government. In the middle was the capital town, used as an administrative centre, and the selection of sites for these towns has already been considered in Chapter 3. As far as can be judged in Britain, the organization of a civitas closely resembled that of the chartered town, with magistrates and a council, but it must be admitted that variations may have occurred both in the structure and in the names used to describe the officers. Yet a quaestor is known from Carlisle and an aedile from Brough-on-Humber.

What then of the status of the civitas capitals? Most, as we have already seen, started as vici attached to forts, and vici they probably remained, despite their often considerable increase in size and importance. There is a little evidence to suggest that some may have been subsequently promoted, but it is not entirely reliable.

Within each civitas there were probably country districts called *pagi*, and additionally there were probably other vici, some of which may have acted as pagus centres. The pagi may correspond to earlier, pre-Roman tribal subdivisions, and some of them are known to have lived on in areas of Brigantia. Indeed one, the Carvetii, was destined for later promotion to an independent civitas. Otherwise there is little evidence for their existence in Britain, but they were possibly the last link in the administrative chain by which instructions were relayed to the great mass of country people. They may well have proved more important in those civitates which remained strongly orientated towards the country, such as the Dumnonii and Cornovii.

We have already seen that two different legal codes, native and Roman, were in force in Britain, certainly down to the early third century; thereafter the grant of the franchise to all freeborn members of the empire should have virtually eliminated the use of native laws. In fact governors were specifically empowered to continue trying cases under local law at their own discretion. In the main these would have been concerned with inheritance, with land-ownership, with the general relationships of servant and master, and landlord and tenant, and with parental and family matters.

Claims have been made that the native laws of Britain were largely later enshrined in a codified version of Welsh law, dating to the tenth century AD. Two principal forms of land-holding have been detected in them. In one, the land was held in common by a whole community, and the apportionment between its members of arable and pasture was governed by changes in the total population and not simply in family groups, so that reallocation took place when someone died or reached the age of majority. In the other, the reverse of primogeniture, the original freeholding was divided equally among all the sons on the death of the father and so on down to the fourth generation, when the cycle was restarted. But it was open to any member to contract out of the system whenever he liked and go off on his own. Indeed it has been claimed that it was the latter system which gave rise to the multiplication of residential blocks in some of the larger villas. Such a system could have brought about a massive fragmentation of the original land-holding, unless a degree of co-operation was secured between members. It is as well to tread delicately on such unsure ground, and remember that, though interesting, these suggestions lack proof. Nevertheless, Celtic law was undoubtedly the mainstay of ordered life for a considerable time in the Roman period of Britain.

Roman law, like so many things in the empire, developed on a piecemeal basis, with its roots firmly established in the republic. It was compounded of a mixture of case law and statute law, with the former predominating to begin with, but with the latter taking over entirely at the end of the empire. In case law, earlier decisions of the courts were binding in subsequent similar cases, unless upset by a superior court; statute law took the form of edicts, issued by the emperors. From time to time, when the weight of case law became overwhelming, codified forms were issued, the first we know of being the Institutes of Gaius, put together in the second century AD and followed much later by the Theodosian Code and the Digest of Justinian, among others. The rulings contained in the latter received legislative force after their publication.

A sharp distinction was made between public and private law. The first regulated the powers and structure of public bodies and their relations to the private citizen, while the second, as might be expected, was concerned with the actions of citizens one with another, but this is not to say that a considerable body of law was not enacted by the state to regulate the latter, and so became part of public law. Within this structure, it is possible to detect three kinds of relationship. There was that of a citizen to the state, an absolute condition which came within the realm of public law; there was that of the members of a family to its head, which was again absolute in its condition, but where excesses were guarded against by further applications of public law; and there was that of one family against another which was the sphere of all private law.

Apart from offences against the state, such as certain types of murder or treason, where the state apprehended and tried the criminal, it was left to the wronged person to bring an action against the malefactor. Many offences, now deemed to be criminal in their content, such as theft and assault against the person, were then considered no more than civil offences, so that, in a wide range of circumstances, someone seeking justice had not only to arraign the accused person before a court, but also to collect the evidence and witnesses. In cases of malicious accusation, a penalty could be enforced against the accuser, often equal in value to the amount supposedly in dispute. These provisions were necessary, since professional informers, especially in cases involving crimes against the state, often hoped to be rewarded on obtaining a conviction from the confiscated estate of the accused.

The different types of court have already been considered above. Civic courts of petty jurisdiction could only inflict minor penalties, mainly fines. Imprisonment was not a recognized form of punishment and was used primarily by magistrates for persons waiting trial and as a method of coercion to arrive at the truth or to extort a penalty. But it would seem that by the late empire, few powers of correction were left to local magistrates in criminal cases. The governor's court technically had power of sentencing to death or to hard labour in state mines or quarries, but ultimately, in fact, almost all death sentences had to be referred to the emperor. There were also different classes of society, the *honestiores* and the *humiliores*. No legal definition of the classes has even been traced, and discretion seems to have been left with the courts to decide. Broadly, however, honestiores were treated more leniently, often being spared the death penalty, certainly in its more extreme forms. Neither could they be condemned to the mines; in place, banishment to a remote province or island, with or without confiscation of their wealth, seems to have been the rule. It should perhaps be remembered that Britain may have been considered a suitable place to which people could have been banished from the central provinces. Humiliores, in contrast, as well as slaves, could be examined as witnesses under torture.

One of the most important applications of the law in Britain must have been in connexion with slavery. Before the occupation, Britain was a slave-owning society and the manacles and slave-chains from the Llyn Cerrig Bach hoard and other sites are eloquent evidence for it. It is likely that the number of slaves increased during the Roman period, and the laws regulating their sale and treatment were many. They had no rights, but were supposedly protected from the worst abuses by edicts issued by several emperors, especially by Augustus and Hadrian, and in time their lot improved. It was open to a free man to discharge a debt by selling himself into slavery, but the supply was chiefly kept up partly by frontier warfare and partly by interbreeding among existing slaves, since the children of slaves were the property of the master and the number could be controlled by the practice of child exposure. The large number of infant burials at the villa at Hambledon, as already noted, implies the existence of a slave-run establishment.

In the later empire, slaves often reached management posts, particularly in the imperial civil service, and many laws had to be enacted to take the new circumstances into account. They could often amass considerable wealth, by means of the *peculium*, or perquisites, and as a result purchase their freedom. Many slaves were also freed by their masters as a gift, while others obtained it on their master's death. But a freedman still had obligations to his ex-master, which, if ignored, might in extreme cases lead to his reduction to slavery. Although many freedmen achieved great wealth, usually as merchants, they still had disabilities, in that certain offices, such as decurion, were not available to them; moreover, even though one freed by a Roman citizen became a citizen himself, he could not•enter the equestrian or higher orders, although his sons could do so. In all, freedmen formed a numerous and important class in society in the empire, frequently occupying prominent positions in the emperor's service; a freedman of Claudius was sent to settle the mutiny of the army at Boulogne in AD 43, while one of Nero was charged with an inquiry into events after the Boudiccan rebellion.

The management of the empire was a continuously developing process, affected alike by imperial edict and provincial attitudes. Many of the changes which reached full flower in the fourth century can be traced back to Hadrian's reform of the imperial civil service. He instituted for the first time a separate career structure for civil servants which did not embrace military service, so bringing about a fundamental change in the types of people holding public office. It undoubtedly brought about greater efficiency and also specialization, but in times of civil war or anarchy, such as in the 190s or later in the third century, put the civil service at a distinct disadvantage. Senatorial provinces had been impotent to interfere in earlier, similar catastrophes, because they contained no garrisons. Hadrian's actions, therefore, theoretically enhanced the power of the army still further.

In Britain, as in some other provinces, the first major changes came about as the result of the civil war of the 190s, and after Severus had retaken the province from Albinus.

The division of Britain into two provinces somewhat naturally caused a duplication in the administrative offices. London remained as the capital of Upper Britain (*Britannia Superior*) under a consular, while York became the seat of the governor of the Lower province (*Britannia Inferior*), but it is probable that the governor of the latter, of praetorian status, combined his duties with command of Legio VI. But the two military commands did not remain entirely separate and legionary vexillations from Superior are known to have served at Corbridge, as well as orderlies from the consular governor's staff at Chesterholm and Greta Bridge.

However, the most drastic changes in the provincial administration came about in the early fourth century, as already indicated. The four provinces which now made up the British diocese were: Maxima Caesariensis, Flavia Caesariensis, Britannia Prima and Britannia Secunda. Each was at first governed by a *praeses*, a man of equestrian rank, whose title had now entirely replaced that of procurator; the title of legate also disappeared. Later, however, Maxima appears to have been promoted to have a proconsular governor. London was almost certainly the seat of the diocesan *vicarius* and also the provincial governor of Maxima. There too would have been the offices which, in the fourth century, partly replaced the old-style imperial procurator's department: the *rationalis rei privatae per Britannias* and the *rationalis summarum Britanniarum*. Between them they continued to collect revenue payable in bullion and to supervise imperial property. Most remaining taxes were by now paid in goods and the organization of the system was combined with the other governmental duties of the praeses.

The separation of military command from civil government was a further measure enforced, together with the reform of the army, as already noted in a previous chapter (Chapter 2). Changes in judicial processes also occurred, summary trials without a jury becoming the norm rather than the exception. Most of Diocletian's new laws intimately affected every person in the empire, particularly those that made employments hereditary. The overall result was to remove all the last traces of fictitious republicanism, fostered since the time of Augustus and to replace it with an undisguised absolute monarchy. Versatility and a slightly amateur approach to administration now gave way completely before more narrowly based, professional specialists; excessive centralization and control became firmly established. The resulting bureaucracy may have been necessary to save the empire from disintegration but in the long run it was hardly beneficial. Indeed it was recorded that the increase in the official class was so enormous that the receivers of public money seemed to outnumber the payers. In the end, tax-collectors were demanding the means for an administration which ruled but could no longer protect, and people who might before have aspired to the rank of decurion, now sought the greater security of comparatively humble posts in the emperor's service.

Not all the measures were, however, successful. Diocletian's edict of prices, which was issued partly to preserve the purchasing power of soldiers' pay in the face of severe price rises, and by which a maximum price was fixed for all the necessities of life throughout the empire, was a complete failure. It had to be withdrawn, despite the savage penalties for breach of the codes.

At local government level there were also many changes, brought about chiefly by interference by the central administration in local affairs. One development was a considerable extension of the system whereby officials of the governor were placed in charge of regions; at first the *regionarii* or *stationarii* were often seconded centurions, later probably civil servants. Their principal duty was probably to see that taxes in kind were correctly returned, but they may also have had some police functions in order to control brigandage; one such centurion is known from an inscription at Bath. The third century had already seen a great rise in the number of *beneficiarii consularis* placed round the provinces, probably for much the same purpose. But, as with so many of the reforms of the fourth century, the beginnings lay much further back in time. Occasionally in the second century, when financial difficulties caused by mismanagement or extravagance beset a town, the emperor appointed a *curator* to clear up the muddle. They were frequently citizens held in high esteem in the town, who perhaps were, or had been, *duoviri quinquennales*. It is possible, also, that the emperor, having remitted taxes to help a municipality, saw the need for some central government control to see that the money was correctly spent. Curatores, therefore, were additional magistrates with special financial responsibilities, appointed first when the need arose. By the third century, however, they had become a permanent feature of the municipal scene, and, since they were appointed by the emperor, assumed seniority over the other magistrates, replacing the duoviri as chairmen of the ordo.

The diminution of the power of the ordinary magistrates went hand in hand with an increase in their burdens. By the fourth century, the ordo was being compulsorily filled from the ranks of those with requisite wealth, and under Diocletian, not only was the office made hereditary, but also more and more laws were passed to prevent decurions escaping their liabilities. Despite the wealth qualification for entry to the ranks, subsequent bankruptcy was no escape. The requirement that held decurions personally responsible for making good the deficits in taxes of certain dependants must have weighed particularly heavily, and it is no surprise that every means to escape was attempted.

In contrast to administrative matters the management of business affairs fell broadly into two classes, public and private.

As we have already seen, the provincial procurator was responsible for most public business, chiefly through the imperial estates. Unfortunately we have no detailed knowledge from Britain of their management, but we can probably assume that they were run no worse than those in other provinces. That being so, it is fair to consider the evidence from the silver and copper mines at Vipasca in Spain, as representing the likely state of affairs in Britain. It is probable that most mining rights were held by the emperor, although the commonly occurring iron ores in Britain may have been exempt, as it meant that a careful control could be kept on production. Since the economy was to a large extent managed and not entirely free, we find that production of metals in Britain was sometimes limited in favour of the Spanish mines.

The evidence from Vipasca comes in the form of two inscriptions, one of which, dating to Hadrian's principate and probably originating in the local procurator's office, gives instructions to the manager on the conditions of mine tenure and operation. They are extremely detailed and all-embracing in their scope, and cover not only tenancy agreements, but also the removal of ore from the mines (only between sunrise and sunset), safety (all diggings to be carefully propped; no props to be removed; rotten ones to be replaced) and drainage (no work to be carried out within a certain distance of the ditch which carried away water from the mines).

The other inscription, probably of the same date, concerns the ancillary services provided by the mining settlement. Even auctions of the metals were carried out under a concession, the concessionnaire taking a percentage of the sale price. Further concessions were made to people who ran the bath-house, acted as barbers or launderers or made shoes. A modern trade unionist might well appreciate the definition of a shoemaker as one who 'drives or sells shoemaker's nails'; other restrictive practices abounded. School-teachers were exempt from taxes, a point of interest to present members of the profession. Also, rights were granted, at a cost, for reworking slag-heaps.

Before leasing a concession to a private individual or company, the procurator had to be satisfied that sufficient working capital was available. This probably accounts for the fact that most silver mines in Britain were at first worked direct by legionary detachments using convict and slave labour. Lead ingots, or pigs as they are usually known, a valuable by-product of the silver industry, have been found with cast inscriptions of Legio II, from the Mendips, and Legio XX, from the Welsh borders. But entrepreneurs were soon in the field and one, C. Nipius Ascanius, probably a wealthy freedman from Italy, was working in Somerset by AD 60 and later in Flintshire. Another, Tiberius Claudius Triferna, had mines in Somerset as well as in the Peak District. By the end of the first century, however, companies were active. One, the *societas Novaec*, was working in the Mendips, while in the second century the *societas Lutudarensis* was heavily engaged in Derbyshire. Another was engaged in mining copper in Anglesey, the *societas Romae*.

These companies, or partnerships as they might be better called, were governed by various laws of contract. In multiple partnerships, two of the members would be appointed executives, as joint *magistri*, and the names of some of the magistri of the societas Lutudarensis appear on lead pigs. In some cases, leases on mines were obtained by the local ordo, or perhaps they were even given the duty of working them, for lead pigs bearing the names of the Brigantes of north England and the Deceangli of Flintshire have been found.

There is one further interesting point concerning lessees of all imperial estates, whether single operators or partners. Normally they had full rights to dispose of their tenancies, or shares in them, for the highest price they could get, simply by registering the transfer with the procurator. But they were not allowed to divest themselves if they were in debt to the imperial treasury. Consequently as taxes became more onerous, more and more people found themselves bound to the land or to the mines, often in time becoming little better than serfs.

It is difficult to trace the activities of other business partnerships in Britain, although they assuredly must have existed; the nearest we can come to suggesting others is probably in the pottery industry. Five different people with the common name of Sextus Valerius made *mortaria* (see Ch. 6) at Colchester and would seem to represent a family business. It is noticeable that in this particular field of manufacture, many of the early producers were Roman citizens, and may either have been sponsored by rich patrons, or were wealthy proprietors in their own right. Towards the end of the second century, one or more German firms from the Rhineland tried, not altogether successfully, to make samian pottery at Colchester. The capital required for such a venture is most likely to have come from partnerships.

Management of shops and other trades must often have been put in slaves' or freedmen's hands. An inscription from Norton, east Yorkshire, mentions a slave running a goldsmith's shop. It has also been suggested that a certain block of shops, built to a standard pattern, at Verulamium in the early years of the town, was leased out to tenants or managed by slaves on behalf of a wealthy, Catuvellaunian land-owner, who had constructed the block as an investment. When it was rebuilt after the Boudiccan fire, fragmentation of the original holding took place, suggesting perhaps that individual owners had bought themselves in.

In the early days of the empire, the state looked with great suspicion on all kinds of free associations, suspecting them of political agitation. Consequently such associations, whether connected with a trade or with a benevolent purpose, had to be registered and the laws controlling them were strict. Yet, flexible in all things, the state then proceeded to make use of those societies which served imperial purposes.

Trade associations, or *collegia*, existed all over the empire, including Britain. Although they were frequently composed of people following the same occupation, at no time were they comparable either to guilds or trade unions. Trade standards, higher wages or improved conditions were no part of their business, and they were primarily intended more as clubs to form foci for social activities on behalf of people with like interests. It is probable that they also acted as burial clubs for their members, which were the commonest types of associations and the only ones permitted to be run inside forts and fortresses. They, therefore, played an important part in society, since they permitted both slaves and freemen to meet on common ground during life and assured them decent burials afterwards. Burial clubs frequently held plots of land in cemeteries (see Ch. 7), and often used communal graves, or *loculi*, in which compartments for cinerary urns or coffins opened off a central space; one has been suspected at Lincoln, where also two guilds formed from districts of the city are known. One of the best-attested examples in Britain is the smiths' club mentioned on an inscription from Chichester. It was sufficiently wealthy to be able to erect a temple to their patron deities, Neptune and Minerva, very soon after the conquest. Here, the authority for recognizing the legality of the club was not the emperor, but the client king, Cogidubnus. The inscription, therefore, provides a useful side-light on the areas of law in which the ruler of a client state was competent to act on his own authority in matters normally reserved for the emperor. In an ordinary province, the legality of a club could not be decided by the governor alone; the matter had to be referred to the emperor, as did Pliny to Trajan when he was governor of Bythinia. Maintaining an illegal society was an act of treason.

The organization of a society or club revolved round a set of rules which were approved at the time of its inception. The names of the officials are reminiscent of municipal magistrates and the titles *quinquennalis, decurio* and *curator* all appear. The latter term, usually taken to mean treasurer, occurs on an inscription from Lincoln. Another inscription from Caerwent refers to a man being excused all further subscriptions, presumably for some signal service, while further inscribed fragments from Silchester attest the presence of what might best be called a Travellers' Club, no doubt to take care of the body, if a member was sufficiently unfortunate to die away from home.

Supreme in the area of management and organization was the Roman army, for which there is a tremendous amount of information from widely different sources. The fundamental organization of the army and its fighting capacity have been considered in Chapter 2, but it remains to look briefly at some closely related matters which went to make it the most efficient army in the ancient world.

Recruits were obtained from many sources, both within and without the empire. Every major acquisition of territory brought its quota of men, and to begin with care was taken to station them away from their homelands, so that Britons are found serving in Germany during the late first and second centuries. In time, however, this regulation was greatly relaxed, with the idea of giving a man a stake in the defence of his own home. Recruits from the outer provinces were normally placed at first in auxiliary regiments, but as time passed greater numbers aspired to the legions, for which, until the early third century, Roman citizenship was the passport. On enrolling, a man had to swear an oath of loyalty and give a statement as to his status. It seems that notes were made in the records of any physical peculiarities, such as scars.

Assigned to his regiment, and equipped, the new recruit underwent a lengthy primary training programme to accustom him to discipline and methods of warfare. Needless to say such training remained a considerable part of peace-time duties. Foot-drill, route marches and swimming in full kit, weighing up to 27 kg., weapon-training, surmounting obstacles, and constructing fortifications were all recommended for infantry, while cavalry likewise trained in squadrons in the principles of attack and retreat. More specialized training probably included exercises such as constructing bridges of boats, or artillery practice with *ballistae* or *onagri*; the former fired an iron bolt, the latter hurled a lump of stone. It was also recommended that recruits and young soldiers should be drilled morning and afternoon, but that experienced men should only have weapon practice once a day. For wet weather, most legionary fortresses had large drill-sheds. No doubt also there were many fatigue duties to be learnt and carried out, and there was always equipment to clean and polish, or clothing to wash and mend.

The logistical problems of the army were immense. The basic foodstuffs were corn, bacon and cheese, supplemented by some vegetables, meat, fish, shellfish, salt and olive oil, together with beer or a thin wine, normally mixed with water. Fodder had to be supplied for animals, timber and other materials for building construction, and leather for tents and clothing. It is not always possible to calculate the quantities which must have been required, although it is known that each soldier was allowed approximately 330 kg. of corn a year, so that the total annual consumption of the army in Britain was of the order of 20,000 tonnes, all of which had to be collected and distributed. The diet also implies the existence of quite large numbers of regular supply ships, carrying wine and oil from Gaul or the Mediterranean. One of the most recent, interesting British finds has been a series of wooden writing-tablets from the fort at Chesterholm, just to the rear of Hadrian's Wall. Dating probably to the end of the first or early second century, they appear to include records of food issues or purchases, but whether as part of the regular diet or for a special occasion is not entirely clear. It must be remembered that soldiers had sums deducted from their pay to cover the cost of their basic diet and also clothing, and they probably had to purchase other foods out of their pay.

On active service and when away from permanent bases, accommodation was in tents made of calf leather. Fragments are found from time to time in water-logged deposits, and, when added to other information, enables us to make some deductions about quantities. It has been estimated that a tent for eight men (the normal arrangement for private soldiers) required some fifty leather panels, and that the skin of one calf would only provide two panels. The second-century garrison in Britain, therefore, possessed tents equivalent to some 200,000 calves. Admittedly they would not all be made at once, and many would have come from overseas, but nevertheless the repair and replacement of worn-out tents must have called for considerable resources of livestock.

It has been calculated that there were 21.7 km. of barrack-walling in the Agricolan legionary fortress at Inchtuthil. Translated into terms of 10 cm. sq. timbers and allowing for roofs and other buildings, it is probable that something of the order of 4000 cu. m. of sawn wood had to be transported, probably from the midlands, to the edge of the Scottish Highlands, i.e. a stack 40 m. long, 20 m. wide and 5 m. high. To that figure has then to be added the 82 main gate-timbers, each about 30 cm. sq. and upwards of 6–8 m. long, and the subsidiary members. In all, about 300 wagons must have been involved to carry such a load. Taking into account the three other legionary fortresses and the 80 auxiliary forts constructed in Wales, north England and Scotland during the late first century, all requiring their quota of timber, perhaps adding up to a further 37,000 cu. m. or more, we can fully appreciate the work undertaken in felling some 5500 mature trees, seasoning the wood, cutting and prefabricating sections, and delivering them to the right place at the right time. A recent calculation has shown that approximately one hectare of natural woodland is needed to produce 9 cu. m. of suitable timber, so that the full amount would have required the felling of some 4500 ha. of forest. Indeed, we can only conclude that the preparation must have been carried out well before Agricola's campaigns and that either stockpiles were kept in readiness, or the forts in the midlands were dismantled sufficiently carefully for much of the timber to have been reused. Such figures, of course, can only be extremely general and tentative, and may indeed be conservative, but they are worth quoting as they can help to quantify the efficiency of the organization which lay behind the operations. We might also remember the 11 tonnes of iron nails of all sizes which could be written off from the stocks at Inchtuthil without a qualm, to save transport when the fortress was abandoned. The order to do so probably caused near heart-failure for some quartermaster, who, no doubt, had to account for their absence in his stock returns.

We know, also, that full records of requisitions and supplies, daily duties, out-postings of men, registers of correspondence as well as accounts were kept, with returns sometimes having to be made in duplicate or even triplicate. Moreover, manpower returns had to be made to show the state of recruitment, and copies of these documents presumably ended up in Rome. One of the most interesting surviving documents from the late empire is the Notitia Dignitatum. It is a list which shows the composition of all the military commands and offices of state and the placing of military units, government factories, and civil service officers. Many arguments have taken place as to the date and origins of the Notitia and, indeed, as to its internal consistency. It seems most likely that not all sections are strictly contemporary and represent dispositions in different parts of the empire at different times. Neither can we be certain that it is an official document, or simply a copy made by someone with access to the records. Nevertheless, it is invaluable in showing the extent of late Roman organization, both civil and military, and reflects the many changes which had occurred. Army administration continued, on paper, as efficiently as before, but we may suspect that the increasing bureaucracy was in the end self-defeating.

Chapter 6

Work

The everyday work of the province, as with the administration, can be broadly divided between military duties and civilian employment, but there is a comparatively large area of overlap, since the Roman army, as already noted in Chapter 2, aimed at self-sufficiency in many matters.

The first duty of every Roman soldier was to achieve proficiency in the art of war. It has long been recognized in all warfare that a few well-disciplined and highly trained men can be more than a match for superior numbers of inferior quality. Consequently the training given to the men of the Roman army always had this objective firmly in mind, and was, moreover, supported by the provision of first-class weapons and armour.

The main offensive weapon of a legionary soldier was a short but broad, double-edged sword, about 0.6 m. long, which was most effective when used for stabbing rather than slashing. Such use is more economical of movement, inflicts the more serious injuries and does not expose the swordsman so much to attack. He was also provided with special throwing spears, or javelins, some 2 m. long, which had a square-sectioned iron point connected to the wooden shaft by a shank of untempered metal. It could be thrown considerable distances and could kill up to about 10 m., but its chief purpose was to lodge in an enemy's shield. The trailing weight of the shaft then bent the soft iron shank, so hooking a large encumbrance firmly to the shield and causing it to be discarded. For his protection, the legionary was given a composite bronze and iron helmet with neck, brow and cheek guards, body armour of overlapping plates attached to leather backing and a rectangular, ply-wood shield curved to fit round the body. It is highly probable that much of this equipment would have been manufactured by the army and certainly maintained by armourers and blacksmiths attached to each regiment.

The weapons and armour of auxiliary infantry and cavalry varied much more. In the first place a cavalryman needed a greater reach and therefore had a longer sword; the rectangular shield would have been cumbersome on horseback and so was substituted by a circular or oval variety. Lances and spears were issued, the different lengths, shapes and styles equating with their use. Specialist regiments of archers, slingers and spearmen were also maintained with their own individual weaponry.

In addition to the personal fighting equipment of each man, the army also deployed artillery in the form of *ballistae* or *onagri*. The former, usually mounted on carts, each with a team of ten men, were not unlike large cross-bows and fired iron bolts with a killing distance of up to a hundred metres or more, while the latter hurled rocks up to 250 kg. in weight for considerable distances. Various other 'engines-of-war' could also be assembled as need arose and were used mainly in sieges or for storming fortified positions.

In Britain, despite its long history of warfare during the Roman period, there is unfortunately little evidence for the sites of battles, or for the ways in which they were fought. The military historian, Vegetius, writing in the late fourth century, tells of tactics and strategy then in use and applies them to battle formations, but in a somewhat idealized form; it is likely also that he was relying heavily on the earlier, now lost account of Julius Frontinus. The latter, governor of Britain in AD 74–8, wrote yet another work, a surviving account on tactics and strategy, which takes the form almost of a training manual for officers. It is more than likely that Frontinus would have practised his tactics in his campaigns in Wales, but unfortunately none can be related to specific sites.

The Roman soldier was most effective when working in close formation on carefully chosen ground. Almost all the serious defeats of the Roman army happened when such tactics could not be followed; the Varus disaster in Germany in AD 9 took place in the Teutoberger Forest, and the defeat of a legionary force in Silurian territory in the early fifties probably occurred in equally difficult terrain.

But the effectiveness of Roman tactics in attacking fortified positions is perhaps demonstrated best in Britain by the battles which excavations have shown to have been fought at the two Dorset hill-forts of Maiden Castle and Hod Hill in the year of the invasion. At Maiden Castle a direct frontal assault was mounted on the complicated structure of the east gate, perhaps after the timbers had been fired by incendiary missiles. There, we can imagine the use of a *testudo*, linked shields held overhead to protect the assault force from missiles thrown from rampart tops. A cemetery of the defenders killed in action produced ample evidence for the power of Roman arms, one skeleton still containing the fatal ballista-bolt embedded in the spine.

At Hod Hill, on the other hand, no assault seems to have been necessary. Instead, an extremely accurate artillery bombardment took place on the chieftain's house which, fortunately for the Roman army, lay within range, at a distance of some 180 m. from the south-east corner. But to carry out the bombardment, a siege-tower at least 15 m. high would have been required to give the gunners, or their observers, visibility over the ramparts. The accuracy of the fire can be judged by the fact that only two bolts appear to have missed the target completely, while eight actually struck the house, causing, so it would seem, an immediate surrender.

Other hill-forts and oppida such as Spettisbury, Old Cadbury, Sutton Walls and Stanwick have shown the Roman army at war, if in less graphic ways. But of the great battles of Romano-British history little is known. Attempts have been made to show that the battle of the Medway in AD 43 was fought near Rochester, that Caratacus was finally defeated near Caersws, in central Wales, that Boudicca's forces were annihilated somewhere along Watling Street near Mancetter, and that Agricola defeated the Caledonians in the battle of Mons Graupius near Ythan Wells in north-east Scotland, but at no site can positive evidence be produced. An altar at Corbridge records revenge taken after the Brigantian rebellion in AD 155, and it used to be thought that the siege works at Burnswark, north of Carlisle, belonged to the same campaigns; but more recent research now relegates them to practice works.

Not all members of the army were actively employed in fighting and the support services were equally important. Foremost among them were the medical orderlies, usually under the command of a non-commissioned Greek officer. The Greeks were noted for their medical knowledge and skill in the ancient world and many entered the ranks of the army. Greek doctors are known from inscriptions left at Chester, Binchester and Housesteads, while a field-dressing station is depicted among the scenes on Trajan's Column. Most medical work was of a highly empirical nature. In battle it would have primarily involved the dressing of physical injuries, amputations, removal of foreign bodies and the recovery of the wounded from the battlefield. Surgical instruments, in many cases of a surprisingly sophisticated design, enabled quite major surgery to be carried out. Good base hospitals, moreover, existed in most forts and fortresses and were equipped with wards and operating theatres. The maintenance of good health among the ranks was a well recognized need and sick-parades must have been a normal feature of peacetime soldiering. The importance of diet in curing ill-health was also known and special diets for invalids were sometimes ordered, while army convalescent stations may have been maintained in a number of provinces, including perhaps one at Bath. It is probable that hygiene also came within the sphere of medical orderlies, who may therefore have controlled the bath-houses and organized sanitary matters.

Although every legionary was something of an artisan, trained carpenters would have been on hand during battles for the construction of siege works or defensive shelters, and if the engagement took place anywhere near the sea, or on a river, special boat parties would have been present, not only to provide transport but also for constructing bridges, and the important parts played by the naval arm in the campaigns of Agricola, or later, of Severus in Scotland must not be forgotten.

It was, however, in peacetime that the full versatility of the Roman soldier became apparent. Some of their duties as administrators have already been considered in the preceding chapter, but beyond that there was scarcely a job, of any nature, that the army could not undertake, in addition to remaining always ready for battle.

Battle-readiness was maintained by an unceasing round of drills, training and manoeuvres. Army drill instructors, of whom one dedicated at a temple at Lydney (Glos), were attached to all legions and had charge of foot-drill and weapon-training, and so instilled that habit of implicit and unhesitating obedience to orders, which is called discipline. In the field, practice camps were constructed as part of training programmes, and good groups of these could once be seen just outside the legionary fortress at York, while they still exist on Llandrindod Common and at Tomen-y-Mur in Wales, among others. Most of the Welsh examples occur near auxiliary forts and were therefore probably constructed by the local regiments. All these camps are small, but nevertheless demonstrate the principal defensive features of Roman fortifications, such as the turf ramparts with rounded corners, the ditches, and either titulate or claviculate entrances. Each camp may have represented a day's work on the part of a detachment of new recruits.

Turf cut to a standard-sized block was commonly employed by the army for defensive fortifications, especially in the first and second centuries in Britain. Certainly practice would be required in its handling, as, clumsily laid, it would slump and peel away from the core. But properly laid and compacted it would give a solidity which is absent from dumped earth or rubble. Great care was therefore taken in selecting good quality turf. At both Glenlochar in south-west Scotland and at Brough-on-Humber it was brought some distance, since the local turf

Fig. 37 Practice camps at Cawthorn, N. Yorks

was too friable. It had the added advantage also that the grass exposed at the outer edges continued to grow, so ultimately rooting the whole surface together and giving increased stability. One of the summer fatigue duties would almost certainly have been cutting the grass on the rampart slopes. Practice camps of an entirely different nature, probably derived from large-scale manoeuvres, can be seen at Cawthorn on the north Yorkshire moors. There a succession of three camps, or forts as they might more correctly be called, was constructed, but never permanently occupied.

At some time, also, a full-scale mock assault was made on the empty native hill-fort at Burnswark, north of Carlisle. The fort occupies a prominent hill in the coastal plain of the river Solway and can only be approached by a steep climb. Military camps were constructed on the lower edges of the slopes on both north and south sides of the hill, and that to the south was also equipped with three projecting ballista platforms, suitable for mounting a preliminary bombardment of the type noted above at Hod Hill. In siege-craft it was often Roman practice to construct a continuous circumvallation around a besieged site. Such a work was carried out at the unoccupied hill-fort at Woden Law in the Cheviots, presumably again as part of a battle-training exercise.

To what extent ordinary soldiers were trained in other fields than martial arts is not entirely known, but the rudiments of carpentry and masonry were probably imparted to all. An inscription from Chesterholm refers to the testing of recruits who, having passed, went on to construct a masonry building. But for the major construction work specialist soldier-craftsmen, under the command of the *architectus*, were at hand to carry out the technical work. It should not be forgotten,

N

0   500 m

Roman earthworks

▬▬▬ Bank
══   Ditch
⧫   Hill-fort ramparts
▭▭▭ Roads
◉   Artillery platforms

North Camp

Hill-fort

South Camp

Fig. 38 Iron Age hill-fort and Roman practice siege works at Burnswark, Dumfries

however, that they were still soldiers and could be called upon to fight if the need arose. But the rank and file legionaries will have provided most of the unskilled or semi-skilled labour, perhaps supplemented by civilian corvées.

Apart from the construction of fortifications of various types and the normal run of military buildings, the army was also responsible, on many occasions, for surveying and building roads, aqueducts, sewers, and even pottery and tile kilns, which they also operated.

For the ordinary legionary, the most fatiguing aspect of all this work was probably the provision of the raw materials: timber, stone, lime, sand, gravel, clay, metals. Every man had in his personal equipment an axe, an entrenching tool, a saw and a basket for carrying earth, and so was basically fitted out for such tasks, and only needed supplementary tools suited to the type of work. For instance quarrying would require heavy hammers, metal and wooden wedges, 'jumpers', crow-bars and lewis or scissor equipment for lifting large blocks by derricks, cranes or shear legs. Quarries used by the Roman army are well attested to the rear of Hadrian's Wall, where the units working them frequently carved their names and those of their officers on the rock face; the Written Rock of Gelt near the fort of Castlesteads is one of the best known examples, and records the activities of a vexillation of the second legion. If Hadrian's Wall had been completed to the full gauge of 3 m., over 1½ million cubic metres of masonry would have been required for the Wall alone. If allowance is made for the reduction in width and for the fact that the masonry is composed of puddled clay or lime mortar as well as stone, it is probably not too rough a guess to suggest that over half a million cubic metres of stone had to be quarried for the work, a proportion of it dressed, and then often carried some little distance before it could be used. Add to that the sand and clay which had to be dug, the stone to be quarried for lime-burning, the mortar to be mixed, and it is not difficult to see why, at first, the employment of three legions was necessary and that they had only progressed a little over half way before the change to turf-work took place to speed up the rate.

Apart from the quarries mentioned above, which, unfortunately, have now been largely destroyed, the best examples of the Roman quarryman's art in the area are to be seen in the sectors where the hardness of the whinstone prevented the full excavation of the fronting ditch. At Limestone Corner, between Chesters and Carrawburgh, can still be seen great blocks of rock as the Romans left them. One such block, which must weigh upwards of 13 tonnes, lies on the northern lip; another, unsplit, still remains at the bottom of the ditch, and the holes cut in the upper surface for inserting the wedges to split the block are visible. Steel-tipped wedges, of a type suitable for such work, have been discovered embedded in the Wall at Milecastle 26, further to the east, while a lewising chisel was found at Chesterholm; heavy hammers are comparatively common finds in Britain. But even given mechanical lifting aids, of which a number of different types were known in the empire, the work must have been laborious and slow and would have called mostly for brute force.

The skilled masons' work would have been no less arduous, and the preparation of several million roughly dressed facing stones for the Wall and its forts would have been a task of considerable magnitude. It also called for more exacting work in the construction of specific buildings, with the preparation of voussoirs for arches, monolithic slabs for sills and lintels, and frequently ornamental work for more important and elaborate buildings. Much of the better masonry was dressed by chopping or by pecking the surface of the stone with a special hammer on which one end was pointed and the other chisel-shaped, but the finer work called for a hammer and a variety of chisels. Plumb-bobs, squares, rules, dividers and straining pegs for lines would all have been necessary equipment, and examples are sometimes found.

Many pieces of the military masons' craft have survived in Britain. As might be expected, they show a degree of workmanlike competence rather than artistic merit, although some of the better examples, such as the Corbridge lions, if they were indeed executed by a military mason, can stand comparison with most provincial art. The fountain-head from the Catterick mansio depicts a dolphin and a sea-horse, somewhat woodenly drawn, but with a pleasant imaginative touch, for one of the front legs of the horse was portrayed so as to be dipping below the surface of the water in the tank; it may have been the work of a mason from Legio VI. It is likely that a large number of the surviving army tombstones were the work of military masons. Some are undoubtedly of better quality than others, but, although they form an interesting and informative collection on their own, they do not fully measure up to the best civilian work. Military altars form yet another corpus of their work, but generally provide less scope for artistic portrayals, although in their own right interesting for the varying calligraphy they display.

We have already seen in the preceding chapter that the demands made by the Roman army for the supply of timber would have been considerable. Timber is at its best when cut down between late autumn and mid winter, a period which would have coincided with the non-campaigning season of the army. Since large stocks must have been maintained, it is likely that much of that time was occupied in felling and preparing the wood. Felling and trimming were presumably carried out with axes, and the work involved in dealing with a mature oak must have been very considerable, with the amount of waste probably exceeding that of today. Saws were certainly in use, but most of those found are too small for felling, and were probably restricted to preparing standards and planks from the trunks. Precisely how this was done is not known, but the longitudinal sectioning of a large, hardwood tree would be no easy job without either circular saws or even large, two-handed saws. The manufacture of the latter, however, were within a contemporary blacksmith's competence, even though none are known, but their use would probably have required saw-pits. Mechanically-driven saws for stone-cutting were known in Germany, and similar devices may have been employed for timber, using either water or animal power. The design and construction of such equipment would again have been well within the ability of Roman engineers, who were familiar with gear-systems and crown-and-pinion equipment; they lacked, however, knowledge of the cam and crank and so were unable to transform rotary into vertical or horizontal motion. Large lengths and sections of sawn timber have sometimes been recovered from water-logged deposits in Roman forts in Britain, so that there is no doubt that the army could manufacture the products, and, in view of the quantities involved, it seems inconceivable that it was done entirely with small, single-handed saws. Admittedly, a single standard could have been cut from one tree by chopping and adzing, but the waste would have been appalling, and the total requirement of trees for the Agricolan building programme would have to be trebled or even quadrupled. But, once again, we might wonder at the amount of physical effort which went into such construction, mainly with somewhat primitive equipment, and anyone who has attempted to cut a single cross-section of a large, hardwood tree with even a modern steel handsaw will be in a better position to appreciate it. We need not doubt, therefore, that a very large number of man-hours went towards the maintenance of the timber stocks and that doing so would have been one of the principal mid-winter duties of the men.

Many timber buildings of the army were made within fairly rigid limits of size, owing, no doubt, to the standard measuring-rods carried by centurions. Consequently a degree of prefabrication could be employed, that was yet sufficiently flexible to allow some variations within the module. All wall uprights could be sawn to standard size with the mortice holes for the horizontal members cut in the correct positions. Wall sole-plates, where used, could likewise be sawn to certain lengths, with the number of specially prepared corner pieces manufactured to a given ratio of side lengths. In the buildings of the Claudian fort at Valkenburg (Holland), where timber survived in the wet conditions, the corner unions of the sole-plates were made with half-lapped joints and the corner post was morticed through the junction to act as a retaining peg. The standard of joinery was, therefore, very high, and numerous carpentry tools, ranging from hammers, gouges, different bits to be used in bow-drills, chisels, rasps, saws and planes have been found in Britain from time to time, many on military sites. Derricks were employed to erect large timbers in a vertical position, and smaller post-holes set beside the main gate-timbers at the fort at Oakwood in south-west Scotland are evidence for their use to haul the larger pieces upright.

There is no doubt, also, that timber was recovered by systematic dismantling when a fort was evacuated. At both Inchtuthil and Fendoch, foundation timbers had been dug out of the ground, and nails removed with a claw, judging from the number of curved and bent examples found scattered around the bases of posts. Such timber was then presumably inspected for rot, and, if sound, returned to stock. Somewhere there must lie extensive compounds used for stores depots, and it is most likely that the large fortified annexes connected with many forts, such as that at Thorpe-by-Newark, which is several times larger than its parent fort, were so used, providing space for storage and parking areas for the numerous carts and wagons employed in the distribution.

Among other building materials produced directly by the army were the metal fittings for woodwork, mostly of iron, and brick and tile. Blacksmiths would have been posted to every unit, while legionary fortresses contained large manufacturing workshops, such as that uncovered at Inchtuthil, with its buried stock of iron nails and spikes. No doubt such men also acted as farriers, and although their duties may have included the manufacture and repair of military weapons, perhaps kept separate from general smithing, it is probable that an equivalent, or even greater, weight of metal had to be turned into structural ironwork. Apart from the wide range of nails and spikes, varying from big, 28 cm. lengths to small, hollow-headed hobnails, all made on a special anvil, large quantities of door locks and hinges, binding straps, ties, hooks and holdfasts would have been needed. Wagons and carts would have required tyres, hub-rims, lynch-pins and chains. Carpenters, joiners and masons needed tools; even agricultural implements may have been manufactured. Bronzesmiths, probably fewer in number, must have worked closely with the blacksmiths, since many pieces were of a composite bronze/iron structure. The two enclosed compounds which were constructed at Corbridge in the early third century seem to have been set up as arsenals for making military ironwork, and the excavators found, in one furnace, a half-completed iron beam which had been in the process of manufacture. The *classis Britannica*, the British fleet, seems to have maintained an iron-smelting works in the Weald of Kent, although the supply of timber for ship-building would have been a useful secondary activity.

The manufacture of brick and tile, which was mainly undertaken by the army during the first and second centuries, called sometimes for specialist depots. The best known of them is that at Holt (Denbighshire) where Legio XX maintained a centre to supply the fortress at Chester. The site consisted of a small fortified enclosure containing at least three barracks and some other buildings, while outside lay a bath-house and a house, perhaps providing accommodation or offices for the officer in charge. There was a range of workshops and drying rooms, besides the firing kilns, which were arranged in a solid bank and served by a single stoking area. The kilns themselves were more elaborate and better constructed than the normal run of civilian types, and possessed sectional floors which could be removed for cleaning the fire chambers beneath. Nearby were the clay-pits from which the raw material was extracted. The situation of the depot close to the river Dee will have enabled the finished products to be shipped by water directly to the fortress.

The kilns, eight in number, not only produced brick and tile, but also pottery, mainly of early second-century types, and including some fine, glazed wares. The site seems primarily to have been established at the time when the Chester fortress was being reconstructed in masonry and the production of pottery was probably introduced as a side-line, although the depot was not finally given up until the fourth century.

It is almost certain that the other two legionary fortresses at York and Caerleon likewise had their own manufacturing centres, and sometimes also auxiliary regiments were similarly equipped, such as the tilery near the fort at Tomen-y-Mur in Wales. Another, worked by Legio IX, has been identified at Scalesceugh, near Carlisle.

We can conclude, therefore, that the Roman army contained competent potters and brickmakers as well as the trades already mentioned. Butchery and tanning will have been an additional qualification for others, as the supply of large amounts of leather, already noted, would have called for works devoted to these skills. It is likely that such a depot existed at Catterick, run by an auxiliary regiment. The Brigantes, with their extensive pastures, and in whose area the fort was placed, would have provided cattle instead of grain as their tax levies. Presumably the live animals were delivered to the depots, slaughtered and skinned. The meat would not be wasted, but was probably salted for later use, while glue and size would have been important by-products. But the skins, when tanned, were the most valuable. The process was a lengthy one, lasting perhaps a year, so some degree of forward planning would have been necessary. The skins were first cleaned of surplus flesh and hair by scraping with convex-bladed knives after treatment with some alkaline material, such as stale urine, lime or ashes. They were then packed in layers in deep pits, each layer being separated by the tanning material, usually wood bark or chips from suitable trees. The pit was kept topped up with water throughout the process. Finally, the tanned skins were washed, and then stretched backwards and forwards over a beam to make them supple. A wooden 'slicker' for this purpose has been found at Chesterholm and suggests, perhaps, the site of another tannery. At Catterick, a long timber structure might be interpreted as a shed for the initial cleaning process,

while a great rubbish-dump, water-logged since Roman times, produced many waste fragments and off-cuts, showing that the manufacture of finished goods was also carried on. Among the rubbish was a
large quantity of animal bones and many discarded boots, shoes and
tent panels. More important, however, for the interpretation of the site,
were some small punches which would have been suitable for embos-
sing patterns on the finished goods.

The construction of roads was, at first, yet another army duty,
although local labour may well have been impressed to assist. As with
streets in towns, roads were invariably surfaced with the best locally
available material, such as gravel, flints, crushed stone, or even iron
slag, but during the fourth century, paved surfaces became more
common, and needed less frequent repairs. During the construction, a
wide strip of land was first cleared of trees and undergrowth and
drained by two ditches dug on both edges of the strip. The size and
position of the ditches could, however, be varied to suit local conditions, the object being not only to create boundaries but also to carry
away surface water, and where necessary to drain the subsoil to give a
firmer base. If very wet or marshy gound could not be avoided, a
substructure of brushwood or baulks of wood was first placed in position, as on Watling Street leading to the Medway crossing at Rochester.
The material excavated from the ditches was then heaped into a raised
mound in the centre to form the agger, which facilitated drainage of the
final surface. Large, heavy stones were usually placed over the agger as
a foundation course and were topped with a rammed layer of finer
aggregate some centimetres thick, which provided the running surface.

Quite frequently, also, numerous quarry pits for providing the
aggregate are to be seen flanking stretches of main road, such as those
by the Fosse Way at Thorpe-by-Newark and Brough. Sometimes,
exceptional methods were employed in the construction, such as the
excavation of a considerable thickness of peat to expose a firm, rock
surface at Blackstone Edge on the borders of Lancashire and Yorkshire
or at Craik Cross (Dumfriesshire).

Wherever possible bridges were constructed over rivers and streams.
In most cases, they were probably entirely built of timber, like that
which carried the Gartree Road from Leicester to Colchester over the
river Nene at Aldwinkle near Thrapston, where huge, iron-shod,
wooden piles, some 50 cm. square had been driven into the river banks
and bed to support the bridge. But in the frontier region masonry
abutments and piers were more commonly used in conjunction with
wooden superstructures, such as those at Newcastle or Corbridge, or at
Chesters, after the bridge had been rebuilt; the latter, in its first stage,
was probably arched, since voussoirs were found to have been incorpo-

rated in the later work. The construction of the piers and abutments will have called for the use of coffer dams, built of timber and carefully plugged with clay, of a type best demonstrated at the bridge which crossed the Moselle at Trier in Germany.

Small streams, or shallow rivers with gently sloping banks, were sometimes crossed by fords, which might or might not have been paved; the crossing of the Trent at Littleborough appears to have been so treated.

Milestones were also an integral part of the arterial road system. Early examples usually took the form of large cylindrical pillars, often standing a metre or more high. Later, however, much rougher blocks of stone were used, perhaps as the result of the repeated cutting down of the original pillar when new imperial dedications were required. Some milestones were uninscribed but most carried an inscription invoking the name of the emperor in whose principate the road works were carried out, so providing valuable evidence of date. Sometimes also the name of the place from which the distance was measured is included, sometimes only the distance was given. Both milestones and bridges are yet further evidence of the work of military masons.

Behind all this construction work of different sorts, however, lay the hand of the army surveyors. Surveying was a skilled and well-practised art in the Roman world and its practitioners must have received some degree of formal training. Apart from laying out the lines of camps, forts and buildings, for which unfortunately little evidence is likely to survive, they were also responsible for road alignments. Despite their normal high standards, errors did, however, occur and it is only necessary to look at the plan of the fort at Fendoch to see how the irregularity in the laying out of its defences had to be repeated in the internal buildings to avoid the barracks impinging on the rampart. But the extraordinarily contorted barrack at Longthorpe is so badly planned that it is hard to conceive it as the work of a qualified surveyor. Indeed, it might be said that the irregular outline was caused by less skilled legionaries trying to put together a prefabricated building and getting the sections inextricably muddled. There seems little other excuse for such irregularity, even given, perhaps, the haste with which the building may have been erected.

It is, however, in the road system where the work of the surveyors can best be demonstrated. One of the most striking roads in Britain is the Fosse Way which links Seaton in Devon with Lincoln in the north-east, a distance of some 320 km. Despite the fact that, like all Roman roads, it was made up of a series of discrete, straight sections, the road never deviated more than 10 km. either side of a straight line joining the two terminal points. This degree of accuracy must have required a consid-

Fig. 39 Road alignments in the Cirencester region

erable knowledge of the local geography as well as the ability to project an established bearing over the whole required distance, which, in the absence of magnetic compasses, could only be done by relating direction to positions of the sun or stars at certain times of the day. Hence some astronomical knowledge was also required.

Study of the Fosse Way alignments is also instructive to show how individual sections were surveyed. Where possible the road clung to high ground, but where this requirement caused deviation from the overall alignment, corrections had to be made from section to section as convenient. North of Leicester, it caused a gradual swing towards the north until reaching the high point of Cotgrave Gorse, where it was returned to the north-east. Further turns in the same direction are made where the road almost touches the Trent at Thorpe and again at Potter Hill, before it finally runs into the southern suburbs of Lincoln.

The same road also provides information on the approach to sharp gradients. In its course across the Cotswolds, several deep coombs had to be crossed and the line was usually adapted to take the road on a more gentle, angled slope down the hill and up again the other side. Yet steep inclines were not unknown and in the approach to Lincoln from the south side, the road climbed directly up the limestone scarp at a gradient of less than 1 in 6.

The instruments used by the surveyors were chiefly the *groma*, a form of cross-staff, and the *dioptra*, a more elaborate sighting device which could be used for measuring both angles and heights. The *chorobates*, a levelling instrument not unlike a huge spirit-level, was principally used for surveying aqueducts, but another form of level could be fixed to the head of the dioptra. A type of hodometer for measuring distances was also known.

Since the fleet was considered an extension of the army, it is not surprising that we also find soldiers undertaking seafaring duties. An altar from York mentions a soldier from Legio VI being seconded for duty as a river pilot, probably on the treacherous waters of the Humber, and the manning of military transports, as opposed to war-ships, was mainly undertaken by soldiers.

In describing the work and duties of the Roman army in Britain, we have to a degree anticipated some forms of civilian employment. This is not entirely surprising since many British tradesmen would first have learnt their craft, soon after the conquest, from army technicians. Broadly, however, civilian work fell into a number of recognizable categories, much as it does today: the professions, such as the law, teaching, possibly medicine, when practised at its higher levels, and some forms of local government service; trade, which included all manufacturers, shopkeepers and commercial travellers; the construction industries, with masons, joiners, carpenters, plasterers, tilers, thatchers, painters, plumbers and floor-layers; seafarers and their ancillary trades, such as sailmakers, shipbuilders and dockers. Consequently, when the total sum of civilian experience is added to what we have already obtained from a study of the army, a fairly full picture emerges, restricted only in certain areas where evidence is scarce owing to the perishable nature of material.

We do not know to what extent the law was practised by British advocates, but it is not unlikely that the province produced its quota of jurists, and Juvenal refers to Britons being trained to plead by Gauls.

Men versed in both Celtic and Roman law would have been needed, not only to act as assessors in court but also to argue cases. At least one British case reached the emperor's courts, and since it involved both legal codes, British jurists would probably have advised on it at one or more stages. We should remember also the many scribes and clerks employed in this, and in other ways, to keep records, write letters and prepare documents. *Styli* for inscribing on wax-covered writing-tablets are exceedingly common site finds in Britain and point to a high level of literacy in most business affairs. Ink-wells are known, although more rarely, and there is also the evidence of impressions on Iron Age (tin) coins showing that papyrus reached Britain before the conquest, and surely afterwards as well. The script employed by these people made use of the Roman capital alphabet adapted for a free-hand style, since no lower-case letters existed; it is referred to as cursive script.

In a province such as Britain, where presumably Celtic and Latin were spoken side by side, and where, in addition, there is evidence for the use of both Greek and Palmyrene, interpreters would often have been required in the courts as well as in daily life. It is interesting, therefore, to record a possible one who was attached to a governor's staff in the late fourth century, and who officiated in the laying of a mosaic floor in the temple at Lydney (Glos).

There must have been teachers since Tacitus mentions that the British learnt readily and that the sons of the gentry came to speak and write passable, if somewhat archaic, Latin. As noted in a previous chapter, Plutarch records a conversation with the schoolmaster Demetrius, who had recently returned from Britain, and who may possibly be identified with the Demetrius who dedicated at York to the gods of the governor's residence. The word *equus* inscribed on a painted wall at Verulamium and *pavo* scratched on another at Leicester, together with other stilted phrases, might suggest somewhat unorthodox writing practice. A stone disc from Dorchester with its repetitive words is also best interpreted as part of a similar lesson.

The practice of medicine at its worst probably gave rise to much quackery and was probably indistinguishable from trade; nevertheless there were respected physicians and surgeons in the empire, often of Greek extraction and frequently freedmen. Many, as we have seen above, enlisted in the army. A case of surgical instruments is reputed to have been found with a burial at Wroxeter, while similar instruments are not uncommon elsewhere in Britain and other provinces; tongue-depressors, artery forceps, surgical needles, retractors, probes and scalpels have all been found, but some of the most interesting are bronze catheters from Baden in Germany and Pompeii. Other common finds are the stamps used for imprinting descriptions, and the instructions for use, on cakes of ophthalmic ointments. Medical information can also be obtained by a study of skeletal remains from burials. A case of gout has been identified at Cirencester; many broken bones were obviously carefully splinted to promote good reunions, while cases of osteo-arthritis, spondylitis and tuberculosis were not uncommon. Medicines were largely made from decoctions of herbs, often taken up in a pleasant-tasting base such as honey or wine. The properties of belladonna, opium, colchicum, henbane, wormwood and many other drugs, often still recognized in modern pharmacopoeias, were well known.

Priests should also, perhaps, be included among the professions. Certainly, as with teachers, they were exempt from taxes. Many of the larger temples must have had residents, and houses closely associated with temples can be observed at Wroxeter and Caerwent. A priestly burial which included ornamental sceptres has been excavated near Brough-on-Humber in Yorkshire, while several ceremonial crowns have been found, including some fine examples from Cavenham, Suffolk. A *haruspex* or augurer is recorded on a statue base at Bath. With the rise of Christianity we know of the Bishops of London, York, Lincoln, probably Cirencester and possibly of Silchester also.

A far larger number of people will have been engaged in commercial or manufacturing activities, and there is much evidence for them. Some were engaged in the import and export trade, such as Verecundius Diogenes and M. Aurelius Lunaris from York, and Antonianus, who dedicated an altar at Bowness-on-Solway before setting out on a trading enterprise, probably to western Scotland. Merchants from the Rhineland came to Britain and one of them, Fufidius, died at Mainz, while another, a pottery merchant M. Secundius Silvanus, dedicated an altar at Westcapell at the mouth of the river. There must have been many firms engaged in the import of samian from Gaul, and one lost a cargo in a shipwreck on the Pudding Pan Rock in the mouth of the Thames. Losses to another merchant were caused by a crate of samian being dropped between the quay and the ship's side in the London dock. If the distribution of some good quality glass vessels is to be taken as a guide, there were merchants dealing directly between the Rhineland and the north of Britain. Trade in wine, oil and condiments, such as fish-sauce, was considerable judging from the large number of amphoras and flagons to be found on British sites. These vessels sometimes bear stamps denoting the origin of the contents, or notes scratched or painted on the walls giving the quantity or quality. For instance a painted example on an amphora from Chesterholm refers to 'prime mackerel sauce', while another gives the tare and total weights of the vessel when filled. One amphora from Chester records in black paint, 'spiced and flavoured, vintage; for the stores', while a stamped example from Cirencester refers to oil or wine from an imperial estate in Spain, imported during the early third century. Yet another, from Carpow, refers to horehound cough mixture for the army, and is a commentary on the British climate.

Metalwork was also imported into Britain in quantity, coming at first from Italian, later from Gallic, workshops. Bronze jugs, candlesticks and brooches, and silver tableware all speak of merchants in what would today be called the upper end of the market. For a brief period during the early second century, enamelled brooches from Britain found a market in the Rhineland, an operation which must have been tantamount to carrying coals to Newcastle. British lead is also known from Gaul, but is more likely to have come from official consignments transported from the imperial mines. But in the same upper bracket there were probably merchants dealing in silk from China, as well as more humble cloths, and a fragment of damask silk has been found in a burial at Holborough in Kent. Cloth-merchants can also be discerned in the mention of British woollen goods in Diocletian's price-regulating edict. Other merchants probably specialized in furs and skins, while oysters from Britain certainly reached Rome, but, although they normally travel well in barrels of salt-water, must have represented a slightly hazardous commercial activity. By way of trinkets, jet ornaments from Yorkshire reached the Rhineland, perhaps carried on return journeys by merchants seeking pottery or glass.

Within the province we can point to many commercial enterprises, and the premises for them have already been considered in Chapter 3. As today, they can broadly be divided into service and manufacturing industries, but with a different emphasis on each category. It must be remembered that most manufacturing was carried out in small workshops which formed part of the premises where the goods were for sale, so resembling many modern eastern bazaars. Only in certain industries, which either required specialist facilities or large open areas of ground, would the two activities have been separated and middlemen sometimes have been brought in to market the goods. Moreover, many manufacturers would have carried on repair work, particularly in the various smithing trades.

The six metals of economic value in Britain all had their own manufacturing areas close to the sources of ore. All except iron are easily smelted in small bowl-shaped furnaces with charcoal as fuel, sometimes after a preliminary roasting to convert the ores to the more readily refined oxides of the metals.

Gold, of course, since it occurs naturally as the metal, requires no such process and, after extraction from the ore matrix, has only to be melted and cast into ingots. The only known mine at Dolaucothi, as already indicated above, was probably under imperial control. The mines themselves were worked both by open-cast and by adit processes, the latter often leading to extensive galleries which were kept drained by means of water-wheels, arranged one above another in series, so that the water was raised from the mine sump to the surface. The work was carried out by convicts or slaves and conditions must have been appalling despite the strict terms of operation; indeed being condemned to the mines was looked upon as being little better than the death sentence. Economy of working was enforced so that, sometimes, little more than the veins of gold-bearing quartz was chiselled carefully from their beds, making the passages narrow and tortuous. Ventilation was occasionally provided by extra shafts in the larger continental mines, but there is no evidence for such provisions in Britain, so that the air must have been foul, the conditions both cramped and wet and the only light was that provided by primitive oil-lamps: both Pliny and Lucretius refer to the bad air in mines.

At Dolaucothi, with its ample water supply from at least two aqueducts, a process known as 'hushing' also seems to have been used. In this, a reservoir of water was accumulated above a slope where ore veins were expected to outcrop. By releasing the water down the slope, soil and vegetation would be carried away, so revealing the ore. The same process could also be used for clearing the mining debris, so exposing new working surfaces.

After the ore had been extracted it was crushed on the dressing-floor and then panned in wooden cradles, of which one was found at Dolaucothi, under running water. The water carried away the rocky detritus leaving particles of gold in the cradle, which could be collected and melted into blocks or ingots.

Despite the fact that most of the gold production went to the emperor, some was sold onto the open market, for evidence for goldsmiths' shops, or working, has been found near the mines, at Norton (Yorks), and at Cirencester, Verulamium and London. The most interesting remains are those from the latter town where a workshop existed in the Neronian period beneath the site of the later palace. A number of crucibles and their lids were recovered, together with the remains of clay luting used to seal the two together. The luting had been stamped with impressions of a lion and a boar within a rectangular panel, and had been intended to give a gas-tight seal for the enclosed vessel; it is likely that the stamp was applied to prevent pilfering of the vessel's contents. These closed containers were used for refining gold, by heating it for a considerable time between layers of brick-dust in the presence of organic acids such as urine. The impurities in the gold were dissolved and absorbed in the brick-dust.

At Verulamium, a goldsmith's shop was identified in Insula XIV, and a number of very small crucibles, some containing residual traces of metal, were recovered from the shop floor. The slave-managed shop at Norton has already been referred to, and the evidence from Cirencester is in the form of a crucible fragment from the market-hall.

Most lead-silver mines appear to have been open-cast and the extraction process will have been closely akin to quarrying. It is, however, claimed that some shaft mines in the Pennines above Swaledale are of Roman date, but no proof is as yet forthcoming. After the ore had been crushed it was roasted and then smelted to give an alloy of lead with a small percentage of silver. In order to extract the silver a cupellation furnace was employed, in which the alloy was remelted in a bowl-shaped container lined with a thick layer of crushed bone ash. A blast of air was directed at the surface of the molten alloy so as to oxidize the lead which, since it was in a molten state, was absorbed by the bone ash, leaving behind a small pellet of silver. In order to obtain the lead, the bone ash mixture was resmelted with further quantities of charcoal. The process is reasonably efficient and desilverized lead from Britain often contains no more than 0.01 per cent silver. Some lead 'pigs' carry the cast inscription *ex argentariis* – from the silver works – from which we may deduce that silver was the most important of the two products.

As with gold, most silver will have gone to augment supplies of imperial coinage, but some again reached the open market. A silversmith's workshop of some size is known at Silchester, where the owner was not only manufacturing, but also cupelling, low-silver alloys. Another is known at Wroxeter, while the goldsmith at Verulamium was also working sometimes in the less precious metal. A glass manufacturer at Leicester was, as a side-line, carrying on the business of separating silver from base silver coins, a process prohibited by law and carrying the death penalty as its punishment.

Lead would have been much more readily obtainable by private individuals and was put to a very wide number of uses. Somewhere, as yet unknown, factories for the manufacture of lead sheet must have existed, for it was the starting point for many finished objects, such as water-pipes, coffins, bath-linings and probably roofing. Water-pipes were made by wrapping narrow strips of lead sheet around a circular former and then soldering together the overlapping edges of the joint; sometimes, as in the case of pipes from Chester, an inscription, cast onto the surface of the pipe, recorded the circumstances of manufacture. The great bath at Bath was once lined entirely with lead sheet, and excavations revealed the small plumbers' furnaces used in its fabrication. Similar furnaces around the Cirencester basilica point perhaps to lead-covered roofs, or to the jointing of large blocks of masonry by means of iron, masons' 'dogs' set in a lead seal. Lead coffins are comparatively common in Britain and are sometimes extensively ornamented. These, together with decorated lead water tanks, are excellent examples of the plumbers' craft. Lead was also a primary constituent of pewter, much used for tableware in the fourth century. A factory for its manufacture existed at Lansdown, outside Bath, where stone patterns, into which the pieces were beaten, or cast, have been found. Another existed at Camerton, and no doubt both were using Mendips lead. Since tin is the other constituent of pewter, and Cornwall the only place where it is found in workable quantities, it is not surprising that stone moulds have also come from St Just, although others have been found as far afield as Yorkshire and Wiltshire.

Copper ores were to be found in Shropshire, and also Wales and Anglesey. Adit mines occur at Llanymynech, but elsewhere collection of ore nodules on the surface appears to have taken place on a local basis. Copper is also an easily smelted metal and industrially can be used either by itself, or as an alloy with other metals, the most commonly occurring being bronze, an alloy with tin. Bronze and copper-smiths must have been almost as ubiquitous as blacksmiths in Roman Britain since the metal was used for many different products, ranging from small personal articles like pins and brooches to large castings for furniture and harness. Manufacturing smiths are known from a number of places: both Verulamium and Catterick have produced evidence for workshops in the form of wooden-lined waste-tubs used for separating bronze filings and waste from lighter dross by flotation in water. The smith at Catterick seems to have been engaged in enamelling and the shop produced several examples of the craft. Bronzesmiths' crucibles of the late first or early second century have been found at Wroxeter, while at least two smiths are known by name, Celatus who was working near, or at, Lincoln and Cintusmus from Colchester. One of the most interesting recent discoveries has been an ingot of brass weighing 9.3 kg. and stamped V.H.ET.B from an industrial area to the west of Colchester, where there was other evidence of practising smiths. Another firm, manufacturing bronze brooches, may have been working on N'or-Nour in the Scilly Isles, perhaps using Cornish tin and copper, although recently some doubt has been cast on this interpretation.

Roman interest in British tin was not great. Spasmodic attempts seem to have been made during the first century to develop the industry but it was not until the fourth century that more deliberate efforts were made to capitalize the resources. Most tin ore was probably obtained by streaming, although limited mining of surface veins probably took place. Smelting, as with copper, is comparatively easy, and at least one tin ingot, possibly stamped with a late imperial imprint, has been found near Camborne. Despite the lack of government interest, considerable quantities of tin must have been required by Romano-British industry for the manufacture of bronze and for coating finished objects, since tinned bronze was a much-favoured material for personal ornament.

Of all the metals in Britain, iron was not only the most commonly occurring, but also the most difficult to extract from its ores, since it melts at a somewhat higher temperature than the other metals so far considered. If melted, cast-iron is produced, and, although Romano-British technologists seldom achieved such high temperatures, they had to reject the product, since they were unable to use it. Consequently the ores, after a preliminary roasting, were smelted with charcoal in either a bowl or shaft furnace. The former was the more primitive device and the rate of extraction was lower, but, providing a high enough temperature was produced, probably with bellows, to liquefy the slag, the end product was a spongy mass of sintered iron with many slag inclusions, called a bloom. Before the bloom was removed from the furnace, the slag would be run off into a separate pit. The bloom was then reheated in a smithing furnace and hammered while still hot to squeeze out the slaggy impurities. The result was a lump, probably weighing about 1–2 kg., of reasonably pure wrought-iron.

Shaft furnaces seem to have been up to 1.5 m. high and 30 cm. in diameter, judging from examples found at Ashwicken in Norfolk, although others of smaller diameter are known elsewhere. They were lined with clay and, at the bottom of the furnace, there was an arched opening for drawing off molten slag and for allowing access of air. The furnace was charged from the top, layers of ore probably being interspersed with layers of fuel. The height of the furnace induced the draught and so increased the temperature, but bellows could additionally have been employed. The slag will have been more fluid and greater extraction would have taken place, while in addition larger blooms were probably produced. Moreover, the higher temperature of operation increased the carbon content of the metal, so making a harder iron. At Wakerley in Rutland, a number of shaft furnaces were found, together with some interesting shallow linear furnaces. The latter would have been appropriate for preparing iron strips, a form in which the metal might most suitably have been marketed.

The art of the blacksmith was practised widely in Roman Britain and some splendid examples have survived, yet strangely enough few blacksmiths' shops have been definitely identified. The inscription from Chichester, mentioned above, indicates that there were enough smiths in the town to form a guild. A tombstone from York depicts a blacksmith with the tools of his trade. Hoards of ironwork have been found from time to time at Silchester, Great Chesterford and Chedworth which illustrate their activities. One fine piece of forging is represented by the great pot-hanger from Cirencester with its three hooked chains fastened to a central rotating pivot. At Cirencester, also, estate blacksmiths may have manufactured and repaired agricultural tools in a smithy associated with a farmhouse inside the town.

Some of the most interesting and largest fabricated pieces are the iron beams made to support hot-water boilers over the stokeholes of bath-houses, often 1.5 m. long and weighing as much as 250 kg. They were made by welding together individual blooms by an alternating process of heating and hammering. But, in fact, examination of their internal structures has shown that the welding only occurred at the outer surfaces and that the interiors of the beams remained very much as separate blooms. Inadvertently, therefore, the smiths had discovered one of the strongest forms of structural support: the box girder. Smiths were acquainted with the process of carburization, whereby the surface of a knife or implement could be case-hardened to form a mild steel. It was also known that tempering, by heating and quenching the metal in water or oil, produced superior quality products. Specialist toolmakers are also known, with a cutler, Basilius, selling his goods in London, while another, Victor, of Vienne, had a market in Catterick; Martinus made chisels which were also on sale in London.

Two other manufacturing processes were normally carried on close to the sources of raw materials: pottery and brick, and glass.

Glass was made in a number of places in Britain during the Roman period, but the quality always remained low and production seems to have been confined mainly to window-glass and the more utilitarian vessels. At no time does fine glass, either coloured or decorated, such as was imported into the province from the Rhineland or the middle east, appear to have been made.

The principal constituent in its manufacture was silica, either in the form of sand, or crushed flint or quartz. This was fused with bone ash or wood ash according to the type of glass required, the former providing a glass with a higher softening temperature. Owing to traces of iron in most of the raw materials, natural glass so produced was usually coloured green or brown, the intensity depending on the amount of iron present. This glass was considered suitable for most ordinary vessels or for windows, although decolourizing could be done by adding traces of manganese salts. Similarly, other colours could be imparted by the addition of different minerals: copper or chromium for green, antimony for yellow, cobalt for blue and finely divided gold for ruby red. None of the colours was apparently used in Britain, although many imported pieces display a wide spectrum.

Glassworks have been identified at Caistor-by-Norwich, Leicester, Mancetter and Wilderspool, mainly through the discovery of suitable furnaces and waste material. The factory at Caistor-by-Norwich was a comparatively large establishment, occupying most of a big house. At Leicester, in contrast, a single furnace was used by the maker in one of the shops of the market. It is not entirely clear what was the total repertoire of these manufacturers, as few vessels can be associated with them, but glass bottles and jars of varying shapes and sizes seem to have been the normal run, in addition to window-glass. Strangely enough, none of the characteristic implements of the glassworker, usually made of iron, has ever been identified in Britain.

Window-glass occurs widely in Britain and was obviously used in considerable quantities for both public and private buildings. Two distinct forms have been detected. The earliest tends to be naturally coloured, rather thick and opaque, with one surface having a sanded appearance. Later, a thinner, colourless and clear material was manufactured, a distinct improvement apparently having taken place in the processing. It used to be thought that the panes were made by casting the glass on sanded surfaces in moulds, so giving the characteristic appearance to the early types. More recently, however, it has been suggested that it was manufactured by first blowing a cylindrical bottle in a mould, after which the top and bottom would be removed and the resulting cylinder cut longitudinally with shears. This cylinder was then placed in an annealing furnace at a temperature just sufficient to soften the glass, when it unrolled and assumed a flat shape. The importance of the process is that it removed the stresses inherent in cast glass which might otherwise have caused it to crack on cooling. It is also thought that, at first, the annealing furnaces were slightly overheated, so causing pitting of the under surface, but as ability to control the process was improved, so the quality improved with it.

Glassware, both imported and locally made, was undoubtedly offered for sale in many towns and settlements, judging from the quantity of broken fragments found on most sites. But only one shop has so far been positively identified in Britain at Colchester. There, at the time of the Boudiccan rebellion, a hardware shop was burnt down. Glass vessels on upper shelves melted and ran down over nests of samian bowls standing on the floor, so sealing all together.

The Romano-British pottery industry, together with the trade which it generated, is probably the best attested of all manufacturing processes, since the material it produced was largely indestructible, although easily broken, so that large quantities, illustrating many different styles, were needed to satisfy the markets. The production of good quality wheel-turned vessels had started in south-east Britain some decades before the Roman invasion, so that the increasing demands made upon the industry, especially at first by the army, seem to have been met without undue difficulty. Fortunately, the distinctive fabrics and forms of many of the vessels enable centres of production to be pin-pointed and the marketing patterns worked out, although much still remains to be done in this direction.

The manufacture of pottery is most conveniently carried out close to the sources of raw materials. Clay, water and fuel are the principal requirements, although access to good transport facilities, particularly by water, is an important secondary consideration. Much pottery is known to have been carried by water in the Roman world, not only because it was cheaper, but also, since pottery is both bulky and breakable, there was less risk of damage and larger amounts could be carried by boat. Readily available supplies of fuel must also have been a decisive factor in the siting of a kiln, as modern experiments have shown that consumption was prodigious. The supply was probably maintained by regular coppicing of woodland. In view of these considerations, it is not surprising that many of the main production centres were situated close to, or within easy reach of, navigable rivers, and it is possible to demonstrate by means of distribution maps that these were often the chief routes to the markets.

The manufacture requires several different processes. The clay has to be dug and then worked up to make it suitable for throwing on the wheel. In the raw stage, certain additives were sometimes included, such as crushed grit, shells or old potsherds, or sand, to make the vessels less liable to crack during firing. No potter's wheel has been found in Britain from the Roman period, since they were probably made of wood, but some objects have been interpreted as spindles. Many vessels were made wholly on the wheel, but a large number of types seem to have been hand-moulded before being finished on it. After throwing, the vessels were allowed to dry to a leather-hard state, at which point decoration or an external coating could be applied. Drying sheds have been tentatively identified at some potteries, but there is little to indicate the actual use of the buildings and many were probably of an ephemeral nature, as indeed were other workshops. One has, however, recently been discovered at Stibbington in the Nene Valley; it consisted of a simple rectangular building, some 6.4 × 12.2 m., with a well outside, and with the bases for four stone-lined tanks, in one of which a quantity of prepared clay, mixed with crushed shell, had been left.

P - Paved Areas

Well

N

Stone
Base

Working
Area?

Clay Pit

Chests for
Clay

P

Kiln

0 1 2 3 4 5 6 7 8 m

Fig. 40 Potters' workshop at Stibbington

While these stages of manufacture were being carried out, other processes, providing the firm had sufficient employees, could have been going on simultaneously, such as cutting wood and preparing the kiln. Remembering that a single small kiln could hold upwards of two hundred medium sized vessels, a reasonable time would have been necessary to prepare for a single firing. But it is likely that many one-man firms were operating in which all the processes would have been carried out consecutively.

The commonest type of Romano-British pottery kiln consisted of three parts. The furnace chamber was dug below ground level and, for obvious reasons of drainage, was usually constructed on a sand or gravel subsoil. The wall of the pit, so dug, was then lined with a thick layer of clay. The furnace chamber communicated with the stokehole area, situated on the same level below ground, through a flue arch, which likewise had to be constructed of stone or clay. The oven, in which the pots were placed for firing, was separated from the furnace chamber by means of a floor supported in one of several ways. In some kilns, a central or off-centre pedestal supported prefabricated fire-bars, which, in turn, carried a perforated clay floor. In others it is clear that the clay floor was carried temporarily by timber framing, and burnt away during a preliminary firing, during which the clay hardened in its place.

Once the floor was made the prepared pots could be stacked upon it and then covered with a bee-hive shaped arrangement of withies over which a clay and straw, or grass, mixture was plastered, leaving a vent at the top. Firing could then commence and might have lasted twenty-four hours or more, according to the size of the kiln, after which it was allowed to cool before the pots were extracted. If red or brown pottery was the desired end product, excess oxygen was allowed at all times, but, if black or grey wares were required, the kiln had to be effectively sealed in the later stages to prevent the admission of oxygen, or, if it accidentally entered, to be consumed by a surplus of fuel.

It is becoming increasingly clear, however, in the light of recent discoveries, that many kilns were built wholly above ground, using perhaps blocks of turf for the walls and prefabricated fire-bars to support the floors, with the top of the oven sealed by a clay lid. Less effort would certainly have been involved in their construction, but, being even less permanent structures, they unfortunately leave little evidence for their presence.

One other type of kiln, common in the Surrey area, is worth mentioning. In this, the stokehole, firing chamber, oven and flue are all situated at the same level below ground. It is not likely, however, to have been more technically advanced, and, indeed, may have suffered disadvantages.

At best all the kilns so far described would have been only semi-permanent, being used for perhaps some half a dozen firings before they were replaced by new structures. That their life was short is demonstrated by a Nene Valley kiln, where the floor had partly collapsed during the last firing, so spoiling a number of vessels.

The principal centres of production were many and altered with the times. At first, the industry seems to have been largely in the hands of small producers, manufacturing primarily for local markets, but from the late first century onwards, mergers seem to have led to an increasing concentration of production in the hands of larger firms, whose products ranged much more widely. The local man never entirely disappeared, however, and, in east Yorkshire for instance, it is possible to find pottery in third- and fourth-century contexts which owes more to continuing, hand-made, Iron Age traditions than to the Romano-British industry.

In considering production centres, it is also possible to look at marketing patterns, although the subject is too large here to be considered comprehensively, and examples will be taken at random. One of the most informative groups of vessels for such an examination is the stamped mortaria of the first and second centuries. Many were made at potteries between London and Verulamium, at Hartshill, near Nuneaton and nearby Mancetter; others at Lincoln, Doncaster and Corbridge to name but a selection of sites. One particular manufacturer, Sarrius, was first producing at Hartshill during the middle of the second century. His markets lay mainly in northern military sites up to and including the Antonine Wall, and it is likely that he had obtained an army supply contract. Later, however, he moved to Doncaster, probably to be nearer his markets and to cut down on transport costs, since the new site had better access to navigable rivers and the east coast sea-routes.

During the first and early second centuries, as already noted above, some military detachments manufactured their own pottery. An abrupt change can, however, be discerned about AD 120, when a new, centralized source of supply replaced the earlier, localized system. The lucky firms to win these valuable contracts seem to have been situated in the Isle of Purbeck, Dorset, or possibly Somerset, and they produced a number of standardized bowls, jars and dishes in a not unattractive, black-burnished fabric. It is not, perhaps, taking the evidence too far to suggest that from AD 120, the legions in Britain, who until then had been the main producers of military pottery, were expected to be more than fully extended in building the new frontier. It is probable, therefore, that they were divested of a purely peripheral activity and the burgeoning British industry given the task of providing the army with pottery. It must have been a decision made at the highest level, since both the Welsh and northern garrisons were henceforth supplied with this ware until the middle of the century, while little of the production reached civilian markets in the south-east.

Some of the most interesting marketing patterns appear in the fourth century, a time which, moreover, saw the concentration of the industry at even fewer centres, such as the Nene Valley, the New Forest, the Upper Thames Valley and east Yorkshire, notably at Crambeck, Castle Howard. Nene Valley pottery, for instance, is seldom found in the south-west or west of Britain, areas normally dominated by the New Forest and Thames Valley industries. There is some degree of overlap between the two latter industries, but it varies according to the type of the vessel. In this respect there was obvious competition between the centres. Also, whereas New Forest pottery is hardly ever found north of the Thames, Oxford wares occasionally travelled into areas dominated by the Nene Valley industry and even reached Brough-on-Humber. The most remarkable concentration of production came in the north in the last decades of the fourth century. There is hardly a site, north of a line from the Humber to the Mersey, occupied at that time, which did not receive Crambeck ware in its supplies. Yet the cut-off line is remarkably sharp, and although a piece has been found at Lincoln, it rarely travels further south. Whether or not this was a return to official manufacture is not known, but the Crambeck potters, supplying both military and civilian sites, must have been successful beyond all their expectations. Yet, despite their extensive range of vessels and the quantities produced, there was still room for Nene Valley pots to be marketed in considerable numbers in the northern areas.

The retail trade in pottery is indicated by the two burnt Colchester shops which occupied sites on one of the main streets, and possibly by a nearby warehouse, stocked with flagons and mortaria. An itinerant merchant is known to have lost his stock of Gaulish samian bowls and Mancetter mortaria in the forum fire at Wroxeter.

The manufacture of pottery was largely in the hands of private firms and individuals, whereas the production of brick and tile seems to have been more highly organized and included public utilities. Brickworks run by the imperial procurator near London and Silchester have already been mentioned, while the municipal works of Gloucester are well known from the number of products stamped RPG (*Rei Publicae Glevensium*). Other companies such as the *Arveri*, or those which stamped IVC DIGNI or TPF on their products also existed in much the same area.

Tile kilns are not as commonly found as pottery kilns, probably because the products were more often fired in large clamps above ground. But a tile kiln near Canterbury, incidentally associated with pottery kilns, was constructed with a long, narrow firing chamber in which the tiles were stacked. All too little is unfortunately known about the processes of manufacture, although we might imagine that considerable cleared and levelled spaces must have been required for moulding the pieces and for laying them out to dry under cover from both sun and rain. The repertoire included the large roof tiles with upturned flanges, possibly moulded, but with the rebated end, intended for interlocking with the next tile on the roof, cut out by means of a knife; curved and tapered tiles for capping the abutted flanges, probably made on some type of wooden or stone former; curved and slotted ridge tiles, made similarly; roughly triangular tiles, often decorated, for fixing to the ends of the roof ribs at the level of the eaves, and a variety of large and small floor tiles and wall bricks, the size depending on their intended use. The latter were probably moulded by hand and trimmed by knife to the required shape.

When production was sufficient for a firing, the items were apparently stacked loosely on the ground until a sufficient pile had accumulated, which was then covered with a thick dome of clay and grass, or straw, apertures being left at ground level for the fires, and vents in the roof. An interesting item relating to the life of one brickmaker was found in London. It was a floor tile on which, while the clay was still plastic, its maker had recorded a message for his master, to the effect that a fellow worker, Austalis, had been absenting himself without leave for the last thirteen days.

The other extractive industries carried on at source were quarrying of different kinds, including coal, and salt production.

Salt was produced, as already indicated (see Ch. 3), by the evaporation of sea-water or brine from mineral springs, a process practised on many coastal sites round the Wash, and the Thames and Severn estuaries. The process requires careful control in order to remove salts other than sodium chloride, since their presence in the final product renders it deliquescent and also unsuitable for tanning. Evaporation seems to have been carried out in large clay pans set over fires, the impurities fortunately crystallizing out before the sodium chloride. Salt was an important item in the Roman economy, being required for preserving meat, fish and skins and as a condiment. In the Diocletian edict of prices, the value was fixed at the same level as wheat, so that it was comparatively expensive.

Outcropping seams of coal were quarried in a number of places in Somerset, south Wales, Nottinghamshire, Yorkshire, Lancashire and Northumberland. It was used on many military sites, both for heating

and for industrial purposes, and considerable quantities have sometimes been found, such as the deposit in the guard-chamber of the east
gate at Housesteads, which seems to have been converted to a coal-
bunker at a late date. It was also used in the Corbridge armaments
depot.

Coal also appears on civilian sites, at considerable distances from the
fields, where it was used for heating hypocausts and baths, and for
sundry industrial purposes. There is a considerable distribution
around the Fens, and it may possibly have been used for the extraction
of salt. It was also used on the altar of the temple of Sulis and Minerva
at Bath, a fact recorded by a contemporary writer, Solinus.

Other forms of quarrying covered the extraction of stone, chalk, clay,
gravel and sand, mostly for building work, of which something has
already been said in considering military duties. But stone quarries are
known just outside the town at Cirencester, while a chalk-pit was
discovered during recent working near Canterbury. Stone from the
better class quarries travelled considerable distances, despite its heavy
and bulky nature. Indeed there must be many more quarries to be
found, since the total amount of stone used in civilian building construction was considerable. Reference was made earlier to the walls of
towns, but it is worth recording that Cirencester alone required some
84,000 cu. m. of masonry for its fortifications, while every time the
streets were resurfaced, which was not infrequent, about 11,000 cu. m.
of gravel or stone rubble were needed. Indeed the total aggregate which
ultimately went into the streets of the town was of the order of 155,000
cu. m., representing a very large quarry hole, 100 m. by 50 m. and 30 m.
deep. Considered in terms of labour, also, a very big task.

Two quarried stones are of especial interest: Kimmeridge shale and
Whitby jet. The former was used extensively for furniture, and some
fine, carved table-legs have been found at a number of places, such as
Dorchester, Verulamium and Silchester. It was also used, as with
Whitby jet, for trinkets. Bangles, for instance, were turned and cut on
lathes and the central discs, removed during the manufacturing process, are not uncommonly found in areas round Kimmeridge.

The quarrying of building materials leads us logically to the construction industry, which, as today, covered a wide field of craftsmen
and technicians, ranging from surveyors to joiners, masons, plasterers,
painters and floor-layers. There is some evidence for all of them in the
civilian industry of Roman Britain. Surveyors' work is difficult to
identify, since it is essentially ephemeral, the quality of the buildings
alone being the surviving guide to their competence. But the surveyors
laying out the apse for the Cirencester basilica had employed special
marked stones as base points, from which the curve could have been

computed by bisecting chords. At Verulamium, also, a wall left unfinished had been marked out by a line secured to a square peg, a feature presumably more normally obliterated by the masonry of completed work.

Wherever possible local materials were used in most domestic construction. Consequently the appearance of Romano-British towns would, as today, have altered according to the part of the countryside where they were situated. In the south-east, where good building stone was hard to come by, a predominance of brick, flint and tile occurred, with occasional public buildings clad in greenish-grey Kentish ragstone. In the Cotswolds, Northamptonshire and Lincolnshire, oolites were extensively employed, giving the characteristic honey colour, or darker brown, to the buildings' external appearance. Sandstones and gritstones further north would again have changed the visual aspect, while at all, it would be right to expect some half-timbering or plastered cob walls.

Some of the more specialized craftsmen probably maintained permanent workshops, but we can envisage most building-work actually being carried out on the site, starting, of course, with the digging of foundation trenches. The material so derived, which, in the case of a large building could be considerable, was normally used to level the site. Lime would have to be burnt and slaked, clay puddled, mortar and plaster mixed, stone cut and finished. At Verulamium, a plaster-mixing pit had been lined first with a wickerwork basket, while plank and joist impressions, on the under surface of a concrete floor in the Cirencester basilica, may indicate a lost mortar-board sealed beneath the floor. At Fishbourne, the masons' yard, where stone for fine wall and floor surfaces was prepared, was identified beneath the palace buildings. Not only were there many waste pieces, but also quantities of silver sand, indicating the way in which the slabs were cut. A metal wire or thin bar was strung horizontally between two pivoted, vertical iron bars. The wire was then swung back and forth over the surface of the stone, on which wet silver sand had been placed, so in time cutting through it. Similar waste material, related to the Temple of Claudius at Colchester, was also found. An outbuilding at Cirencester had a neat stack of sandstone roofing-slates set upright against an external wall and ready for repairs.

Of the building workers themselves we know very little. A sculptor, Sulinus, set up altars at both Cirencester and Bath, and may have had a workshop in the former town. Certainly, a group of sculpture found there might be attributed to him, while other pieces from the same town indicate that he was not the only sculptor in the field, the standard of execution sometimes being remarkably high. Priscus, a native of Gaul, was a mason employed at Bath; his presence indicates that craftsmen from other provinces were attracted by, or imported to, work in Britain, and there must also have been a monumental mason at South Shields who was familiar with eastern art styles, for an elaborately carved tombstone was set up there to Regina, British wife of a native of Palmyra (Syria), called Barates. In an altogether more specialized class was a man at Bath who carved semi-precious gemstones with mythological and religious scenes for setting in signet rings.

It seems that mosaicists also came to Britain from time to time as work was required, and that by the fourth century, if not before, provincial workshops had been set up in a number of places. Of these, four have so far been identified at Cirencester, Dorchester, Water Newton and possibly Brough-on-Humber, but they are not necessarily all contemporary; indeed, there is sound evidence to suggest that the Cirencester firm had gone out of business before the Dorchester workshop was set up, while a fifth firm, in the Colchester-Verulamium region, is suspected of operating in the second century.

The first of the fourth-century firms to start work was that at Cirencester, and they developed a highly characteristic design incorporating Orpheus with his animals and trees, which was not only used in Cirencester itself but also in several villas in the neighbourhood, such as Woodchester. Interestingly also, a similarly patterned pavement, clearly originating from the same designer, is known from the imperial capital at Trier in Germany, suggesting perhaps that the master-craftsman had himself emigrated. The Brough-on-Humber firm seems to echo some of the Cirencester patterns, if in slightly cruder forms, and this perhaps points to an employee of the Cirencester workshop setting up on his own in another part of the country after the firm had ceased to trade. Some fifty mosaics have now been attributed to the Cirencester factory, and something approaching saturation of the area with its products must have been reached, a state of affairs only to be resolved by movement elsewhere.

It is sometimes possible to work out the manner in which mosaics were laid by observing the guide-lines that were often inscribed on the underlying concrete surface. It is also possible that some of the more intricate panels were made up in the workshop and laid in a piece, with the intervening areas being filled in on the spot by standard geometric and floral patterns or plain tessellation. The four seasons mosaic at Cirencester is perhaps the best example of what could happen when an apprentice, or less skilled craftsman, was given the opportunity to try his hand at figure work. Summer and Autumn are set in braided roundels and are well up to standard; Spring is not and was clearly produced by a junior member of the firm.

In a number of places, the debris of mosaic floor layers has been identified, usually in the form of rough cut tesserae, which could be either chopped or sawn. A particular type of fine-grained oolite, found not far from Cirencester, breaks naturally into small, rough cubes, and was exploited. Other materials used were brick – both yellow and red – sandstones, ironstones, slates, and even coloured glass and chips of samian, according to the colours required in the pattern. Considerable quantities were found in the forum at Cirencester and also in another house near the town walls. At the villa at Rudston, noted for its primitive mosaic of Venus, heaps of tesserae of different sizes and colours were found in an outbuilding.

Plasterers were also highly skilled, and the white lime finish they produced on wall surfaces was fine enough to have paint applied directly to it. If the colour was applied when the surface was still wet, the process was called fresco and the pigment became bonded more firmly with the lime. Further colours could then be painted on, using white of egg, or milk, as size, a process known as tempera. Plasterers were also called upon occasionally to execute decorative stucco work, examples coming from the Fishbourne and London palaces and from the villa at Gorhambury, near Verulamium, where human figures seem to have been part of the design.

The wall-painters of Britain must have relied to a great extent on pattern books for their designs, as did their colleagues, the mosaic floor-layers, although many of the themes were freely adapted to suit individual tastes or skills. The laying-out lines can sometimes be detected on the plaster surfaces, and, although the standard of execution was normally quite high, frequent faults in perspective can be seen, of a type that so often occur in classical wall-paintings. The pigments employed were of mineral origin, some, such as bright blue, being prepared artificially from a copper frit. Occasionally, small lumps of pigment are found on excavation, together with the flat stone palettes used for grinding them to a fine powder.

Other technical processes, which would have required permanent premises, were those connected with tanning and cloth manufacture. Unfortunately no civilian tanneries are known in Britain although there are some suggestive details. A deep pit in a timber-framed building at Alcester may have been so used, while a dump of ox-jaws beneath a later building at Silchester could represent the refuse dump of another factory, since it was customary to leave the heads on the skins, for identification, but to remove the jaws before steeping. A similar dump of cows' heads lying on the floor of a derelict house in Leicester might similarly be interpreted, although another possibility is a horn factory.

Shoemakers' or leatherworkers' shops are equally difficult to identify, although a simple rectangular building, lying between the Bath Gate and the amphitheatre at Cirencester, had many hobnails lying about the floor and may represent a boot and shoe factory. As in the military areas, leather is not an uncommon find from water-logged deposits on civilian sites, but mainly turns up in rubbish deposits and not in the relevant shops. Nevertheless there is ample evidence to illustrate the leatherworkers' skills both in the boot and shoe trade and in the manufacture of other products. The former were normally made with openwork uppers of calf-skin or other supple leather and were sometimes ornamented with embossed patterns; they laced up round the ankles. The soles were usually made of multiple layers of oxhide, sometimes giving a thickness of up to 6 mm., and waterproofed with a mixture of iron salts and soot. If hobnails were used, they were occasionally applied in the form of a pattern. Leather was used for garments, and the bikini pants from a well in London are a good example. It was also the covering for many pieces of upholstery and a fragment of cushion, once embossed in gold, came from London.

The textile industries involved a number of different processes, each of which probably had its own practitioners: spinning, weaving, fulling, dyeing. The first two operations seem mainly to have been carried on as a home industry, spindle-whorls, distaffs and sometimes loom-weights from vertical looms being found on domestic sites, although at least one government clothing factory is known to have been placed in Britain, according to the Notitia Dignitatum, and is thought to have been at Winchester. Fulling and dyeing, however, required more specialized equipment, but, as with tanning, it is almost impossible correctly to interpret the pits, troughs, tanks and ovens which must have been used, in the absence of the materials themselves. Consequently, although a dyer's shop is suggested at Silchester, and, from time to time, fulleries are implied by small concrete-lined tanks in certain villas, such as Darenth, nothing can be proved, since the organic materials associated with the processes have, in every case, failed to survive.

The process of fulling, which was used to remove grease from new woollen cloth, involved its treatment with stale urine, so saponifying the fat and enabling it to be washed out. Fullers, therefore, usually operated the jars placed at street corners for the convenience of passers-by and, moreover, from the time of Vespasian, had to pay a tax for the privilege. Since the process also required large quantities of water, their workshops were usually placed close to an aqueduct, so that they could make use of the surplus flow. After the cloth had been treated and washed, it was dried and roughened with teazles, then bleached with sulphur fumes and finally clipped to give an even nap. The huge cropping-shears from Great Chesterford, 1.34 m. long, must have come from a fuller's workshop. Since much the same process removed dirt from soiled clothing, fullers also acted as launderers.

Dyers made use of various vegetable and animal pigments, and, as far as we know, most specialized in only one colour. Some of the plants needed have already been mentioned, and it is likely that quite large quantities had to be grown or collected to satisfy requirements. Madder, wild lotus, meadow saffron, and dyers' bugloss among many others were all used.

Woollen cloth must have been by far the commonest in circulation, although there is evidence for the use of linen for shrouds at York and for containing cremated ashes at Caerleon, and flax may well have been grown in Britain, despite the fact that Spain was the chief supplier.

Agricultural and horticultural workers must also be included among the productive industries, although much of the work which they did has already been detailed in Chapter 4. As today, most of their work will have depended on the seasons; ploughing and seeding, along with herding, will have alternated with hedging and ditching, wood cutting, reaping, threshing and parching grain, tree pruning, or wool clipping according to the time of year and to the nature of the farm on which they worked. Herdsmen, for instance, probably lived with their flocks on the hills during the summer grazing period, only returning to the farm in winter.

From the productive industries we can turn to the so-called service trades, remembering that many manufacturers also repaired goods. Among these trades, also, must be included such people as municipal and provincial slaves. We know of one of the latter at London, although his duties are obscure. The former, however, will have been responsible, under the appropriate officers, for maintaining public utilities, such as the aqueduct, and for cleaning out sewers and probably roadside ditches; the great sewers at Lincoln were equipped with man-holes for this purpose. They probably also ran the public baths, stoking the boilers, clearing the flues and hypocausts, and cleaning out the accumulated scum in the baths themselves. Sweeping up litter in the markets would have been another task, during which they may have been able to enrich themselves by picking up lost coins, and the cleansing of the forum at Cirencester continued long after the floor had worn away. Although we have no evidence for individuals among such people in Britain, as a class they must have existed, since we must assume that these jobs were done by someone.

But by far the biggest group of service trades will have been the suppliers of food and drink. Ale must have been brewed in considerable quantities, although, as with all trades dealing in organic materials, the evidence is very slight. Who is to say, now, what a large oven, capable of supporting a vat of considerable size, was used for in the absence of more specific information? It could have been for baking, brewing, or dyeing, or steeping flax, or cooking, but Gallic beer is listed in Diocletian's edict and was probably not dissimilar to the British product.

Wine was imported in quantity and must have been available in most towns. A wine shop has been inferred on a corner site near the forum at Verulamium from the number of broken flagons and amphoras which it contained. It is possible that, after the emperor Probus relaxed the laws relating to the growing of grapes in the provinces during the third century, vines were grown and wine made in Britain, but proof has still to be found; however the increasingly wetter climate of the third and fourth centuries will not have favoured it.

Fruit and vegetables must have been marketed in large amounts and grape-pips, fig seeds and the stones of various fruits indicate what was available, perhaps, in the case of imported fruits, in the dried state. Elsewhere, vegetables used in Britain have been mentioned (see Ch. 4).

Butchers' shops, fortunately, leave better evidence in the form of bones, cut and sawn during the preparation of carcasses. At Cirencester, two pits, filled with such bones, close to the market, imply the presence of butchers, and it is possible that that part was used as a meat market. In the row of shops opposite, almost every one had an oven, perhaps suggesting that they were providing cooked meats. Another butcher's shop, or sausage factory, has been suggested at Verulamium, not far from the London Gate. The by-products of these shops, chiefly bones, were not wasted and bone implements of many types, ranging from hair-pins to inlays for wooden boxes, were commonly used. Shops dealing with these materials have been found at Catterick and Wroxeter, while a child's burial at Colchester contained a wooden box, or possibly dolls' furniture, which had been inlaid with bone.

Fish shops, especially those selling oysters or other shellfish, can likewise be more readily identified, in particular where the product was consumed on the premises, and a merchant appears to have occupied one of the shops leased out by the town in the forum at Caerwent, where numerous oyster-shells were found. Oysters, judging from the ubiquity of their shells on almost all sites, must have been one of the commonest items of diet.

Flour was normally ground in the home for immediate use, on a pair of hand millstones. But commercial bakeries also existed, where the bakers probably ground their flour on a larger scale. Big hour-glass shaped millstones, driven by donkeys, have been found at London and Canterbury, and military, water-driven mills have been identified on Hadrian's Wall. Other mechanically-powered mills existed at Lincoln, Great Chesterford and Wanborough, but we cannot be sure that flour was the product. An iron slice for removing loaves from the oven has come from Verulamium and a stamp for impressing a pattern on a cake, or loaf of bread, was discovered at Silchester, but, since the design shows a religious scene, it may have been used for a special occasion.

Money-lenders and bankers also figured among the population, and a room in the forum at Silchester, where many coins were found, has been suggested as the office of one of them. Money-lending operations, however, chiefly figured in the early years of the Roman period, when some senators were said to have advanced large sums to Britons struggling with the expenses of romanization.

There must also have been various inns and restaurants, separate from those provided for imperial officials, but again, in the absence of detailed evidence they are hard to identify and even more difficult to distinguish from shops only selling food.

The transport industry was divided between road, river and sea-going traffic. Harness fittings from draught animals and also metal parts of carts and wagons illustrate the first category. Horses, mules and donkeys undoubtedly drew light vehicles, used primarily for passengers, and examples can be seen depicted on masonry reliefs in the Rhineland. Horses also provided the motive power for larger wagons in many cases, although oxen may also have been employed. If British vehicles were anything like those used in Germany and Gaul, there was probably a basic, four-wheeled wagon with low sides, drawn by three or four beasts, in addition to a much wider variety of two- and four-wheeled carts, gigs and chaises. Pack-horses may well have provided extra carrying capacity.

The rivers of Britain were no doubt plied by numerous barges, usually with flat bottoms. In the almost complete absence of native evidence, it is again possible to look at examples from across the North Sea, where, in the Netherlands, barges of this type are known from the Roman period. Some were as much as 35–40 m. long, but medium-sized craft of about 20 m. would have been more suited to British rivers. In most cases these boats were probably drawn by animal or human power along the banks, and evidence for mast-steps in some of the surviving examples should not necessarily be taken to mean the existence of sails, since towing-masts are known to have been common features. By so raising the towing-rope, bankside obstructions and other vessels could be more easily cleared.

Sea-going vessels are, however, known from Britain. A small, carvel-built ship, found beneath County Hall, London, can be dated to the later third century. The method of construction shows that the builder was acquainted with Mediterranean types of vessels, although the ship can only have been built in northern Europe. Another sea-going craft found at Blackfriars, London, sank, presumably in dock, while about to unload a cargo of building stone from Kent.

Harbours and docks are known in many places, one of the most impressive being the quay which flanked the waterfront of London on the north bank of the Thames and which was constructed of a box-frame of sturdy timbers. An ancillary to any harbour is a lighthouse, and at Dover there still stands on the Castle Cliff most of the tower of one of a pair which once marked the entrance to the harbour below between the two bluffs of the cliff. But Dover was more probably a naval base, and it is not known if civilian ports in Britain were similarly equipped. Ancillary also to any dock were the derricks and cranes used for lifting heavy cargoes, and a large stone foundation on a quay just outside the legionary fortress at York has been interpreted as the base for a crane. A baling-hook of Roman date from London, in addition, reminds us of the dockers who unloaded the ships, and who on several occasions carelessly dropped goods overboard.

We may also look with profit at the domestic duties of housewives, and their servants and slaves, if they were fortunate enough to possess them, since the duties of cleaning and cooking will then have passed to them. Floors must have been swept, scrubbed and even polished, and one mosaic in a house at Dorchester had limber-holes left in the walls at floor level to allow washing water to escape. Lamps had to be cleaned and filled and wicks provided; fuel had to be supplied for braziers or hypocausts and the fires had to be stoked. Shale furniture must also have been kept polished with oils or waxes, since it is liable to split and flake unless this is done. Wooden furniture was also subject to attacks by wood-boring beetles, and fleas, bedbugs and probably clothes moths had to be combated; a bedbug has been found at Alcester, while a carbonized wooden object attacked by furniture beetle comes from Brough-on-Humber.

Cooking was carried out mainly on grid-irons, such as that from Silchester, or on tripods over open fires, although various types of closed oven are also indicated. Most of the utensils were of pottery, but in the richer households, bronze and iron pots, frying pans or skillets were additionally used. Kitchen knives, ladles and flesh-hooks, two or three pronged hooks for pulling boiling meat away from the bone, are comparatively common finds. The wide variety of food available has already been discussed above and in many cases may have been supplemented by hunting. The food itself, if we are to judge by contemporary authors, contained many items where the combination of flavours and textures would seem strange to most modern palates; sweet-and-sour dishes appear to have been great favourites.

While all these household duties were being undertaken, the lady of the house, if she was not herself engaged, was able to spend hours over her toilette, helped probably by a slave girl. Personal trinkets, depilatory tweezers, perfume flasks, mirrors and combs have all been found in Britain, illustrating this side of daily life, and a head of hair surviving from a York burial shows not only the careful braiding which was kept in place with jet pins, but also the artificial reddish tint which had been applied. Neither must we forget that the master of the house, in the days before Hadrian, when beards once more became fashionable, had to be shaved with fine bronze or iron razors and his hair, and later, beard trimmed with small shears. It is not unlikely, also, that men of fashion had their hair waved and set, following the manner of Nero, as is so obvious from representations on his coins.

In these days of job comparability and wage and price freezes, it is informative to look back to another occasion when an attempt was made to regulate not only wages but also prices: Diocletian's Edict of maximum prices, published early in AD 301, by which he sought to fix ceilings on prices and wages throughout the empire. The attempt was a failure and, despite invoking the death sentence for breach of the code, had ultimately to be repealed, mainly due to the difficulty of enforcement. But at least it provides us with some comparative values.

The basic agricultural wage for a day labourer was 25 denarii, but he also received the fringe benefit of food. Four days' wages, therefore, were required to buy 9 litres of wheat, if it was being sold at the maximum price. A shepherd received marginally less, but a carpenter and baker twice as much. Shipwrights earned the same as a carpenter if aboard an inland vessel, but slightly more if sea-going. A barber could charge 2 denarii per customer, but since shaving was a lengthy process, he would be hard put to make a fortune. This compares with the charge of 6 denarii per animal which a veterinary surgeon could make for hoof-trimming. Teachers were graded according to the level of tuition, an elementary teacher being allowed to charge up to 50 denarii per boy per month, so requiring some fourteen pupils to equal the income of an agricultural labourer, whereas a teacher of rhetoric could charge five times as much; a jurist pleading in court could, by contrast, command a fee four times as much again. A tailor could charge up to 60 denarii for a first-quality cloak, but only 20 for a pair of breeches, and this seems to compare unfavourably with the cobbler's price of 120 denarii for a pair of farmworker's boots (hobnails extra). From this it can be seen that the farmworker had to labour for five days before he could buy a pair of boots. Somewhat surprisingly also, a pair of patrician's shoes cost only 150 denarii.

These figures must, of course, be viewed with some caution, since it is possible that the charges actually made were less than the maximum.

But, if it is also remembered that business opposition was largely responsible for the edict's repeal, it is likely that the figures given were more often than not being exceeded. Moreover, all but one of the inscriptions which carry information on the edict come from the eastern empire, and we cannot know how the figures applied to the west, although there was probably a close similarity. Nevertheless, they do allow us to put the value of work in perspective, and equate them approximately to the cost of living.

Chapter 7

Superstitions and Beliefs

Man has always been a superstitious creature. The more he is at odds with his environment, and the less control he feels he has over it, the greater his belief in unseen powers, and it is when these basic superstitions are channelled into recognizable forms that they become religious convictions.

In antiquity, man's fears and hopes were expressed in a variety of ways. An altar erected in Roman Britain to the *Genius Loci* – the spirit of the place – simply means that on some occasion a person coming home one night, slightly drunk from the pub, was frightened out of his wits by a barn owl or other natural phenomenon; consequently the place attracted a reputation for being haunted and subsequently an altar or altars were erected to placate the ghost, since it was recognized that the spirit of a dead person was helpful if propitiated, but spitefully destructive if neglected, and could, in extreme cases, even take possession of the living. Similarly, a promise made for the erection of an altar to a favourite deity might inspire a hope for a successful journey or business venture. There was therefore a strong contractual element in most early religions.

British religion before the arrival of the Romans was highly fragmented, consisting of little more than a collection of local superstitions, which might, though different in place or name, bear strong resemblances to one another according to their attributions. However, some of the more advanced Iron Age tribes appear to have had patron deities who watched over the welfare of the people, their crops and animals. The only indication of a more truly corporate religion was that provided by the Druids, who, from their centre in Anglesey, held some sway over almost all the tribes in the midlands and south-east. They were implacably anti-Roman in outlook, having, by their political interference in Gaul, already been outlawed by the edicts of several emperors. Consequently, we may imagine that the hard core of Druidism fled to Britain as refugees and provided a stiffening to resistance in AD 43.

Roman attitudes to the Druids were governed by two main factors: apparent dislike of the Druids' human sacrifices and disapproval of their involvement in political and educational affairs. We may indeed wonder about the relative importance of these two reasons, since some modern writers tend to favour the first as the real cause for the Roman hounding of the Druids. It might be thought surprising, in view of the numerous instances we are given of Roman attitudes towards 'blood' sports of a human kind, that they would have any such objections; they were not a noticeably queasy race. Neither must we forget that an aggressor will often invent purely cultural reasons to excuse his actions against the aggressed. Even now, it is still one of the commonest forms of pretext for making unprovoked attacks in order to achieve seemingly desirable political objectives. We can also remember the unmentionable acts attributed by certain pagan writers to early Christians in Rome, and so accept that the Romans' expressed dislike of Druidic sacrificial practices was the excuse, partly to salve the Roman conscience, partly for external consumption, for the violent suppression of a sect which acted as a focus for disloyalty and a foment for disobedience. This view is even more acceptable, if the general Roman tolerance towards foreign religions is compared with it. The Romans themselves were just as superstitious as other people in the ancient world, and they were far too cautious to risk running foul of nameless deities in remote areas; so cautious, indeed, that a specific temple, the Pantheon, was erected in Rome, just in case some such nameless deity had been left out of the official reckoning. Only if religious practices became mixed with politics did the state intervene, and, although disgust might from time to time be expressed about the rites of some of the more esoteric cults, little action was taken against them, providing they stayed within the law. But Druidism and Christianity, and on occasion Judaism, owing to their political involvements, were seen as enemies of the state and treated accordingly. A Roman, accused of religious intolerance in such a context, would have roundly protested his innocence, claiming the purely civil nature of the crime of the early Christians, the refusal to take the oath of loyalty to the emperor.

Apart from Druidism, the areas of Britain in the south-east which were subjected to Belgic influence before the conquest were probably affected by other superstitious beliefs. It may be that the concept of a central tribal deity then arose, and there is certainly a marked similarity between certain classes of temple in these parts of Roman Britain and those in parts of north-west Gaul. Indeed, the prototype for these temples in Britain has been claimed to lie in the even earlier Iron Age, at Heathrow, and was excavated when London Airport was constructed.

Tribal intercourse may also have led indirectly to the establishment of other religious centres, albeit probably of a more local nature. It is possible to point to many sites which appear to coincide with tribal boundaries and which, during the Roman period, developed as combined religious and trade centres, so probably continuing earlier usage. There took place fairs and markets and the late Sir Ian Richmond so admirably described them: '. . . associated with ancient sanctuaries whose deity hallowed the transaction and gave to the market or fairground a sacred peace which folk no less superstitious than quarrelsome would not violate by quarrels and brawls'. If commercial enterprise was to continue in times of inter-tribal unrest, such centres would have been essential.

Apart therefore from the suppression of Druidism, the religious beliefs of the British were at first untouched by the Roman invasion. But, even though the empire was polytheistic in outlook, the cult of the imperial house had been grafted on to the basic cults of the classical world, ostensibly to act as a unifying force in an otherwise religiously heterogeneous community. Consequently, one of the first acts of the new government in Britain was to introduce the imperial cult. As far as is known, this first took the form of an altar, a massive temple and a provincial centre at Colchester. Much has been written about the original dedication of the temple, since emperors were not normally deified until after death, and Claudius is known to have discouraged an attempt in Egypt to proclaim him a god; most other emperors acted likewise. So that it would have been unusual, not to say bad form, for the Colchester temple to have been dedicated to Claudius in his lifetime. There are reasons, however, for not so believing, and it is now considered more likely that the temple itself was not completed until after Claudius' death. That being so, the dedication to *Divus Claudius* would have been perfectly correct.

Although the temple was destroyed in the Boudiccan rebellion, it must have been rebuilt, since we cannot envisage the ruins being left as a lasting monument to Boudicca. The temple was large and imposing, so much so that it excited interest even in Rome, and was surrounded by a colonnaded court. It was constructed in the best classical manner on an elevated podium and with an octastyle portico approached by a flight of steps. In front of the steps, in the courtyard, was the main sacrificial altar, surrounded by a screen and flanked by statues. Here would have been conducted all public ceremonies, since the temple itself was simply the repository for the cult statue of Claudius, probably well above life size.

In the provinces the imperial cult was served by a council elected, or appointed, by the native peoples, and in Gaul and Britain it represented the tribal groups or civitates. This provincial council nominated annually the chief priest, whose task it was to reside in the cult centre and arrange all ceremonies and festivities connected with it. The cost was considerable and had to be met by the office-holders, so it is not surprising that Tacitus mentions various complaints in the period before the Boudiccan rebellion, when civitates were few and the costs therefore fell across only a narrow sector of the British people. But the provincial council also had the power to communicate directly with the emperor and to some extent, therefore, represented a safeguard against an over-zealous governor or procurator, even if that power was seldom used.

There seem to have been buildings in Colchester associated with the temple, and therefore presumably acting as the administrative head-quarters of the provincial council, but it has often been claimed that the cult centre was transferred to London by the end of the first century, by which time London had also become the administrative capital. A fragmentary inscription from London, now lost, invokes the *numen*, or spiritual power of an emperor, on behalf of the province of Britain. Even if such an inscription had come from a temple, it is not, in itself, sufficient evidence to show that the principal temple of the cult was then in London. Indeed, it would be surprising, cult centre or not, if there were no dedications to the emperors by the province in its capital. The fact, provided by a tombstone, that the wife of a provincial slave was buried in London, at best shows the presence of the council in the capital, and need not relate to the cult, for it is not unknown in the empire for the two to be separated. There is no reason to believe, therefore, that Colchester ever ceased to possess the principal temple in Britain devoted to the imperial cult.

Despite, therefore, the initial resistance to the cult, which played its part in the background to the Boudiccan rebellion, it came ultimately to be accepted in a variety of manifestations. In the chartered towns, other than Colchester, temples to the cult will almost certainly have existed, although only at Lincoln is the site of one possibly suspected. Nevertheless, M. Aurelius Lunaris, *sevir Augustalis* of both York and Lincoln is testimony to its practice in both places. At Chichester, the *domus divinae* – the deified dynasties of the emperors – is invoked in one dedication of a temple of Neptune and Minerva and in another is coupled with Jupiter. At Brough-on-Humber a similar formula was used in the dedication of a new *proscaenium* for the theatre, and illustrates what may be appropriately called the secular side of the imperial cult, which called for expressions of loyalty in many everyday matters. Hence the frequent references in building dedications to deified members of an emperor's household. Such expressions were also forthcoming in another way. In order to circumvent the difficulty of worshipping a living emperor who had refused divine honours, provincials fre-

N

V Vaults

Steps

0   10   20   30 m

Drain

Altar

Fig. 41 Temple of Claudius at Colchester

quently invoked his spiritual power, the *numen Augusti*, and altars and inscriptions which include this formula, either on its own, or coupled with another deity, are comparatively common, suggesting that in time the cult became reasonably popular, even extending to the countryside. In the area around the Fens and the east Midlands some small bronze busts, usually identified with certain second-century emperors, have been found. They are of a size to fit a staff or ceremonial sceptre, and may have been part of the regalia of priests whose country temples included the imperial cult.

Along with the imperial cult came the other official observances of the Roman empire, enshrined in the deities of the whole classical Pantheon: Jupiter, Neptune, Pluto, Juno, Minerva, Mercury, Venus, Mars, Apollo, Diana, together with immortals such as Hercules. Abstract concepts such as Fortune, Fate or Victory were also personified in the form of deities. In classical theology, a temple was considered the residence of the deity to which it was dedicated, but the ceremonies celebrated at different temples might in time grow apart, giving rise to recognizably separate forms of the cult. So we find Jupiter Capitolinus, named after the temple on the Capitoline Hill in Rome, Jupiter Dolichenus from Doliche in Commagene, and Jupiter Heliopolitanus from Baalbek (Heliopolis), both in Syria.

There is evidence, either in the form of inscriptions or of statuary, for the practice of almost all the main classical cults in Britain. Certainly the army, with its official observances to the Capitoline Triad – Jupiter, Juno and Minerva – as well as to other deities will have been primarily instrumental in their introduction, and secondarily, by a process of diffusion, to the higher centres of romanization, such as London, the chartered towns and civitas capitals. We have already noted the temple at Chichester jointly dedicated to Neptune and Minerva, while at Lincoln, worshippers of both Apollo and Mercury were organized in guilds. Jupiter, in a north-western provincial guise, appears at Cirencester, Chichester and probably Wroxeter and Catterick as well. Minerva appears in Bath and again in London, but in both places linked with other deities, and, indeed, it is not common to find unadulterated classical cults in civilian centres of Britain.

It is, therefore, in the military versions that we find the best evidence for these cults. The army possessed a calendar of well-regulated, religious events which were observed corporately by each unit. These would include the annual oath of loyalty to the emperor and to other gods, notably Jupiter. It was the custom on such occasions to erect new altars to the deity on the edge of the parade ground, the discarded pieces being ceremoniously buried, and a cache of such altars dedicated to Jupiter was found at Maryport (Cumbria). Each unit also maintained a shrine in its headquarters building in which would be placed the appropriate imperial statues and also the military standards when not in use. The obligations to carry out these observances to the letter were very real, in view of the contractual nature of the religion. Any backsliding or slovenly performance on the part of the celebrants might have been deemed to be breach of contract by the deities invoked and, so it was thought, might have threatened the whole safety and welfare of the empire and its rulers.

But the Roman army, containing men from many parts of the empire, all with their own beliefs, and certainly no less superstitious than resident Britons, not only introduced new cults to Britain, but also did not hesitate to make appropriate gestures to the local cults they found here. Consequently, there grew in time a broad spectrum of religious beliefs which incorporated both classical and native deities, in which gods and goddesses of one canon were often identified or equated with those of the other. So it can be seen that an almost infinite number of conjoint deities became possible, and, in the process, Celtic beliefs received a classical veneer, while at the same time classical cults became acceptable to the Britons. Such a union would not have been possible unless both forms of religion had contained an underlying, common creed, and the people practising them a common basic spiritual need. It is interesting that, during the Roman period, the only religions which did not, or refused to, integrate with the general run, were those possessing a completely different theological approach, such as the monotheism of Christianity or Judaism.

Examples of the fusion of beliefs are many and occur in all contexts. At Bath, Minerva was equated with Sul, or Sulis, the local deity of the hot springs and commemorated in a great temple of classical proportions set within a precinct which also contained the bathing establishment. Much of the temple pediment has been recovered and was decorated with winged victories and also, in the centre, with an hirsute face. The latter is often identified as the Medusa head, an attribute of Minerva, although its portrayal, even on a classical building, owes much to Celtic art. It seems far more likely, therefore, especially in view of the prominent position which it occupies, to be a representation of Sul, which, in Old Irish meant eye or sun, so accounting for the flame-like locks of hair and beard, looking not unlike the corolla of the sun. As the guardian of a hot spring it would be an appropriate representation.

In another guise Minerva is equated with the patron goddess Brigantia on a relief from Birrens, near Carlisle, where the latter deity is decked in the attributes of the former. Mars became a favourite deity in the Celtic field and was equated with many different native godlings, and surprisingly his field of influence, which in the classical religion was that of a war god, became greatly modified, sometimes appearing as a healing figure. Such an example is Mars Rigonemetos from near Lincoln, or Mars Medocius from a temple outside Colchester. Some of these mixed deities were themselves imports into Britain, such as Mars Lenus, or Ocelus, from near Trier, which occurs at Caerwent and Carlisle, or Mars Rigisamus from Aquitania who was worshipped at West Coker (Somerset). Mapon was equated with Apollo in the north-west and has left a legacy in the modern place-name Clochmabenstane on the north shore of the Solway. Silvanus, a classical god who ruled the wild, appears as Callirios at Colchester and Vernostonos at Ebchester, near Durham. Jupiter is sometimes depicted as Taranis, the wheel god.

The fused religions were recognized by Roman and native alike. To the former it was an essential part of the romanizing of provincials, being called the *interpretatio Romana*; to the latter it was but an extension of an already multitudinous system. Somewhat naturally, also, the further away from centres of romanization, the stronger remained the Celtic flavour, and in many remote country places in Britain, the old religious beliefs and superstitions continued virtually unchanged throughout the Roman period. Yet, fortunately for us, they were sometimes romanized to the extent that sculptures or inscriptions recorded the presence of a deity who would otherwise have remained nameless and without form. From time to time, some of these local deities achieved a wider popularity, probably on account of their supposed powers, and the large and splendid temple with its accompanying guesthouse and bath-building at Lydney in Gloucestershire, was dedicated to Nodens, a god of healing and finding, whose fame had certainly spread across the Bristol Channel and perhaps even as far as Silchester.

One important Celtic manifestation was widespread over both Britain and Europe: the concept of the Mother Goddess, or Earth Mother, or in the classical canon, Ceres. It was essentially a fertility cult, and, since she was considered a most powerful deity, was sometimes portrayed in a triple or, more rarely, a quadruple form. In most religions, including Christianity, the number three has a mystical importance, which was sometimes used to denote the power of the deity and its all-embracing activities. In Britain, the cult of the Matres was widespread and some excellent sculptured reliefs have been found at London and Cirencester. At Cirencester, and again at Bath, the cult was of a form which took the title the Sulevian Mothers, and on one sculptured plaque they appear as three severe-looking matrons, sitting upright on a bench and nursing baskets of loaves and fruit.

In the main, however, Celtic deities remained essentially local manifestations, such as the water-nymph Coventina at Carrawburgh on Hadrian's Wall. There, a small shrine was erected around the spring which gave rise to the myth and was decorated by sculptures picturing Coventina, sometimes singly, sometimes in triplicate. Into the basin, which collected the water from the spring, were thrown the offerings of suppliants to the deity; mostly these people were of humble origin and the small coins, bronze pins and brooches were the best oblations they could afford, and considerable numbers accumulated over the years. Another similar local god, Antenociticus, was worshipped at Benwell, also on the Wall; he was represented by a splendid head in stone of a handsome young male, which was nevertheless executed in a highly Celtic artistic style. A nameless but complicated deity, formed of a combination of an owl, a bull and a female bust, presided over a temple erected in the long-deserted hill-fort of Maiden Castle during the late fourth century. In this context, it is interesting to record the returns frequently made to places with old associations during the fourth century probably as a reaction to burgeoning Christianity. Maiden Castle was not the only hill-fort reimbued with religious significance at that time and Lydney and Chanctonbury Ring (Sussex) are but two other examples. The association of cults with places, affectionately remembered in the imaginations, lore and legends of the native peoples, is hardly surprising.

Reference was made at the beginning of this chapter to the unspecified *genius loci* and the place which it probably occupied in the minds of the inhabitants. It can probably be connected with a somewhat similar manifestation, which is more normally depicted in a nameless form as a series of little hooded figures – the *genii cucullati* (*cucullus* = a hooded cloak). They are recorded in several parts of Britain and there is a fine relief from Housesteads, showing the three figures full face; it is not possible to determine their sex, and this is a common feature of these illustrated versions. Benwell, not so very far from Housesteads, has produced an altar to the three witches, and there is something remarkably witch-like about the portrayals at Housesteads. From Cirencester comes an even more remarkable piece of sculpture illustrating the same theme, on which the figures are represented with such severe simplicity and in such low relief that it is little more than a cartoon, but a cartoon endowed with all the verve and movement that such basic treatment can often impart to a subject. The trio this time are shown in side view and their faces and figures, but for the lower legs, are completely concealed by the all-enveloping cloaks, so introducing an element of anonymity and mystery. The cult seems to have been popular in the country around Cirencester, and several similar, but less inspired, sculptures have been found, some of which contained four, or even five, figures.

They appear not only on sculptured reliefs, but also on pottery, and one of a number of interesting vessels, probably manufactured at Colchester, displays a group of genii cucullati, some apparently floating through the air, and being chased by a hunchback; physical deformities such as this, or a squint, are often viewed with superstitious fear by primitive peoples. Another pot depicts several animal-headed men picking grapes.

It is when we arrive in a world peopled by witches and little hooded figures, by hunchbacks and animal-headed men that we approach the very roots of superstition in Roman Britain. Such creatures are the basic apparatus of all folklore and legend: the world of dwarfs and goblins, of fairies and the wee people, of witches and wizards. There can be no doubt also that the fear engendered by an abstract concept takes on a less menacing appearance if it is endowed with a physical personality. Hence the very necessary invention of all these characters. Nowadays, they only inhabit children's stories, and their menace has largely been neutralized in civilized societies; only a residue of somewhat humorous superstition lingers on. But to the inhabitants of Roman Britain, they would have represented very real forces for good or evil, to be propitiated with gifts and libations and to be treated with respect.

Such feelings were indigenous to Britain and Rome alike and it was only in the outward expression that differences occur. We have looked at some of the native examples, and to them we can add an example of a purely classical method of averting the evil eye: the phallic symbol which was a good luck emblem of high potency. Such devices seldom occur in Celtic religious contexts, so that their introduction to Britain will have occurred after the Roman invasion. It was a device, however, which achieved considerable popularity and was rapidly absorbed into the general catalogue of mystical symbolism. Quite frequently, the phallus was endowed with limbs, and appears so on pottery vessels from Colchester, while an extraordinary miniature sculpture from Wroxeter depicts a phallus drawing a chariot. Remembering the interest of Celtic religions in the human head, it is likely that, where a phallus is given a face or head a combination of classical and native concepts has taken place.

The worship of the more formalized deities took place at many different types of temples and shrines. Although classically styled temples are known in Britain, they tend to be rare and restricted to cities and towns, and, of course, include the great temples of Claudius at Colchester and Sulis and Minerva at Bath. A little has already been said of these two temples and their precincts, but it is from Bath that we obtain most information about a British example of a classical temple.

Fig. 42 Bath

The temple at Bath lay in an enclosure, or precinct, formed by a double portico, with the hot spring rising in the south-east quarter, and with the baths, therefore, forming a separate wing which extended beyond the enclosure in that direction. The temple sat on its podium approximately in the centre of the precinct, and seems to have been of pseudo-peripteral form with engaged columns of the Corinthian order on back and side walls, and with a tetrastyle portico at the front. Fragments of the pediment with its portrayal of Sulis, held aloft within a wreath by winged Victories, in the centre of the tympanum, have already been mentioned above. Within the precinct was another ornamental façade, making use of the Doric order and apparently incor-

porating the Four Seasons supported by attendant Cupids. The principal altar stood well before the flight of seven steps leading up to the
temple and immediately north of the hot spring; it was decorated with
figures of deities at the four corners among whom Bacchus, Hercules,
Jupiter and Apollo have been identified. In front of the altar stood at
least two statues, one of which had been given by L. Marcius Memor,
augurer of the temple.

The basin into which 2.25 million litres of hot water flowed daily
from the spring, at a temperature of about 50°C, interrupted the line of
the precinct porticoes at the south-east angle. From this basin the flow
was divided in two, part running through the main outfall and part
being channelled successively through the Great Bath and its sub-
sidiaries. In addition to the naturally warmed waters, two other
bathing-wings were included, heated by more conventional hypocausts, one at each end of the Great Bath.

There can be no doubt that the water was endowed with magical,
and, consequently, curative properties. It seems to have been used by
Britons as well as by people from other provinces, and may, as already
noted, have acted as an official convalescent station for the Roman
army, since many dedications by, or tombstones of soldiers are known
at Bath. But neither the waters nor the deities could cure old age and an
unknown decurion from Gloucester died there, aged eighty. The spring
which served the Great Bath of the Romans, now known as the King's
Bath, was not the only source and it is not often realized that there were
at least two other hot springs in close proximity, both of which seem to
have been invested with the same religio-medical function. Both the
Cross Bath and the so-called Hot Baths seem to have been dedicated to

Fig. 43 Classical temples at: a) Verulamium forum; b) Corbridge

a   V   Vaults   0   5   10   15   20 m

the same deities, Sulis and Minerva, while the Hot Baths has addition-ally produced an altar to Diana.

Other classical style temples are known at Corbridge, where a group of at least five cluster beside the north-east angle of one of the military arsenals, whose exterior wall was diverted to avoid the sacred sites. Two temples were added, one on each side of the council chamber, to the south-west range of the forum at Verulamium during the middle of the second century, and seemingly appear classical in conception, since they were incorporated in the architecture of the forum colonnade. There was also an interesting small temple at Wroxeter in Insula VIII. It had been constructed in an area once occupied by shops which were burnt down in the mid second-century fire, and may have been associated with a house constructed alongside it, perhaps as a residence for a priest. The dedications are not known, but masonry fragments found in the area included the chariot-pulling phallus referred to above, and also pieces suggestive of horses.

By far the commonest type of temple in Britain, however, was one that had a distribution which coincided with the Celtic parts of the Roman empire; consequently it is called the Romano-Celtic type. Consequently, also, they are only found in Britain roughly south of a line drawn from the Wash to mid Wales. In ground plan they have the appearance of one square within another, or, less commonly, of concen-tric circles or polygons. When restored to their original appearance on paper, it seems likely that the inner unit, no matter what its shape, rose as a tower above a surrounding portico, and acted as the repository for the cult figures; its interior would have been lighted by clerestory windows. Occasionally, also, additional wings or porticoes seem to have been added, as in one of the principal temples near the centre of Verulamium, which was enclosed within its own precinct walls and later associated with the theatre. Sometimes also the inner chamber is provided with an apse which projects across the portico to the rear, as at Caerwent, where a temple was situated across the road from the basilica, and where the precinct is provided with an entrance hall and possibly a priestly residence as well.

The positioning of temples, often eccentrically within their enclos-ures, shows that, in many cases, they were of secondary importance and that pride of place went to some totem which has since disappeared; it may have been a tree. Sometimes also there is evidence for continuity between Iron Age and Roman times, and both these factors can be demonstrated at the Trinovantian religious centre at Gosbecks Farm just south of Colchester. A massive ditch outlined an almost exactly square area in the pre-Roman period and was ultimately filled during the first century AD, when the enclosure was enlarged and marked anew by a double colonnade or portico. In the south-east corner of the original ditched enclosure, a Romano-Celtic temple was constructed, implying that whatever it was that had given the site its religious significance in the Iron Age, still survived into the Roman period. As at Verulamium, this temple was associated with a theatre and with two other big enclosures. Since, also, a fine bronze statue of Mercury was ploughed up in a nearby field, it seems probable that he was included in the dedication. Mercury was the god of trade, so the existence of a

Fig. 44 Romano-Celtic temples at: a) Chelmsford; b) Caistor-by-Norwich; c) Springhead; d) Silchester; e) Verulamium

A   Ambulatory

C   Cella

fairground combined with temple and theatre, as already suggested above, was simply continuing a practice which certainly originated in the Iron Age, if not before.

In some towns and other settlements, temples were grouped together, such as at Caistor-by-Norwich, where two lay side by side north of the forum, or at Springhead where there were four within a precinct. At Silchester, a sacred site of some importance lay just inside the east gate and was connected to the forum in the town centre by what

Fig. 45 Small shrines at: a, b) Brigstock; c) Housesteads; d) Bowes; e) Springhead could be interpreted as a processional way. At least two, and possibly more, temples occupied the precinct, in addition to some other buildings. Such arrangements are reminiscent of the large temple complex at Trier in Germany, where a considerable number of religious buildings were congregated, some within their own precincts.

Simpler forms of shrine and temple are also known in Britain. They were normally small, and could be rectangular, such as that at Springhead, or the centurion's shrine dedicated to Silvanus on Scargill Moor, near Bowes. Sometimes, this type terminated in a semi-circular apse, as in the temple of Antenociticus at Benwell, or the *nymphaea* at Chedworth or Housesteads. Many were circular, such as those at Maiden Castle and Frilford; the latter was one of the number where combined religious and commercial activities took place on the borders between one civitas and another. It was certainly preceded by a circular Iron Age building of probably similar function, as was the temple at Maiden Castle. In these cases the native antecedents of the type are not in doubt and clearly followed a different line of development from that which produced the Romano-Celtic temple. Unrelated to them, therefore, is the circular shrine of the prefect of the first cohort of Thracians which was a companion to the centurion's shrine near Bowes; both were dedicated to Silvanus or his local variant, Vinotonus. Polygonal forms are also known, such as those favoured by the Coritani at Brigstock (Northants) and Collyweston (Rutland). In both places they occur in conjunction with circular temples. Inside the hill-fort at Chanctonbury, on the South Downs, there was, in addition to a Romano-Celtic temple of normal plan, a horseshoe-shaped building which may have been yet another shrine.

All these temples lacked the external portico of Romano-Celtic types and would have been simple roofed edifices. It is usually more difficult to detect in them evidence for internal arrangements. The hexagonal temple at Collyweston appeared to have a bench running round three sides, while sundry pits and post-holes appear in others. The two shrines at Bowes were equipped with altars, but not apparently with statues of the deity. There must have been many priests to serve these temples. Their ceremonial regalia is found from time to time, like the bronze coronets, with their attached silver plaques depicting deities, from Cavenham (Suffolk) and Hockwold (Norfolk), or the sceptres from a priestly burial at Brough-on-Humber.

Among the cults introduced to Britain were also those that originated in the eastern empire or beyond, an area noted for its exotic religions. As in Britain, where Celtic beliefs became infused with classical leanings, so in the eastern empire there was to some extent a similar fusion between classical and eastern cults.

In most cases the deities were introduced to Britain by soldiers or merchants. One of the most popular seems to have been the cult of Jupiter Dolichenus, and evidence for his worship appears on northern military sites such as Corbridge, where parts of a statue and architectural fragments from a temple or shrine have been identified. The temple of the Dolichene cult was planned on eastern house-styles and required several rooms. An altar from Corbridge, erected by a centurion of Legio VI, joins Jupiter Dolichenus with Caelestis Brigantia. Since Juno Caelestis was the official consort of Jupiter Dolichenus, it can only imply the equation of Juno with the patron deity of the Brigantes, and this admirably demonstrates the way in which widely differing cults became mixed up. We have already seen that, at Birrens, Brigantia was, in contrast, linked with Minerva. Juno Caelestis was also sometimes called the Syrian Goddess (*Dea Syria*) under which guise she is mentioned on an altar and on a statue base at Carvoran; the latter contains a dedication in verse made up of ten iambic senarii, and in reality represents the apotheosis of Julia Domna, Syrian-born wife of the emperor Severus, who was sometimes accorded the honour. Both Jupiter Dolichenus and Jupiter Heliopolitanus are mentioned on other altars from the same place. Since the fort was for a time occupied by a regiment of Syrians, the association of the deities is not surprising.

Other deities from the same part of the empire are also found in Britain, such as the cult of Astarte and her consort Heracles (Syrian Hercules) practised at Corbridge, where two companion altars with dedications in Greek have been found; one was set up by a priestess of the cult, Diodora. But its orgiastic nature did not make for its popularity, and more widespread in Britain was the cult of Cybele, the Great Earth Mother, and her consort Attis, also of Syrian derivation; dedications or attributions to one or other are known from places as widely spaced as Chester, London, Carrawburgh and Gloucester, where an anthropomorphic altar carved to represent Attis playing pan-pipes has been found. No shrine has yet been positively identified with the cult, but the triangular temple near the London Gate at Verulamium has been tentatively associated with it. It is an unusual building whose shape was more probably dictated by the available ground at a road intersection than by any theological requirements, but the occurrence of imported Italian pine seeds, the cones of which were used for burnt offerings having pleasant olfactory properties, caused the suggestion to be made.

Egypt was also a fruitful source of cults which reached Britain. A shrine to Serapis existed in the colonia at York and a fine dedication by a legate of Legio VI has survived. The building appears to have been apsidal, and situated not far from the imperial palace; it may have been founded by the emperor Severus, when he was based at York, and who was enthusiastic about the cult. Heads of the god have been found at Silchester and at London, where it was associated with the temple of Mithras (see below). Isis was also worshipped at a temple in London, possibly across the river in the suburb of Southwark, while a shrine to Osiris may have existed at Rochester, where a small terracotta head of the god was found.

But of all eastern deities imported into Britain, the best attested is Mithras. As a religion, Mithraism was different from most ancient, contractual cults, since it demanded certain standards of conduct from its followers, who therefore had to undergo various processes of initiation, involving tests of physical and moral fortitude. Theologically, Mithras was a derivative of the Persian worship of Ahuramazda, and was a cult in which the deity, depicted as the power of light, or good, was considered to be waging a constant battle against the power of darkness, or evil. In this he was aided by two torch-carrying acolytes Cautes and Cautopates, representing dawn and twilight. The mythology is complex and, since it was essentially a mystery religion, not always easy to grasp. The subduing of wild creation, in the form of a bull, was attributed to Mithras, who, by slaying the animal, released its blood and so gave rise to all useful plants. Consequently, the principal portrayals of the god illustrate the bull-slaying scene, but add also the serpent and scorpion, creatures of the powers of darkness, who attempted to defile the life-giving flow. Another apparition shows Mithras' birth from a rock, or, less commonly as at Housesteads, from an egg. He was, also, frequently invoked on altars in conjunction with his main ally, the Sun, so that inscriptions might record *Sol Invictus* as at Rudchester or *Deo Soli Mithrae* as at Castlesteads.

In view of its nature, it is not surprising that the cult appealed most to certain classes of society, such as soldiers and merchants, and the Mithraea known in Britain were placed where they could draw their congregations from among such people. Membership was achieved by means of initiation into several different grades which were individually named, such as Lion, Raven, Bridegroom, Soldier or Father, and the ceremonies included ordeals by fire, water or fasting.

The principal Mithraea in Britain were those at London, where no doubt merchants were among its devotees, Caernarvon, Housesteads, where the sanctuary was contained in a cave, Carrawburgh and the three legionary fortresses; there are, however, indications of others in several places, and recent excavations have disclosed a possible temple at Leicester. In the main, the cult had more attraction for legionary than auxiliary soldiers and, at Housesteads, the primary dedicators, whose altars occupied the place of honour at the head of the temple,

Fig. 46 Temples of Mithras at: a) London; b) Carrawburgh

were respectively a centurion and an orderly on the governor's staff. Even in London, the donor of the bull-slaying panel was a veteran of Legio II Augusta.

The temples themselves were usually quite small, rectangular buildings, sometimes, as in the case of London, with an apse at one end, or, as at Carrawburgh, with a recess, in which the principal altars and other iconographic pieces could be placed. The main body of the temple was divided in three longitudinally, so that a central aisle was usually flanked by raised platforms on which the benches of the worshippers would be placed. A screen normally separated the temple proper from an ante-chamber, or narthex, which in the Mithraeum at Carrawburgh had been equipped, at one stage, with a hearth set beside a sunken, coffin-shaped 'ordeal' pit.

It is not surprising, also, that the character of Mithraism, with its belief in the powers of good and evil, its symbolism and the demands made upon its adherents, brought it into abrupt collision with Christianity. In Britain, it was late to develop so that it was at its most powerful at just the time when Christianity was also in the ascendant, and Christianity, like Mithraism, must be seen as an oriental import into the province.

The difference in the treatment that was at first accorded to both these religions in the Roman empire was conditioned by the refusal of early Christians to take the oath of loyalty to the emperor. Consequently Mithraism was permitted and tolerated whereas Christianity was banned and its followers persecuted. But it must be remembered that refusal to take the imperial oath was as much a secular as a religious offence, so it could be argued that persecution was not an act of religious intolerance, but punishment of a treasonable crime which struck at the very unity of the empire. Almost all stories of the early

martyrs come from Christian literature and we may be sure were
heavily coloured with propaganda; the desire for martyrdom on the
part of the people concerned cannot either be overlooked, since the
Christian ethic placed as much, if not more, emphasis on the after-life
as on life in this world. It is also important to remember that the Roman
empire was always suspicious of people who banded together for whatever purpose, no matter how innocent, and regulated such associations
closely. So what appeared to the government to be a secret society
whose members, additionally, refused to take the loyal oath would,
from the first, be marked down as extremely undesirable.

Naturally there is little evidence for early Christianity in Roman
Britain since, before the Edict of Toleration in AD 313, any references
would have been covert, with openly expressed convictions attracting
punishment. But there is an interesting cryptogram from Cirencester in
the form of a word-square:

R O T A S
O P E R A
T E N E T
A R E P O
S A T O R

It had been carefully scratched on the painted surface of some wall-
plaster, which stylistically belongs to the second or third century. For
many years it was not thought to have any special meaning other than
perhaps some magical significance. Translated it means: the sower
Arepo guides the wheels carefully. Symbolically the wheel can be taken
as a reference to eternal life, but it appears in both pagan and Christian
mythologies. However, it has been shown that if all the letters are taken
and rearranged they form a cross with a common N, each bar being
made up of the word PATERNOSTER, the opening words of the
Lord's Prayer, with two A's and two O's left over. In early Christian
symbolism AO, or Greek AΩ, was adopted to represent the 'beginning
and the end' of the Revelation of St John. We need not doubt, therefore,
that Christianity was being practised in Cirencester at a time when
open references might have attracted persecution. Apart from this we
cannot say where, or to what extent, it was followed in the years before
it became a permitted religion.

Nevertheless, by AD 314, only a year after the Edict had been
promulgated, no fewer than three British bishops, the metropolitans of
three of the provinces, from London, York and Lincoln, together with
the representatives of the fourth, probably from Cirencester, attended a
council of the Church at Arles. So we might conclude that the British
Church was well organized for some time before the Edict and wasted

Fig. 47 Silchester church

no time in coming into the open. For the fourth century, there is, however, more evidence, although much of it comes in the form of Christian symbols, such as the chi-rho (☧) monogram, on personal possessions; this monogram is made up of the first two Greek letters of the word *Christos*.

One building with probable Christian significance is the so-called church at Silchester. It is a small, temple-like structure close to the south-east corner of the forum and it cannot have been constructed before the middle or later part of the third century. Consequently, if it is accepted as a church, for which, it must be admitted, there is no absolute proof, it is more likely to have been built during the early or mid fourth century, after the Edict of Toleration.

The building possesses a nave, side aisles, a narthex, an apsidal west end and two transeptual-like rooms at the heads of the aisles. The floor of the nave was covered with plain brick tesserae with a black and white chequerboard mosaic panel in the apse. Outside to the east lay a base, perhaps for a basin, and a carefully constructed soak-away pit, which together have sometimes been considered as a detached baptistry. Despite the fact that, if a church, the orientation is reversed, such arrangements are not unknown in the empire, but there are difficulties in accepting this interpretation, not least of which is an apparent disuse before the end of the fourth century. Yet none of its features are entirely inconsistent with a Christian building.

More certain is the identification of a timber-framed church of late fourth or early fifth century date inside the Saxon Shore fort at Richborough. This too possessed an external baptistry, with the font sunk in the ground and lined with waterproof cement.

The most striking evidence for a building of Christian worship, however, is the domestic oratory constructed in a suite of rooms of the villa at Lullingstone. Their attribution is in no doubt since wall-plaster recovered from the rooms produced fragments of painted ☧ monograms surrounded by floral wreaths. Moreover the rear wall of the main chapel was decorated with a frieze containing praying figures each set in a columned niche. Various identifications have been given to the figures, since they are by no means identical, and the excavator considered them to represent the household.

Taken as a whole, there is probably more evidence for Christianity from villas than from urban sites. In addition to Lullingstone, there was the hallowing, by the sacred monogram, of the water basin at Chedworth. A mosaic incorporating the same device is known from a villa at Frampton, near Dorchester, where it was amalgamated with a rollicking pagan scene associated with Neptune. Most important perhaps is the mosaic from Hinton St Mary, on the borders of Dorset and Wiltshire, with its portrayal of Christ, together with, probably, the four evangelists and animals gambolling in Paradise. Remarkably also, another part of this pavement depicts Bellerophon mounted on Pegasus slaying the mythical beast, the Chimera. The same scene is utilized in the main dining-room at Lullingstone and its apparent association with Christianity has led some authorities to suggest a symbolic significance, which enabled a pagan scene to be incorporated in Christian iconography. A number of villas such as Walesby (Lincs), Icklingham (Suffolk) and Wiggonholt (Sussex) have produced sizable lead tanks bearing the Christian monogram. It is not certain what purpose they served, although it has been suggested that they acted as baptismal fonts.

The rise of Christianity engendered a reaction, confirmed by the emperor Julian in AD 355. In Britain it is to be seen in the number of late pagan temples which appear in rural places, such as Maiden Castle and Lydney, in contrast to the apparent strength of the Church among the gentry. Whether this, therefore, represents a social as well as a religious reaction on the part of the lower classes is a possibility, as we may read into it a desire to return to freer times. This re-emergence of paganism in the countryside can to some extent be contrasted, also, against apparent acts of Christian iconoclasm against temples situated in or near towns or forts. The Mithraeum at Carrawburgh seems to have been systematically levelled and used as a rubbish-dump, while at least one temple west of Colchester was similarly treated, with the walls being razed to ground level. But care must be exercised in making such assumptions, since not every derelict pagan temple need have been subject to the attentions of Christian vandals.

Britain also had its share of early Christian martyrs, of whom perhaps the most famous was St Alban, executed at Verulamium probably during the principate of Severus, although earlier arguments attributed his death wrongly to the long persecution under Diocletian in the early fourth century. A *martyrium* was reputedly built on the place where he was executed, on a hill-top overlooking the town, and legend would place it under St Alban's Abbey. Two other martys, Aaron and Julius, are also recorded from Britain, but less is known about where and when they met their deaths.

The early Christian Church was from time to time rent by schisms. One of these was the Gnostic sect which, while denying Christ, seized on the idea of a universal redeemer. The noted mosaic pavements in the villa at Brading in the Isle of Wight contain portrayals of various aspects of this cult. More serious, however, was Pelagianism, started by a Romano-Briton, Pelagius. It involved the doctrine of divine grace and seems to have been strongly supported in Britain even though its protagonist early left the province. It was particularly damaging in the fifth century after official Roman government had ceased, and it caused serious rifts which assumed political importance in the subsequent control of the country. The official Church was sufficiently aware of the damage being caused for St Germanus, bishop of Auxerre, to be sent to combat the heresy in AD 429 and again some fifteen years later. While in Britain, he visited Verulamium and was also, on one occasion, able to lead an attack on a band of marauding Saxons, putting them to flight in the so-called Allelujah Victory. Indeed it has been argued that Pelagianism was one of the major contributory causes for the ultimate decline of Roman Britain.

Two further interesting aspects of superstitious beliefs may be considered; the use of magical amulets to protect the wearer from certain ills, and the wish to cause harm to one's adversaries by putting up an appropriate curse, inscribed on lead or bronze plates, in a prominent position near a shrine or temple. Even now, people wear lucky charms, but would probably be loth openly to ascribe any specific function to them, despite their private feelings. So much more force then would similar charms have had in antiquity, when people were a prey to more primitive superstition. It is certain that numerous small phallic objects, manufactured as pendants or brooches, were worn as good luck charms, and even in some instances attached to horse-harness. An infant burial at Catterick had six such objects accompanying it; they were so fashioned as to have formed a necklet on a leather strap. Small bronze swastikas, with the arms in the reverse position to the Nazi emblem, were likewise considered as protecting the wearer and sometimes appear as brooches. Occasionally, also, metal plaques are found bearing an almost meaningless jumble of letters, like a lead disc from Brough-on-Humber, which, in addition to the necessary 'spell' was also inscribed on one side with a crude representation of male, and on the other, female genitalia.

Some amulets, or tokens, were intended to be more specific. A particularly interesting one comes from the villa site at Lockleys (Herts). It is an intaglio of a hard, haematitic material, probably originally mounted as a locket to hang round some part of the body, or else to be enclosed in a leather or fabric pouch. Both sides are carved, the obverse including portrayals of the Egyptian deities Isis and Bes, together with a representation of the human womb and a seven-toothed key, all enclosed within a border of a snake devouring its tail, which in Egyptian mythology was a symbol for Eternity. The reverse carries a representation of a sacred beetle, or scarab, while both sides have encircling legends in Greek letters, which in either magical or palindromic form make up invocations to Typhon, an elemental force, to Orōriouth, a spirit providing protection in cases of gynaecological disorders, and Iaō, the equivalent of the Jewish Jehovah. Amulets of this type are referred to by classical authors and appear to have been used especially to shorten or relieve the pains of childbirth. The conflation of Egyptian, Semitic and Greek superstitions is clearly magical rather than religious.

Another amulet which makes use of Hebrew words intermixed with Greek comes from Caernarvon and was inscribed on a rectangular piece of gold leaf. On it some deliberate religious invocations are mixed with magical alliterations and symbols and followed by a prayer: protect me Alphianos.

Curses were normally scratched on lead sheet, as being an easily impressed medium and then probably nailed to a post in a prominent position in a temple or a shrine. Quite a large number are known from Britain and cover a wide variety of circumstances. In order to increase the power the same inscription was sometimes scratched on both sides of the sheet. One from London reads: 'I curse Tretia Maria and her life and mind and memory and liver and lungs mixed up together, and her words, thoughts and memory; thus may she be unable to speak what things are concealed, nor be able . . .'. There the sheet is broken, but not before poor Tretia Maria has received some unpleasant prognostications as to her future, presumably for threatening to reveal secret information. Another from Old Harlow reads: 'To the god Mercury, I entrust to you my affair with Eterna and her own self, and may Timotheus feel no jealousy of me at the risk of his life-blood', an overt threat to Timotheus not to interfere in the abduction of his wife, girl-friend, daughter or sister.

Most curses, therefore, were appeals to a deity or supernatural force to inhibit physical or mental processes of the cursed, such as eating, sleeping, drinking or thinking; or they can invoke damage to some physical organ of the body. In the main they seem to fall into four classes: those which involved unfaithful consorts, or rivals in amatory affairs, those which might affect the performance of athletic rivals, or rivals at law, and those which condemned thieves. One of the most interesting in the last class is a curse from the temple of Nodens at Lydney, which therefore must date to the late fourth century. It reads: 'To the god Nodens, Silvianus has lost a ring, he promises half its value to Nodens. Let him not grant health among those of the name Senicianus, until he brings it back to the temple of Nodens', and then additionally, 'curse renewed'. It seems probable that both Silvianus and Senicianus had gone to Lydney, hoping that the deity would cure them of some disease or physical ailment. No doubt both stayed in the guesthouse, from which, no doubt also, the latter walked off with the former's ring. An appeal to the god by Silvianus to withhold the request for health by Senicianus would, in the circumstances, make excellent sense, until the ring was returned. Strangely enough a polygonal gold ring, bearing an intaglio labelled Venus, has been found at Silchester. Moreover, subsequently it had scratched on the outside the legend: 'May thou live in God, Senicianus', a form of words which is typically Christian. Was this the same Senicianus, who finding his journey to Lydney had done him no good, subsequently embraced the Christian faith? What then also of the curse being renewed? Such evidence, when it occurs, illuminates the personalities of Roman Britain with a sudden, bright light, revealing their hopes and fears, ambitions and failures, which were not so very different from people today. We shall never know the full story behind this curse and the ring, nor the circumstances in which the two protagonists passed their lives, but, for one short moment, they stand revealed in all their human weakness.

A deep-seated belief in some form of survival after death was common to both Classical and Celtic worlds, so that the introduction of Roman burial practices into Britain, as with classical religion, placed no great strain upon the recipients of the new ideas. In the Roman world, as represented by Vergil, Hades was recognized as a place, which not only punished evil-doers in Hell but also rewarded others in Heaven. Nevertheless, this was perhaps a restricted view which not all people shared, even if they believed in the survival of the spirit, probably underground in the region of their final interment. Burial rites, therefore, grew up to take account of these convictions, which were sometimes coupled with the idea of a resurrection into the vegetable kingdom. It is not surprising, also, that they were easily grafted onto indigenous customs, since fundamentally there was little difference in the beliefs.

In Britain at the time of the conquest, both inhumation and cremation were practised, with a greater predominance of the latter in the south-east, where large cremation cemeteries appear at such places as Swarling and Aylesford in Kent, or Welwyn in Hertfordshire. Within a particular rite, however, it is possible to detect evidence of social stratification from the quality and quantity of grave goods included with the burial. Some were extremely richly furnished with all the trappings of life being included for the life-hereafter; they were clearly graves of the aristocracy and were in some instances surmounted by a barrow. But the very poorest graves seldom contained more than a cooking-pot for the ashes, and perhaps one other vessel, intended to hold food for the journey to the next world.

Both rites were likewise practised in the Roman world, but cremation seems to have been undoubtedly the most popular among immigrants to Britain after the conquest. From the middle of the second century, however, there was a gradual change to inhumation, which seems to have been brought about more by altering fashion than by any fundamental change in belief. It certainly cannot, as is sometimes done, be related to the rise of Christianity. Such changes are detectable in Britain before then and by the late third century, the rite of cremation was seldom being carried out.

The laws relating to the burial of the dead in the Roman empire were governed principally by the old republican statutes which forbade the interment of bodies or cremated ashes within the boundary of a town or fort, the only exception being children under ten days old, who had no legal existence. Consequently if burials other than those of infants are found apparently inside a town or fort they take on a special significance; either they represent foul-play followed by secret and hasty interment, or they relate to earlier or later boundaries of the settlement concerned. That being so, it is sometimes possible to use the distribution of cemeteries as indicators for urban boundaries, perhaps in those times before they became crystallized by the construction of defences. For instance, at Canterbury, little is known of the boundary before the fortifications were built in the late third century. Yet we may conclude that it never greatly changed over the years, since, on most sides, earlier cemeteries run right up to the walls, but do not appear within them, with the possible exception of an area beyond the river Stour which may have been omitted from the town when the defences were built.

Major urban cemeteries are, therefore, to be found outside towns and most frequently lining main roads; in this respect they follow Roman practice, but whether by accident or design is not so easily determined.

Given the legal requirements, graves and tombs would be most accessible if placed beside a road, and would interfere less with agricultural or other uses. Some well-attested examples occur outside many major cities and towns in Britain such as those which lined the main road to London outside Colchester, or the Tadcaster road leading out of York.

Individual cremation burials were often marked by an upright gravestone on which was usually inscribed a suitable reference to the dead person and, normally, either a pictorial representation taken from his life or the scene of his funerary banquet. Many are known from Britain of both civilian and military forms. A much-favoured piece of iconography from the latter was the cavalryman's tombstone depicting an armed horseman riding down a fallen enemy, who lies, or crouches, at the feet of the horse. The tombstone of Rufus Sita from Gloucester shows him in such an act, and since he appears to be unclothed it is probable that the stone was originally painted. Below this representation is an inscription recording his name, his regiment, the sixth cohort of Thracians, his age at death, forty years, the fact that he had served twenty-two years in the army and a customary phrase to show that his heirs had erected the stone according to his will. Then follows the abbreviated form of *Hic Situs Est, H S E*, to denote that he was buried at the spot where the stone was erected. The latter formula is usually restricted to the first century but had some real meaning, since the H was omitted from a tombstone of a sailor from Chester, who died in a shipwreck; presumably his body was not recovered, so that the stone was more of a memorial than a tombstone.

Civilian tombstones of this type often show a family group and are frequently accompanied by a more elaborate invocation. The stone to commemorate Flavia Augustina and her children at York shows the whole family, father, mother, a boy and a girl, while another, erected for a thirteen-year-old girl, Corellia Optata, contained an invocation to the spirits of the underworld in verse form, and was put up by her father.

The information to be gained by a study of these tombstones is considerable. Not only do we learn of the people themselves, the positions they occupied and the lengths of their lives, but also details of their clothing and furniture which is so often illustrated as well. It has, however, been argued that they do not form a sound basis for calculation of life expectancy, since tombstones are, by their nature, the product of a supposedly limited social class. Yet, it is perhaps not so strange that the one instance in Britain, at York, where statistical comparison can be made of age at death between the better off and the poor, produces much the same result for both.

Other methods of marking cremation burials were either by the erection of an earth mound over them or by placing them in masonry mausolea, and, indeed, it may be that the former is the forerunner of the latter, since it is likely that some mausolea were topped off with a mound of earth. Certainly, both forms have much the same distribution in Britain, both lying south-east of a line running roughly from Dorset to the Wash. Roman barrows can normally be distinguished from those of other periods by their pronounced conic shape and sometimes also by a low bank ringing the mound within the ditch. Moreover, they usually occur in groups beside main roads, such as those at Badbury (Dorset), Bartlow (Essex) or Stevenage (Herts). Occasionally, single barrows are found in the neighbourhood of villas, such as that at West Mersea (Essex), which was contained within a masonry circle, reinforced by internal radial walls and external buttresses, to retain the weight of the earth filling.

The full development from barrow to masonry tomb is perhaps best demonstrated by the mausoleum at Keston (Kent), where a buttressed wall enclosed a circular space about 9 m. in diameter. A door led into the interior and it is probable that the latter had once been equipped with niches to contain cinerary urns. Sometimes several such tombs, or *columbaria*, were placed within a walled enclosure, like that at Lockham (Kent), which may have been the property of a rich family or of a burial club, the existence of which, in Britain, is attested by inscriptions.

The poorer classes, however, could probably only afford a post or some other means to mark the site of a burial, so that it could be visited to provide the necessary libations for the dead. It is likely that, in some instances, the neck of the cremation vessel, left projecting above the ground, acted as a marker; by covering the top with a flat slab of stone or tile, adequate protection could be given and, at the same time, libations of wine or honey or other material could simply be poured in after the lid had been lifted.

The actual cremation of the body was carried out in special areas, sometimes, as at Riseholme (Lincs) incorporated under the burial mound, or else, as at York, situated in the middle of a busy cemetery. The ashes would be collected in a container which varied according to the wealth of the person and which could range from a humble cooking-pot to a glass, pottery or lead vessel, or a combination of one or more. At Chichester, a wooden box was sometimes inverted over a burial, or, elsewhere, it might be contained in a stone or brick-lined cyst. Sometimes, also, special provision for making libations was incorporated in the form of a pipe running from the surface to the canister, as in the Caerleon pipe-burial.

The change from cremation to inhumation led to a corresponding alteration in methods of burial. The body, usually in an extended position, was sometimes contained in a wood, lead or stone coffin, or sometimes in a combination of wood and stone or lead and stone. Elaborate stone sarcophagi, sometimes ornamented and inscribed, replaced the earlier, upright tombstones. Ornamental examples were clearly not intended for burial, but rested above the ground or in a recess in a tomb. It is not surprising, therefore, that they are sometimes found to be occupied by a person who cannot be identified with the commemorative inscription. More often than not, however, no coffin was used, the remains being interred perhaps in a sack or shroud. Certainly in the cemeteries of the poorer people, such as that at Trentholme Drive, York, or near the amphitheatre at Cirencester, bodies seem to have been treated in a most unceremonious way, with later often interfering with earlier burials, even where decomposition was not complete. They must, therefore, have presented a somewhat gruesome and unhygienic appearance, with partly rotted and dismembered limbs lying around.

A custom, which grew in Britain with the increasingly used rite of inhumation, was partial embalming by pouring liquid plaster of Paris around the body in the coffin, so that, on hardening, it recorded impressions of the deceased, their shrouds and sometimes other perishable objects which had been included in the burial. Frequently, also, this process preserved heads of hair, as with that from York (see Ch. 6). The custom appears to have been mainly restricted to those areas where gypsum is found, such as York and Dorchester (Dorset), although it is not unknown elsewhere in the empire, having apparently originated in north Africa. In Britain, it has been claimed to represent a Christian burial rite.

Grave goods were, of course, included in both cremation and inhumation burials, the quantity and quality reflecting roughly the wealth and social class of the dead person. They will normally have included refreshments for the journey to the underworld and the person's most valued possessions. Flagons, amphoras, bowls and dishes commonly occur; occasionally something more valuable is included as at Winchester, where two joints of meat had been placed on a beautifully incised shale trencher. There was the army veteran's child at Colchester who was buried with the much-loved toys, that included not only many pottery and glass vessels, and terracotta animals, but also human figurines intended for giving dolls' dinner-parties, while a terracotta head and shoulders of a young child can only have come from a rag doll of a type which is still made today. Sometimes a coin was placed in the mouth of the corpse; it was the fee to Charon, a ferryman of the river Styx, to carry the person to the underworld. It was so placed because both hands would have been encumbered with cakes for the two heads

Key:
- Hill-fort bank
- " " ditch
- Mausolea
- Ditched enclosures
- Lead or stone coffins
- Dug graves
- Limits of cemetery
- Settlement - Early
- " Late

Map labels: ? Road, Aqueduct, N

Scale: 0 20 40 60 80 m

Fig. 48 Poundbury cemetery, north-west of Dorchester

of the dog Cerberus, guardian of the underworld. Women's graves were frequently equipped with toilet articles, such as mirrors, depilatory tweezers, nail-cleaners and -parers, and bottles of scent or other cosmetics. Personal ornaments are commonplace, since they were probably left on the body at burial, and include a wide variety of pins, bangles, rings, bracelets, necklaces and brooches, some of which may, of course, have been used for fastening the shroud.

The rise of Christianity, however, brought about a decline in the use of grave goods, since the Christian ethic was concentrated on the more spiritual side of the life-hereafter. Christian cemeteries can usually be distinguished from other inhumations by the uniform east-west orientation of the graves. The Poundbury cemetery at Dorchester (Dorset) and the Lankhills cemetery at Winchester are excellent examples. The former has been estimated to occupy some 2 ha. with a density of some 2000 graves per hectare. Most of the burials were contained in plain wooden coffins, with the head placed to the west, and with few grave goods. Some apparent family groups were distinguished which contained two adults and one or two children, with one of the interments in each group embalmed in plaster of Paris in a lead-lined, heavy wooden coffin. There were also a number of rectangular mausolea, at least two of which had handsomely painted walls and vaulted roofs; human figures are represented in the decorations and appear to be portraits of important and distinguished people taking part in some ceremonial. The burials in these mausolea were also grouped and were placed in more elaborate lead or stone sarcophagi, again with the bodies often being embalmed in plaster of Paris. They seem to represent, therefore, a development of the 'family group' burials, perhaps on the part of richer or more prominent people.

The Winchester cemetery, although possibly Christian, is interesting for the items of late Roman military equipment which it contained, and which must represent elements of the town garrison in the late fourth or even early fifth century.

Group cemeteries also occur in another form, where compartments, or *loculi*, for containing caskets or coffins, open out in rising tiers from a central corridor. A possible example of this mode of burial was found at Lincoln, where several stone coffins in close juxtaposition came to light north of the town; it was probably the property of a burial club.

One last type of monument has to be considered in this context: the war memorial, or, as it should more correctly be called, the triumphal monument. These were erected not so much to commemorate the dead, as today, but to record a major victory on the part of the Roman army. Several are known in Britain and the most famous is undoubtedly the great triumphal arch at Richborough, erected late in the first century, probably to commemorate the final and successful establishment of the British province. It was a four-way arch, placed on a massive foundation, over 10 m. deep, to prevent the weight from carrying it into the soft, underlying sand. Unfortunately, it was almost entirely destroyed when the Saxon Shore fort was built in the late third century, but enough fragmentary pieces survived to show its plan and to demonstrate that the structure had once been clad in white marble, imported from Italy. The top of the monument would have been ornamented with trophies of victory, and inscriptions, probably in letters of bronze, would have recorded the circumstances of its erection.

Evidence for two further, similar monuments comes from the north-ern frontier region. Two fragments of an inscription, found in Jarrow church, almost certainly once belonged to a prominent memorial erected on Tyneside to record the completion of the Hadrianic frontier. Its position is most likely to have been in advance of the termination of the Wall at Wallsend. It refers specifically to the frontier works as a consolidating feature and speaks of Hadrian's desire to keep the empire within its limits.

Another, in the form of a circular, domed shrine, once existed north of the Antonine Wall beyond Falkirk. Known as Arthur's O'on, it was dismantled in the eighteenth century and the stone used for a mill-dam, but it appears to have been associated with Winged Victories and legionary eagles. It is set in a prominent position and it would have been visible for many miles; it is, therefore, likely to be more than an ordinary shrine. Its position would suggest that it commemorated the successful completion of the Scottish war conducted by Lollius Urbicus (see Ch. 2) which culminated in the construction of the Antonine frontier.

Chapter 8

Leisure

One of the most popular myths concerning Rome relates to the pleasure-loving habits of its inhabitants, which, if taken at its face value would lead us to believe that no one, not even the common people, except the slaves, ever did any work. The reverse was, of course, the case, and most people, throughout the empire, worked a seven-day week, which had been known from the time of Augustus, and which was relieved only by holidays granted on the occasion of various religious festivals. Each day, from dawn to dusk, was divided into twelve hours, so that the length of the 'hours' varied according to summer or winter. Work normally began at daybreak and continued until midday – the sixth hour – although many businessmen and shopkeepers probably continued until dark, or even later. Consequently, if a man or woman was fortunate in his employment, it is probable that he had a certain amount of free time. In contrast, retirement was an admired, but seldom achieved concept, and most people probably continued work, either till they dropped, or were prevented from doing so by some incapacity.

The amount of time available for recreation for most people was, therefore, not unduly small and could be spent in a number of ways.

One of the commonest ways of relaxation, and in towns probably also the most universal, was a visit to the public baths. Most bathhouses in the Roman world were equipped with an open space, the *palaestra*, as at Silchester, or, more appropriately for the British climate, a covered hall, as at Wroxeter or Leicester, in which a variety of ball-games could be played or very strenuous exercise indulged in, such as running, wrestling and boxing. After this exercise a bath would be taken in the normal manner, or, if the weather was clement, a dip in the open-air swimming-bath, as at Wroxeter, although these were not on the whole popular in Britain. Certainly, if the size of most urban public baths in Britain is taken as a guide, there was accommodation for a considerable number of bathers at any one time. It is probable, also, that itinerant food sellers would have displayed their wares in and around the palaestra, so that it would have been possible to take a snack or a drink, in much the same way that ice-cream or hot-dog vendors

PA   Palaestra
L   Latrine
La   Laconium
F   Frigidarium
T   Tepidarium
C   Coldarium
B   Plunge bath
R   Praefurnium
D   Drain
S   Service
A   Apodyterium

Fig. 49 Plans of bath-houses at: a) Leicester; b) Wroxeter; c) Silchester

now frequent places of public recreation and entertainment. Some towns appear to have had smaller, probably privately-run bath-houses, as at Canterbury, but in the main these were probably little better than the 'massage parlours' of today.

Another, more polite way of enjoyment among the wealthier classes was the fashionable dinner-party, given at the ninth hour, in the afternoon. Tacitus refers to sumptuous banquets and, given the readily identifiable dining-rooms in houses, it is inconceivable that this form of entertainment did not take place. It was customary in the better circles for readings or recitations to take place during dinner, or for dancers, jugglers or acrobats to perform afterwards. The child's toys from the Colchester burial (see Ch. 7) included figures made to recline at a dining-table, while others read from scrolls. The questioning mind of a child would have undoubtedly asked what they were doing, and it is to be assumed the answer was readily forthcoming. It was also customary after a dinner-party to spend the evening drinking, either at the same house or at the home of one of the guests. Since, however, dinner was the only real repast of the day, and was usually restricted to no more than three courses, the popular idea of orgiastic gluttony, often attributed to the Roman world, is largely the product of modern imagination battening on the views of one or two ancient satirists.

The apparatus of the dinner-party is well known in Britain and includes pottery vessels graded in size accordingly for drinking wine or beer and sometimes decorated with an appropriate motto such as 'long life', or, 'give me neat wine'; normal practice was to dilute wine with water, and to drink it unmixed was considered the action of the intemperate. We might, therefore, wonder about the bibulous habits of the man who owned that particular beaker at Verulamium. Glass, pewter, and even silver, drinking vessels are also known. Samian ware, and later pewter, was undoubtedly used for dinner-parties, but exceptionally the very rich could afford silver dishes and plates, like those which were found at Mildenhall (Suffolk) and which were probably imported from an eastern province.

There is little doubt, also, that conversation pieces were provided in dining-rooms, in the form of a mosaic or wall-painting, since the best mosaics were usually placed so as not to be covered by table or couches. Vergilian references occur in one medium or the other in several villas, as well as at Silchester, indicating at least some degree of familiarity with classical literature on the part of the owners. The cultured man was therefore expected to show an interest in the arts, which he might encourage by commissioning a sculpture, mosaic or painting.

For the less well-to-do, who could not afford, or did not belong to the social class that gave, dinner-parties, there was almost certainly an abundance of cafés, wine and ale shops and brothels to suit all pockets in most towns and lesser settlements. But in this respect the countryman was at a distinct disadvantage when compared with urban inhabitants, apart from the fact that he may well have had to work longer hours.

Various games of skill or chance were also played extensively among, seemingly, all classes of society. Many northern British sites produce quantities of flat, round discs, cut from stone, pottery or brick. Considerable variations occur in size, and the large majority are unmarked, and it is just conceivable that they were stoppers for flagons or amphoras, kept in place by a seal of pitch or resin. On the other hand, they could equally have been used as the pieces in some quite elaborate game, whose rules and form of play have long since disappeared. Board games of various types certainly existed, and, at Silchester, a tile inscribed before firing with chequerboard patterns, was probably manufactured as the result of idle moments in the brickworks; although, of course, they could have been made deliberately for sale as gaming boards. Gaming pieces of glass, pottery, stone, bone and lead occur widely and usually in quite large numbers, although such objects could also have been used as aids in arithmetical calculations. Sometimes the pieces are inscribed with numerals or letters and three from Silchester bear the letters FVR (thief), MAR (abbreviation for *martialis* – warlike) and PRIMVS (first). It is difficult to visualize the game played with them but several possibilities can be imagined, the most probable being some sort of battle-game. Sometimes, also, different coloured glass was used to denote opposing factions and these can be marked, on occasion, with spots to give the numbers. A fine glass set occurred with a rich burial at the Lullingstone villa, together with bronze angle pieces indicating the one-time presence of the gaming board 48.3 cm. square. There were fifteen white and fifteen brown pieces, but no dice; nevertheless the pieces all displayed differing numbers of spots, so that a more complicated game than draughts may be envisaged.

Another set, denoting perhaps an even more intricate pattern of play, was found in Bermondsey, London. There were twelve pieces carved from bone combining the word SEXTIII with other varying devices.

But such games were not restricted to the Roman world and a fine set, together with indications of a board, came from an Iron Age burial at Welwyn Garden City (Herts). It included twenty-four glass counters, arranged in colour groups of six pieces each – white, blue, yellow and light green – and also six fragments of glass beads or bracelets. Experiments with the latter showed that, if thrown like dice, they could only fall with a flat or rounded surface uppermost, and therefore, they were probably used in their place. That being so, it is likely that the whole set represented a race-game for four players, perhaps not unlike backgammon.

Dice, usually carved from bone, and sometimes of slightly eccentric shape, are similarly common finds, and indeed the sport became so popular in the empire that edicts were promulgated against it; loaded dice are not unknown. Bone counters from Leicester were worn in such a way as to suggest tiddleywinks.

Music must also have played its part in leisure-hours. Bone pipes have been found in London, and mouthpieces from bronze trumpet- or horn-like instruments also turn up from time to time in Britain, although they may have come from military sources. A small bronze statuette from Silchester shows a girl playing a single pipe, although double-pipes are sometimes displayed in other contexts, as, indeed, are multiple pan-pipes. Stringed instruments were also known, and a thin fragment of ivory from Cirencester may have come from a *cithara*, a lyre-like instrument. But it is probable that, in Britain, and apart from the army, most musical activities would have been restricted to religious ceremonies or theatrical performances.

Hunting and fishing appear to have been popular sports, but again it is difficult to gauge the extent of their followings in Britain. The Celtic peoples were great hunters on horseback. Moreover Britain was famed for its hunting dogs, of which there were probably several kinds, before the Roman invasion, and small bronze statuettes or depictions on sculpture show breeds ranging from mastiff and greyhound-like animals to Scotch terriers. Hunting scenes were commonly illustrated on certain types of decorated pottery vessels, notably those produced around Colchester and Water Newton during the late second century, to which the name Hunt Cup has been given. Hounds chasing deer are the most familiar representations.

Apart from deer, wild boar was almost certainly hunted in Britain, providing excellent, if somewhat dangerous, sport. A splendid altar dedicated to Silvanus and set up far out in the country on Bollihope Common (Co. Durham) records the death of a 'boar of remarkable fineness which many of my predecessors had been unable to bag'. It was dedicated by G. Tetius Veturius Micianus, prefect of a cavalry regiment, stationed at Lancaster. The nearest fort to Bollihope Common is at Binchester, and it has been suggested that Micianus was visiting, perhaps while on leave, the prefect there, and was invited to take part in a hunting expedition.

It is likely that bears were also hunted in Britain, both as game and also for capture for use in the amphitheatre. But coursing for hares was probably commoner, and a sculptured relief from Bath illustrates the moment when the hare has just been put up and the dog is about to be unleashed. Game-birds were also shot with bows and arrows or trapped with nets or bird-lime, and the pheasant was probably a Roman introduction to Britain. Finally, it should not be forgotten that most weapons found on civilian sites in Britain would have been for hunting, since, by law, it was one of the few occupations in which a man might appear armed.

It is likely that fishing was practised more for a livelihood than for a recreation; nevertheless it is mentioned as a sport in contemporary

Fig. 50 Plans of theatres at: a) Canterbury; b) Gosbecks Farm, Colchester;
c) Verulamium

Roman literature, and barbed fish-hooks of bronze have sometimes
been found on British sites. Weighted nets were also used, as were
three-pronged fish spears, or tridents.

The principal entertainments of the Roman world were, however,
provided by the theatre, amphitheatre and circus and they have been
introduced in Chapter 3. In Britain the theatre seems to have been a
rare diversion which was, in most cases, connected with a temple. The
juxtaposition of temple and theatre was common in the Graeco-Roman
world, and usually indicates the presence of a deity popular enough to
attract large crowds on festival days. Consequently, theatres are not
only to be found on urban sites, but can exist just as easily in a rural
setting, as the one at Gosbecks Farm, south of Colchester. The theatre
there represents the romanization of a site of ancient native sanctity,
which may at one time have been the prime religious centre of the
Trinovantes. At first it was built with wooden walls retaining raking
banks of earth, on which the seating would have been placed, the banks
being arranged in a near semi-circle around a similarly shaped central
space, or orchestra, across the diameter of which was placed the stage,
also built of wood. An entrance into the orchestra led through the banks
on the opposite side to the stage. Although the main walls were rebuilt
in buttressed masonry by the middle of the second century, the stage
seems to have remained entirely of timber. The orchestra was used for
the seats of important people.

Another, very much smaller, 'theatre', of similar nature to that at
Gosbecks Farm, has been discovered at Catterick, on the north bank of
the river Swale, where it was situated beside a trapezoidally-shaped

temple. A theatrical mask, made of pottery, and probably manufactured in the Nene Valley, was found with the buildings and may have
been used in the performances.

Despite the existence of a temple-theatre at Gosbecks, the colonia at
Colchester possessed its own urban theatre according to Tacitus, who
refers to it in the events he describes as leading up to the Boudiccan
rebellion. The site is not, however, known, although it may be suspected. It is likely that other theatres have still to be found in the
remaining coloniae and also at London. An inscription from Brough-
on-Humber mentions the gift of a new stage building, but a theatre in
such an out-of-the-way place must almost certainly have been, once
more, related to a temple.

The theatre at Canterbury, on the other hand, is a much more
imposing building, although marginally smaller, than that at Gosbecks
Farm, and may have been of the true urban variety, although, even
now, we cannot be sure that it was not related to a temple. The first
structure to be erected, *c*. AD 80–90, was, however, a compromise, in
which one building was intended to do duty as both theatre and
amphitheatre. This can be seen as a wise precaution on the part of a
municipality, which was not too rich, nor too certain of the support that
newly introduced theatrical shows might receive. It was, however,
replaced by a much more substantial building of more classical plan in
the early third century.

The best-known theatre in Roman Britain is probably that at Verulamium. As at Canterbury, this had first been built to a compromise
plan, incorporating both theatre and amphitheatre in one building.
Consequently the orchestra, instead of being semi-circular in shape,
was almost a full circle, with the stage buildings forming a chord across
it between the curving arms of the seating banks. But also, as at
Canterbury, later alterations tended to give it a more classical profile.
At Verulamium, however, we are left in no doubt of the association of
the theatre with one of the principal temples in the town. Indeed, before
it was built, towards the middle of the second century, an open space,
presumably for religious gatherings, occupied the same area in front of
the temple. The provision of a theatre can, therefore, be seen as an
attempt to accommodate the spectators in greater comfort, as well as
enabling better crowd control to be practised.

It is exceedingly difficult to visualize what was performed in those
theatres connected specifically with temples. The rituals will, presumably, have varied from deity to deity, but would normally have
included scenes depicting the particular functional attributes of the god
or goddess concerned, and will have been composed of part thanks-
giving and part invocation. Attendances at such festivities were obvi-

ously considerable, since a theatre as large as that at Gosbecks Farm
would have accommodated perhaps up to 5000 or more people. The
requirements of the crowd would have been catered for in other ways as
well, with stalls and booths selling food and drink, or small commemorative trinkets relating to the deity, such as the bronze votive
figures and miniature sacrificial axes from the rural temple site at
Woodeaton (Oxon). The further association of such places with fairs
and markets has already been mentioned, and the overall effect will
probably have been not unlike some modern places of religious pil-
grimage.

In urban theatres, however, performances will normally have consisted of pantomimes, mimes or recitations. The former employed
actors who, by changing their clothes and face-masks, were able to
represent different characters, who performed with a chorus and
instrumental accompaniment to an audience that was probably familiar with most of the themes. Mime, from which the modern pantomime
is descended, employed stock characters who performed highly topical
sketches, more often than not of a ribald and coarse nature.

In Britain, as in other provinces with large garrisons, the
amphitheatres tended to fall into two types. The military
amphitheatre, or *ludus*, was used, not only for entertainments, but also
for training exercises, drills and parades. Since the size of the audience
was known from the first, they did not have to be constructed to contain
more than the necessary number of seats, and, at Caerleon, the central
arena therefore occupies a larger percentage of the total area of the
building. In contrast, in civilian amphitheatres, a much higher proportion had to be devoted to seating. This can easily be appreciated
by comparing the civilian amphitheatre at Cirencester with that at
Caerleon.

In general, both types consisted of a central, elliptical arena entirely
surrounded by raked earth banks for the seating, normally retained
between masonry walls. The entrances to the arena penetrated the
seating banks at both ends of the long axis; it is probable that they were,
for part of their length, vaulted so that the seating could be carried over
the top, as at Cirencester. In many cases, the masonry walls were
preceded by timber, as at the legionary ludus at Chester, although
occasionally as at Dorchester (Dorset), such wooden walls were not
replaced. There, a Neolithic henge monument on the southern edge of
the town was pressed into service as an amphitheatre. Consequently it
did not follow the standard pattern, and possessed only one arena
entrance; the retaining walls of the arena, which included perimeter
passageways, were never replaced by masonry.

Access to the seats was probably, in most cases, from external

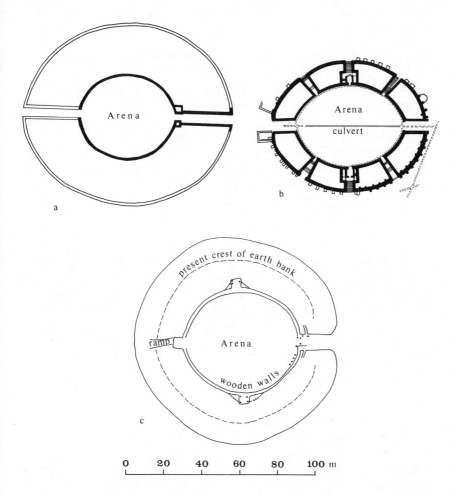

Fig. 51 Plans of amphitheatres at: a) Cirencester; b) Caerleon; c) Dorchester

staircases. Quite often, also, there appears to have been provision made, in the form of special boxes, for eminent people. They were normally situated immediately on a level with the top of the arena wall at either, or both, ends of the short axis, and sometimes, as at Caerleon, were placed over shrines to various deities, such as Nemesis or Fortune. Shrines, alternatively, could be placed in small chambers on each side of the arena entrance, as at Chester and Cirencester. A shrine at Chester had an altar to Nemesis still standing in it when excavated, while a lead curse (see Ch. 7) found at Caerleon read: 'Lady Nemesis, I give thee a cloak and a pair of boots; let him who wore them not redeem them except with his life's blood.'

It is unlikely that the seating of amphitheatres in Britain was often protected from the elements, although both theatres and amphitheatres in the Mediterranean region often had canvas awnings hoisted to ward off the sun rather than the rain. There is, however, a suggestion that Caerleon may have been so equipped.

Both legionary fortresses at Caerleon and Chester had their amphitheatres, but that at York has yet to be identified. Neither, for that matter, has any amphitheatre been discovered at fortresses of an earlier date, such as Exeter, Gloucester or Wroxeter. Nevertheless, some forts, such as Tomen-y-Mur were provided with them, although of smaller and more appropriate size for an auxiliary regiment. In the civilian sphere, almost all chartered towns and civitas capitals will have possessed them, although, as yet, none are known at the former sites. Among the civitas capitals, amphitheatres still stand, as grass-covered mounds, at Cirencester, Dorchester, Carmarthen and Silchester; others are known at Chichester and Caerwent. Normally they were constructed on the outskirts of a town, since they required large areas of ground; consequently they were often excluded when fortifications were built. That at Silchester, which was within the late first-century defences, but not within the later wall, and at Caerwent, which was constructed inside the walls, are the only exceptions in Britain. Other amphitheatres are known at the minor settlements of Charterhouse (Somerset) and Richborough. Another possibility, at Leicester, is suggested by a sherd of pottery found there with a graffito carved on it and reading: 'Verecunda actress; Lucius gladiator'. It may have been dropped by a member of a company of travelling players.

The types of displays performed in amphitheatres will have varied enormously, ranging from gladiatorial combats to cock-fighting or bear-baiting. The former were expensive, since the fighters had to be hired from a contractor, who trained and kept them. No training establishment has ever been identified in Britain, but a heavy, bronze helmet of typical gladiatorial pattern has been found at Hawkedon in Suffolk. It may well have been part of the loot taken from Colchester during the Boudiccan rebellion. In Britain, commoner shows probably involved wild animals fighting together, and the province could produce bulls, wild boars, bears, wolves and dogs. Occasionally, wild-beast hunts may have been simulated, but it is doubtful if more exotic animals such as lions or tigers often figured, since the price would have been exorbitant; certainly no instance of the recovery, on excavations, of the bones from such animals has been recorded. Sometimes, also, animals may have been tamed to perform circus acts, and it should not be forgotten that public executions were often carried out in the arena. Boxers, wrestlers, jugglers and acrobats may all have taken part, and a colour-coated piece of pottery from Water Newton depicts a female acrobat performing her feats on top of animals with two gladiators fighting nearby.

Apart from the existence of the buildings themselves, an interest in theatrical and amphitheatrical performances was displayed in many other ways. One theatrical mask from Catterick has already been mentioned. Parts of another, of tragic mien, have been found at Baldock, while another miniature mask, carved of ivory, was discovered near the legionary bath-house at Caerleon. There is a marked contrast between the styles of the latter and the Catterick mask, as might be expected. Caerleon, with its strong citizen body, would have required performances measuring up to the true Roman standards; consequently the mask shows all the classic features to be expected. The Catterick mask, on the other hand, with its lentoid, rather than round, holes for the eyes, its straight nose, and narrow slit of a mouth, comes largely from a Celtic world.

A further interest in theatricals might be implied from the Leicester wall-paintings, where at least two tragic masks were included, together with a simplified architectural illustration resembling a proscaenium. Another probable face-mask was depicted on a wall fresco from Cirencester.

Scenes from the arena were often used to decorate glass and pottery vessels. Although the latter were almost certainly imported, the former were frequently made in Britain and therefore imply a first-hand knowledge of the shows on the part of the potters. The colour-coated Colchester vase shows a fight between a heavily armed gladiator (*mirmillo*) and a man armed only with net and trident (*retiarius*), and names them as Secundus Memnon and Salvenus Valentinus respectively. There is also a reference to the thirtieth legion, stationed at Xanten on the Rhine. It is possible that the vase, which probably dates to the second century, was made as a souvenir or commemoration piece to record the visit to Colchester of a troupe from Xanten, but, since the legionary reference has been scratched on after firing, presumably by the owner, we cannot be certain.

One of the mosaics from the Bignor villa illustrates a scene of nine winged cupids dressed as gladiators and undergoing training with three instructors standing by. It is a lively scene, depicting different types of combat; in one, a retiarius lies wounded on the ground. Another scene of a gladiatorial battle is shown on one of the mosaics from the villa at Brading (I.O.W.).

Small portable articles, such as the ivory handle of a pocket-knife, carved to represent a gladiator, from South Shields, or the bronze statuette of another from London, may represent souvenirs sold by itinerant traders during the course of the games. A bronze statuette of an athlete, found in a bath-house at York, may on the other hand have been used to decorate the palaestra, and so be more symbolic of exercise there, than of an arena scene.

The last of the three principal forms of amusement in the Roman world, the circus, is not well attested in Britain, and no building related to this entertainment has yet been positively identified. Normally, they were long, but comparatively narrow, buildings with a central spine set lengthwise down the middle, round which the races would be run; seats were provided on the perimeter and stables were usually situated at one end. Nevertheless, horse- and chariot-racing, the sports carried on in them, could also take place wherever there was a large enough area of level ground. Remembering the Celtic love for hunting on horseback and both Roman and Celtic love of gambling, it would be surprising if racing had not become an accepted sport in Britain. At the villa at Chedworth, an inscription had been roughly scratched on a wall, referring to a 'green company'. In Rome, the four racing colours, each belonging to a different faction, were red, white, blue and green, so that the Chedworth inscription may be an allusion to horse- or chariot-racing, perhaps at nearby Cirencester. Two more references come from Lincolnshire, one from the colonia itself, in the form of a fragmentary stone carving showing a boy charioteer, the other from the villa at Horkstow, where a mosaic graphically depicts a combined horse and chariot race in progress. One chariot, in turning the corner at the end of the straight, has hit the central wall and lost a wheel, so tipping out the charioteer, who is being helped by a dismounted horseman. It may be, however, that the latter scene is not so much topical as allegorical, since it is combined with an Orpheus mosaic. Glass beakers were also imported to Britain showing circus scenes, presumably as companions for those on which gladiators fight. A small bone plaque, found in a burial at York, was inscribed with a phrase, the language of which is appropriate to gladiators or charioteers.

In the context of horse-racing, there is an interesting building which appears to belong to a temple at Wroxeter. Among the deities venerated in the temple was certainly a god or goddess associated with horses, since fragments of a life-size stone head of a horse were found in it; a small cast bronze horse's head, and parts of a bronze headstall may also have come from it, although there is the possibility that they originated in the earlier, military layers. In Celtic mythology, the principal horse goddess was Epona, although it is probable that others like her also existed. To the rear of the temple was a large and unusual enclosure, which has not yet been fully excavated; it was approximately rectangular with rounded corners and may well have extended for over a hundred yards as far as the town fortifications. There was a large central space surrounded by twin parallel walls, some 4 m. apart, on which, it has been suggested, wooden seating could be erected, and opinion so far seems to favour its interpretation as a primitive amphitheatre. But if the principal deity of the temple was connected with horses, it seems far more likely that races or other forms of equestrian activity were practised on festival days, and the building would have been more appropriate for this purpose.

Leisure implies more than just time spent in pleasurable pursuits; it can also imply idleness and the unseemly acts which sometimes spring from it. Consequently, it is of interest to note one of the first recorded cases of senseless vandalism of a deserted building in Britain, at Leicester. The house which contained the fine painted wall-plaster appears to have been unoccupied and possibly roofless in the late second century. Parts were taken over by various manufacturers, and a deposit of cows' heads was found on the floor of a room, after it had been stripped of its mosaic floor. But, apart from the industrial workers, other less desirable people seem to have visited it from time to time and scrawled upon the walls; one such graffito mentioned a mare's arse, another had a clear reference to sodomy. When the building was ultimately demolished, the clay walls were tumbled to the ground, carrying much of their painted plaster with them, which was then recovered in the course of recent excavations. After one of the main panels had been restored, it was found to have three gaps in it, which started at ground level and rose no higher than the height of an average man. These gaps coincided with the three main decorative features of the panel: two groups of human figures on either side of an architectural perspective. We must assume, therefore, that the plaster from these gaps had been deliberately destroyed before the building had been demolished, otherwise the fragments would have been found, as with the rest. But a vandal, intent on destruction, is most likely to pick the centrepieces of an ornamental display for immediate attention, and we may conclude that this had happened at Leicester.

Other acts of wanton damage, as opposed to religious, or official, vandalism which was more commonplace, are difficult to identify, and appear mostly as minor incidents, such as the graffiti which were scratched on the walls of the council chamber in the basilica at Caerwent, presumably after law and order had broken down. Indeed, graffiti written on plastered walls are not uncommon, and in many cases were probably scrawled by children while the houses were still occupied. The word EQVVS, together with a 'pin' chicken emerging from a highly distorted egg, from a house at Verulamium were probably so caused by a child in an idle moment.

Taken as a whole, therefore, there is no lack of evidence of the way in which spare time was spent in Roman Britain, although some of it is not as satisfactory as that from other provinces.

Chapter 9

And after the Romans?

We saw in Chapter 1 how the Roman invasion of Britain came about as the result of the coincidence of a number of events. So in the end, many factors contributed to the decline of Roman Britain, not all of which are yet fully understood, as, from the end of the fourth century onwards, if not before, the evidence becomes less, and much more difficult to interpret. The forces at work were partly internal, partly external, and appear at times almost as a death-wish on the part of the empire. It has been said that every great institution carries within it the seeds of its own destruction, and this is probably true of the Roman empire.

It is extremely difficult, if not entirely impossible, to point to a particular stage in the decline of fourth-century Britain, and say that at that moment the rot started. The peak of general prosperity, which had started early in that century, was probably reached within the reign of Constantine I. After that it is possible to trace at first a very gradual decline, relieved by minor recoveries from time to time and place to place, until the worsening military situation culminated in the barbarian conspiracy (see Ch. 2) of AD 367. Even then all was by no means lost, and given different people and different circumstances thereafter, a totally different outcome might have resulted.

Then came, in AD 383, the British revolt led by Magnus Maximus against the central authority. As has so often been the case in history, the ambition and greed, the success and failure of only one man can alter the whole course of subsequent events. So it was then, and from AD 383 the rate of decline in Britain became more precipitous, partly because a considerable reduction in garrison strength caused less money to circulate, partly because repressive measures implemented after the rebellion probably removed permanently from the scene many of the most able people in the provinces. Further events, ending with the military reorganizations of AD 395-401, accelerated the process, by which time the garrison strength had again been severely reduced. Growing dissatisfaction with the officials of the central government in Britain, who could no longer fully control events, also brought its repercussions, and between AD 405-7, the diocese threw up, in turn,

✱	Legionary fortress
▲	Fort
▫	Shore fort existing in **3**rd cent.
▪	" " added in **4**th cent.
●	Signal station
◇	Walled town
‿‿	**100**m contour

0   100   200Km

Fig. 52 Fourth-century Britain

three usurper emperors. The last of these, Constantine III, responded to the confidence expressed in him by the Britons by taking almost all remaining army units to Gaul in order to expand his own sphere of influence and to expel marauders; once more, personal ambition had intervened. In disgust, the British leaders threw out Constantine's remaining officers and also the last officials of the central government.

The hiatus of government which followed, during which the Britons were presumably managing their own affairs, culminated in official instructions being issued by the emperor Honorius, probably as the result of a request for help, that they must conduct their own defence. The letter was sent to the civitates of Britain, and it is to be assumed, therefore, that the decurions had assumed ultimate responsibility. But it is not surprising that, in such circumstances, strong men would come into their own, and among them one called Vortigern appeared upon the scene; his name, in fact, means 'high king'. It would appear that he was devoted to Pelagianism, the Christian heresy which was strongly represented in Britain (see Ch. 7), particularly among the ruling class. It is interesting that he adopted a purely British and unromanized name, and it has been suggested that he was the leader of the anti-Roman party, intent on maintaining the independence of Britain. To do so, he appears to have traded land, especially in Kent, but possibly also elsewhere, with the Saxons in return for armed protection.

The most dangerous enemies of Britain at the time were the Picts and secondly the Irish, and settlements of Saxon federate soldiers seem to have been placed by Vortigern at strategic places on the east coast and also inland, such as at Dorchester-on-Thames.

But the orthodox Church also had a strong following, and eventually Vortigern was outmanoeuvred, partly by the visit of St Germanus to combat the heresy in AD 429 and, later, partly by a serious rebellion of his Saxon troops. After this, he appears to have been displaced by Ambrosius, a member of the orthodox party, and it is probable that it was he and his supporters who, appalled by the progress being made by the Saxons, directed the final appeal for help to Rome, the so-called Groans of the Britons: 'To Aetius, thrice consul, come the groans of the Britons . . . the barbarians drive us into the sea, the sea drives us back to the barbarians; between these two means of death we are either killed or drowned.' Dated to between AD 446 and 454, most probably to the former year, it is the last firm date which we have in the dissolution of Roman Britain. The appeal, however, went unanswered; Rome had no longer time for a sometime, remote province.

Perhaps surprisingly, in the period under discussion, no great and immediate decline occurred in the Romano-British way of life, beyond that which had already come about in the late fourth century. Almost all the evidence now being produced tends to show that, in most areas, life continued much as before. Indeed Bede, admittedly writing two centuries later, refers to it as a time of peace and prosperity, after the Britons had ejected the Roman officials. There were changes, certainly, but they were caused more by abandonment and decay than by war-fare, and many of the buildings which were left to fall down were those which were now superfluous to contemporary requirements. The first sufferers, as already indicated in Chapter 4, were the isolated farms and villas, bereft of their markets in towns because the highways were no longer safe or kept repaired. But it is important to distinguish individual cases, as some places were seemingly more resilient than others. Yet many towns appear to have survived in full operation even when deprived of their chief sources of supply. It is probable that they relied, in the end, on local produce, and the corn-drying oven, inserted into a farmers' house at Verulamium, is eloquent evidence of what was happening. But despite the restrictions on food supply, Verulamium still had a functioning aqueduct and water distribution system, and moreover, new masonry buildings were still being erected, while the forum at Cirencester seems to have been used as a market-place until at least AD 440. But, by that time, it is necessary to draw distinctions between one area and another. For instance, the areas of east Kent, east Anglia and the middle Thames Valley were probably most affected by the rebellion of Saxon federates, and it is likely that by the mid fifth century those areas had disappeared under Saxon subjugation. There is evidence from Canterbury, and at some other towns, of Saxon mercenaries being given an insula in the town for their own dwellings, presumably in return for military service, while at Caistor-by-Norwich there is a cremation cemetery which was used mainly by federate soldiers of like kind.

   Although slow decay rather than violence at the hands of enemy raiders seems to have been the main cause of destruction, there were, nevertheless, places where the end came with fire and slaughter. Probably early in the fifth century two of the signal stations on the Yorkshire coast so suffered, while the sack of the two frontier forts of Birdoswald and Chesterholm must mean that Hadrian's Wall was no longer an effective barrier to Pictish invasion. Isolated villas, such as North Wraxall (Wilts) or Lullingstone (Kent) went up in flames and at the former, two bodies were thrown down a well. No doubt they had attracted the attentions of a raiding party, or even of rebellious peasantry, and the apparent presence of troops at the former may well have provided the reason. On the whole, however, Britain does not seem to have suffered, as did parts of Gaul, from social upheavals which led to open rebellion of slaves and labourers.

   In such circumstances, it is probable that villa-owners abandoned their homes to their fate and, at first, sought sanctuary in the nearest walled town or settlement. But as the pressure of Anglo-Saxon settlement increased, so whole areas may have been evacuated by the upper classes, who fled westwards. What then happened to the slaves and peasants is not known; some, like their masters, may have fled also, but those remaining would probably have fared no worse under Saxon than under Romano-British domination had they stayed on, and many may have done so. There is, for instance, a record of Celtic-speaking Britons remaining in the Fens as late as the eighth century.

So long as towns could provide enough inhabitants to man their defences and had enough food, they were largely safe from Saxon assault. The Saxons had neither the equipment for breaching fortifications nor the tenacity to mount a siege; nevertheless they could destroy all standing crops, so that periodic famines may have resulted. It is somewhat surprising, therefore, to find some towns being deserted for no very obvious reason, often, as in Wales and the west country, in favour of a nearby Iron Age hill-fort, which was refortified, as at South Cadbury or Dinas Powys. Alternatively, it seems that, at Cirencester, the nearby amphitheatre was fortified as a stronghold. But by this time, each place has to be considered on its own merits. With communications unsafe, or cut altogether, as seems to have happened to the main road from Silchester to Dorchester-on-Thames, each town and village tended to become a small isolated enclave of surviving Romano-British customs and institutions. What happened at one, therefore, was not necessarily common to all.

But the end when it came, if not violent, could still be abrupt. At Cirencester, for instance, a new ditch dug beside a main road in the town centre remained unfilled with road silt, an indication that traffic had ceased; instead it collected decaying leaves and grass – and two unburied corpses. At Silchester, attempts seem to have been made to protect, or delimit, an area round the town by means of large dykes. These appear mostly on the side facing towards the Thames valley. Since one of the earliest rebellions, and consequent takeover of an area, on the part of Saxon federate troops, seems to have centred on the garrison town of Dorchester-on-Thames, the dykes probably represent an attempt by the townspeople of Silchester to restrict the rebels.

What then led the inhabitants of towns apparently to abandon their safe refuges ultimately in favour of less desirable places? A combination of factors was almost certainly responsible and together caused a depopulation so serious as to render the defence of most large towns an impossible task; hence the removal by the survivors to smaller, more easily fortified sites. Among the reasons, we might include flight to more distant places of safety, famine, rebellion and ultimately a major pestilential epidemic.

By the middle of the fifth century, therefore, parts of eastern and central Britain had been taken over by the rebel Saxon federate troops, reinforced probably by other migrants from across the North Sea. But other movements had also taken place. In Wales and the west, the first half of the fifth century was marked by raids from across the Irish Sea, and to help combat them Cunedda, a chieftain from the Votadini, whose tribal area was situated south of the Firth of Forth, was transferred with a body of supporters to north Wales. Ultimately the trouble was settled by a fortuitous marriage between the opposing factions and the increasing strength of Christianity in the Celtic parts of the British islands.

It would seem, therefore, that until troubled by the totality of events in the middle of the century, some form of central control had been successfully retained. Thereafter, the disintegration became faster, and may be seen as being linked with the final collapse of overall authority and the eclipse of almost all surviving traces of Romano-British culture and institutions.

Vortigern was replaced by Ambrosius, and he some time after by the even more shadowy figure of Arthur. But it did not all go the way of the Saxons, despite some local successes on their part. Towards the end of the century, the Britons, who still could command cavalry, rallied and inflicted a major defeat on the Saxons at the unidentified site of Mount Badon. After it there ensued another period of peace and stability which is reputed to have lasted for two generations. Into such a stage of equilibrium might best be fitted the Silchester Dykes.

By the middle of the sixth century, the Saxon advance had been resumed, perhaps with an added impetus caused by the arrival in Britain of an epidemic of bubonic plague which was affecting most of the Mediterranean world. By the end of the century most remaining areas of Britain, excluding the Celtic regions of the south-west, Wales and northern Scotland, had been over-run. In those regions there sometimes survived a legacy of Roman Britain, such as the Latin loanwords taken into early Welsh, and possible systems of land-tenure. Elsewhere, the institutions which had nourished Britain for nearly four centuries were extinguished. If Roman towns became English towns, it was largely the accident of geography which so decreed it, and apart from possible continuity of settlement in them, they were completely changed. Villas sometimes coincide with English villages, but again it is probable that the ideal situations which they normally enjoyed were those which equally suited villages. Yet, sometimes in those later years there comes an echo of a vanished era, such as the Anglian *praefectus Lindocolinae civitatis* who governed Lincoln in the seventh century. But it is only an echo, with no substance in it; Roman Britain had passed into history.

Bibliography

I have attempted, as far as possible, to restrict the bibliography to monographs, which are likely to be more readily obtainable by the average, interested reader who wishes to pursue the subject further. But the very large mine of material in periodical literature should not be overlooked and references to this can be most easily found by consulting one of the appropriate volumes cited below. In addition there are the annual summaries of recent discoveries contained in the periodical *Britannia*.

GENERAL

J.P.V. Balsdon (ed.), *The Romans* (London, 1965).
A.R. Birley, *Life in Roman Britain* (London, 1964).
W. Bonser, *A Romano-British Bibliography* (Oxford, 1964).
British Museum, *Guide to the Antiquities of Roman Britain* (London, 1958).
A.R. Burn, *The Romans in Britain* (Oxford, 1969).
R.G. Collingwood (ed. I.A. Richmond), *The Archaeology of Roman Britain* (London, 1969).
R.G. Collingwood and R.P. Wright, *The Roman Inscriptions of Britain, I* (Oxford, 1965).
S.S. Frere, *Britannia* (London, 1974).
F. Haverfield, *The Romanization of Roman Britain* (Oxford, 1915).
K. Jackson, *Language and History in Early Britain* (Edinburgh, 1953).
M.G. Jarrett and B. Dobson (eds), *Britain and Rome* (Kendal, 1965).
A.H.M. Jones, *The Later Roman Empire* (Oxford, 1964).
N. Lewis and M. Reinhold, *Roman Civilization, Sourcebook II: The Empire* (New York, 1966).
J. Liversidge, *Britain in the Roman Empire* (London, 1968).
London Association of Classical Teachers (Original Records No. 4), *Some Inscriptions from Roman Britain* (London, 1969).
Ordnance Survey, *Map of Roman Britain* (4th ed., 1979).
I.A. Richmond (ed. P. Salway), *Roman Art and Archaeology* (London, 1969).
I.A. Richmond, *Roman Britain* (London, 1963).
I.A. Richmond (ed.), *Roman and Native in North Britain* (London, 1958).
A.L.F. Rivet, *Town and Country in Roman Britain* (London, 1965).
P. Salway, *The Frontier People of Roman Britain* (Cambridge, 1965).
C.H.V. Sutherland, *Coinage and Currency in Roman Britain* (Oxford, 1937).
J.M.C. Toynbee, *Art in Britain under the Romans* (Oxford, 1964).
J.M.C. Toynbee, *Art in Roman Britain* (London, 1962).

CHAPTER 1

Caesar, *De Bello Gallico* (Harmondsworth, 1957).

B.W. Cunliffe, *Iron Age Communities in Britain* (London, 1974).

J. Forde-Johnston, *Prehistoric Britain and Ireland* (London, 1976).

S.S. Frere (ed.), *Problems of the Iron Age in Southern Britain* (London, 1961).

D.W. Harding, *The Iron Age in Lowland Britain* (London, 1974).

D.W. Harding (ed.), *Hillforts* (London, 1976).

C.F.C. Hawkes and S.C. Hawkes (eds), *Greeks, Celts and Romans* (London, 1973).

Margaret Jesson and David Hill (eds), *The Iron Age and its Hill-Forts* (Southampton, 1971).

Ordnance Survey, *Map of Southern Britain in the Iron Age* (Chessington, 1967).

A.L.F. Rivet (ed.), *The Iron Age in Northern Britain* (Edinburgh, 1966).

CHAPTER 2

P.T. Bidwell, *The Legionary Bath-house and Basilica and Forum at Exeter* (Exeter, 1979).

E. Birley, *Research on Hadrian's Wall* (Kendal, 1961).

E. Birley, *Roman Britain and the Roman Army* (Kendal, 1963).

A.R. Burn, *Agricola and Roman Britain* (London, 1953).

R.M. Butler (ed.), *Soldier and Civilian in Roman Yorkshire* (Leicester, 1971).

J. Collingwood Bruce, *Handbook to the Roman Wall* (12th ed., I.A. Richmond (ed.), Newcastle, 1966).

B. Cunliffe (ed.), *Excavations at the Roman Fort at Richborough, Kent, V* (Oxford, 1968).

D.R. Dudley and G. Webster, *The Rebellion of Boudicca* (London, 1962).

D.R. Dudley and G. Webster, *The Roman Conquest of Britain. AD 43-57* (London, 1965).

S. Johnson, *The Roman Forts of the Saxon Shore* (London, 1976).

M.J. Jones, *Roman Fort-Defences to AD 117* (Oxford, 1975).

J.C. Mann, 'The Frontiers of the Principate' in H. Temporini (ed.), *Aufstieg und Niedergang der Römischen Welt, II. Principat, 1* (Berlin, 1974).

V.E. Nash-Williams, *The Roman Frontier in Wales* (2nd ed., M.G. Jarrett (ed.), Cardiff, 1969).

R.M. Ogilvie and I.A. Richmond (eds), *Cornelii Taciti. de vita Agricolae* (Oxford, 1967).

Ordnance Survey, *Map of the Antonine Wall* (Chessington, 1969).

Ordnance Survey, *Map of Hadrian's Wall* (Chessington, 1964).

R.C.H.M. (England), *Eburacum, Roman York* (London, 1962).

A.S. Robertson, *The Antonine Wall* (Glasgow, 1968).

G. Simpson, *Britons and the Roman Army* (London, 1964).

C.E. Stevens, *The Building of Hadrian's Wall* (Kendal, 1966).

F.H. Thompson, *Roman Cheshire* (Chester, 1965).

G. Webster, *The Rebellion of Boudica* (London, 1979).

G. Webster, *The Roman Imperial Army* (London, 1969).

D.R. Wilson, *Roman Frontiers of Britain* (London, 1967).

CHAPTER 3

G.C. Boon, *Silchester, the Roman Town of Calleva* (Newton Abbot, 1974).
R.M. Butler (ed.), *Soldier and Civilian in Roman Yorkshire* (Leicester, 1971).
B. Cunliffe, *Roman Bath* (Oxford, 1969).
S.S. Frere, *Verulamium I* (Oxford, 1972).
S.S. Frere, 'Verulamium and the Towns of Britannia' in H. Temporini (ed.), *Aufstieg und Niedergang der Römischen Welt, II. Principat, 3* (Berlin, 1975).
M.R. Hull, *Roman Colchester* (Oxford, 1958).
R. Merrifield, *Roman London* (London, 1969).
W. Rodwell and T. Rowley (eds), *The Small Towns of Roman Britain* (Oxford, 1976).
M. Todd, *The Roman Settlement at Margidunum* (Nottingham, 1969).
J.S. Wacher (ed.), *The Civitas Capitals of Roman Britain* (Leicester, 1975).
J.S. Wacher, *The Towns of Roman Britain* (London, 1978).

CHAPTER 4

S. Appelbaum in H.P.R. Finberg (ed.), *The Agrarian History of England and Wales* I. ii (Cambridge, 1972).
H.C. Bowen, *Ancient Fields* (London, 1961).
K. Branigan, *The Roman Villa in South-West England* (Bradford on Avon, 1977).
B. Cunliffe, *Fishbourne, a Roman Palace and its Garden* (London, 1971).
I.Ll. Foster and G. Daniel (eds), *Prehistoric and Early Wales* (London, 1965).
W. Gardner and H.N. Savory, *Dinorben* (Cardiff, 1964).
G.W. Meates, *The Lullingstone Roman Villa* (London, 1955).
D.S. Neal, *The Excavation of the Roman Villa in Gadebridge Park, Hemel Hempstead, 1963-8* (London, 1974).
John Percival, *The Roman Villa* (London, 1976).
C.W. Phillips (ed.), *The Fenland in Roman Times* (London, 1970).
R.C.H.M. (England), *Westmorland* (London, 1934).
A.L.F. Rivet (ed.), *The Roman Villa in Britain* (London, 1969).
A.L.F. Rivet, 'The Rural Economy of Roman Britain' in H. Temporini (ed.), *Aufstieg und Niedergang der Römischen Welt II. Principat, 3* (Berlin, 1975).
A.C. Thomas (ed.), *Rural Settlement in Roman Britain* (London, 1966).
K.D. White, *The Agricultural Implements of the Roman World* (Cambridge, 1967).
K.D. White, *Roman Farming* (London, 1970).

CHAPTER 5

G. Askew, *The Coinage of Roman Britain* (London, 1951).
M.I. Finley, *The Ancient Economy* (London, 1973).
Michael Grant, *Roman History from Coins* (Cambridge, 1968).
E.G. Hardy, *Five Roman Laws* (Oxford, 1912).
A.H.M. Jones, *Studies in Roman Government and Law* (Oxford, 1960).
R. MacMullen, *Soldier and Civilian in the Later Roman Empire* (Harvard, 1963).
M. Rostovtzeff, *The Social and Economic History of the Roman Empire* (Oxford, 1957), 2 volumes.
P.M. Schisas, *Offences against the State in Roman Law* (London, 1926).
F. Schulz, *Classical Roman Law* (Oxford, 1951).
A.N. Sherwin-White, *The Roman Citizenship* (Oxford, 1973).
G.H. Stevenson, *Roman Provincial Administration* (Oxford, 1949).

C.H.V. Sutherland, *Coinage and Currency in Roman Britain* (Oxford, 1937).
I. Tenny-Frank (ed.), *An Economic Survey of Ancient Rome* (USA, 1933-40), 5 volumes. The British section occurs in Vol. III.

CHAPTER 6
R. Chevallier, *Roman Roads* (London, 1976).
N. Davey, *A History of Building Materials* (London, 1961).
O. Davies, *Roman Mines in Europe* (Oxford, 1935).
A. Detsicas (ed.), *Current Research in Romano-British Coarse Pottery* (London, 1973).
O.A.W. Dilke, *The Roman Land Surveyors* (Newton Abbot, 1971).
R. Duncan-Jones, *The Economy of the Roman Empire* (Cambridge, 1974).
M.I. Finley, *The Ancient Economy* (London, 1973).
W.F. Grimes, *Pottery and Tilery of the XXth Legion at Holt* (London, 1930).
B.R. Hartley, *Notes on the Roman Pottery Industry in the Nene Valley* (Peterborough, 1960).
H. Hodges, *Artefacts* (London, 1964).
E.M. Jope (ed.), *Studies in Building History* (London, 1961).
R. MacMullen, *Soldier and Civilian in the Later Roman Empire* (Harvard, 1963).
I.D. Margary, *Roman Roads in Britain* (London, 1967).
E.W. Marsden, *Greek and Roman Artillery* (Oxford, 1969).
H.M.D. Parker, *The Roman Legions* (Cambridge, 1961).
I.A. Richmond, *Hod Hill*, Vol. II (London, 1968).
F.H. Thompson, *Roman Cheshire* (Chester, 1965).
R.F. Tylecote, *Metallurgy and Archaeology* (London, 1962).
Vitruvius, *The Ten Books on Architecture* (translated by M.H. Morgan, New York, 1960).
G.R. Watson, *The Roman Soldier* (London, 1969).
R.E.M. Wheeler, *Maiden Castle* (Oxford, 1943).
R.E.M. Wheeler, *Roman Art and Architecture* (London, 1964).
J.P. Wild, *Textile Manufacture in the Northern Roman Provinces* (Cambridge, 1970).

CHAPTER 7
M.W. Barley and R.P.C. Hanson (eds), *Christianity in Britain, 300-700* (Leicester, 1968).
B. Cunliffe, *Roman Bath* (London, 1969).
W.F. Grimes, *The Excavation of Roman and Medieval London* (London, 1968).
E. and J.R. Harris, *The Oriental Cults in Roman Britain* (Leiden, 1965).
M.R. Hull, *Roman Colchester* (London, 1958).
M.J.T. Lewis, *Temples in Roman Britain* (Cambridge, 1966).
Stuart Piggott, *The Druids* (London, 1975).
Anne Ross, *Pagan Celtic Britain* (London, 1974).
J.M.C. Toynbee, *Art in Roman Britain* (London, 1962).
J.M.C. Toynbee, *Death and Burial in the Roman World* (London, 1971).
L.P. Wenham, *The Romano-British Cemetery at Trentholme Drive, York* (London, 1968).
R.E.M. and T.V. Wheeler, *Report on the Excavations of the Prehistoric, Roman, and Post-Roman Site in Lydney Park, Glos.* (Oxford, 1932).

CHAPTER 8

W. Beare, *The Roman Stage* (London, 1950).
A.J. Butler, *Sport in Classic Times* (London, 1930).
J. Carcopino, *Daily Life in Ancient Rome* (London, 1941).
Gunter Fleischhauer, *Musikgeschichte in Bildern; Band II*, 'Musik des Altertums' (Leipzig, 1964).
B. Flower and E. Rosenbaum (eds), *Apicius: the Roman Cookery Book* (London, 1958).
G. Jennison, *Animals for Show and Pleasure in Ancient Rome* (Manchester, 1937).
H.J.R. Murray, *A History of Board Games other than Chess* (London, 1952).
V.E. Paoli, *Rome, its People, Life and Customs* (London, 1963).

CHAPTER 9

L. Alcock, *Arthur's Britain* (London, 1971).
J. Morris, *The Age of Arthur* (London, 1973).
J.N.L. Myres, *Anglo-Saxon Pottery and the Settlement of England* (Oxford, 1969).
E.A. Thompson, *The Early Germans* (Oxford, 1965).
A.W. Wade-Evans (ed.), *Nennius' History of the Britons* (London, 1938).

Index

Trier, 224, 232
  bridge at, 188
  mosaics, 208
triumphal monuments, 54, 102, 247–8, pl.
  6
turrets, *see* Hadrian's Wall

Upwell, 132
urbs, 65

vandalism, 238, 261, pl. 25
Vegetius, 177
Vergil, 241, 251
Verulamium, 113, 163, 206, 207, 209,
  212, 251, fig. 18
  Boudiccan onslaught at, 38
  civitas capital, 69
  farm in, 125, 265
  fortifications, 70, 96–7, 99
  forum, 75, 76, 229, figs. 21, 43
  houses, 79, 103, fig. 22
  industries, 91, 194–6
  Iron Age *oppidum* at, 20, 24, 26
  market-hall, 90, 101
  martyrium at, 239
  mint, Belgic, at, 20
  mosaics, 82, pl. 26
  municipium, 67
  sewers, 77
  shops, 77, 88, 91, 171, 194, 196, 211–12
  temples and shrines, 83, 229, 233, 255,
    figs. 43–4
  theatre, 84, 101–2, 229, 255, fig. 50
  triumphal arch, 102
  wall-paintings, 79, 261
  water supply, 77, 104
vicarius, 55, 67
vici, 48–9, 52, 65, 71, 87, 88, 101–2, 103,
  141, 161, 163, fig. 13
villages, 16, 51, 57, 62, 85, 128, 129, 130,
  132, 135, pls. 4, 43–4, figs. 3, 23–4
Villa Publica, Rome, 111, 126
villas, 111–24, 127, 130, 131, 133, 135,
  143, 145–7, 167, 210, 224, 232,
  238–9, 259–60, 265, 267, pls. 37–40,
  fig. 29
  aisled, 122, 125, 133
  courtyard, 119, 122
  definition of, 111–12

distribution, 119, 123, 127, 133, fig. 30
fortified, 133
siting of, 121, 130
Villa Faustina, 130
Vipasca, mines at, 170
Vortigern, 264, 267

wages, 215
Wakerley, iron-smelting at, 197, pls. 55–6
Walesby, 238
wall-paintings, 79, 89, 91, 114, 121, 151,
  251, 259, pls. 25, 40
  graffiti on, 191, 236, 261, pl. 68
Wanborough, 87, 103
warfare, 16, 20, 60, 96, 146, 176–8
Water Newton, 88, 103, pl. 27
  mosaicists at, 208
  pottery industry at, 94, 200–4, fig. 40
  villas round, 113
wells, 121
West Brandon, 140
West Coker, 224
Weston-under-Penyard, 93
Wiggonholt, 238
Wilderspool, 91, 199
Winchester,
  beneficiarius at, 156
  cemetery at, 247
  civitas capital, 69
  fortifications, 70, 96
  weaving mill at, 210
Witcombe, 119
Woodchester, 119, 127, 146, 208, fig. 29
Woodcuts, 130
Woodeaton, 256
workshops, *see* shops
Wroxeter, 99, 191, 226, fig. 20
  bath-house, 100, 103, 249, pl. 24, fig.
    49
  beneficiarius at, 156
  circus (?), 260
  civitas capital, 70–1
  forum, 90, 100, 103, 204, pl. 21
  industries, 195–6, 211
  legionary fortress at, 39, 70
  market-hall, 90, 101
  streets, 73
  temples, 192, 222, 229, 260
  water supply, 77
Wycomb, 87–8, 95